DIRECTORY OF
BROOKLYN
ARTS
ORGANIZATIONS

D1246332

Brooklyn Arts Council (BAC)
55 Washington Street, Suite 218
Brooklyn, NY 11201

Printed in the United States of America, 2008

Library of Congress Cataloging-in-Publication Data is available upon request.

ISBN 978-0-9800018 0 8
ISBN 0-9800018-0-3

DEAR FRIENDS OF THE ARTS,

As Speaker and Cultural Affairs, Libraries & International Intergroup Relations Chair of the New York City Council, we take genuine pride in introducing the 2008 *Directory of Brooklyn Arts Organizations*. The book you hold in your hands demonstrates Brooklyn's ever increasing relevance to the cultural life of our city, state, and country. In assembling this updated and expanded directory, the Brooklyn Arts Council (BAC) has proven that it continues to be an able steward of our borough's cultural renaissance.

For several years now, Brooklyn has been the site of an unparalleled increase in artistic activity, establishing itself as a destination for both artists and arts tourists from all over the world. Capturing Brooklyn's extraordinary range of arts organizations in one accessible, user-friendly volume is a valuable accomplishment that the Brooklyn Delegation of the New York City Council proudly supports.

A cultural resurgence like Brooklyn's wouldn't have been possible without a lot of carefully-laid groundwork beforehand. For over forty years, BAC has been doing that groundwork by promoting and sustaining Brooklyn artists and arts organizations. In all that time, BAC has fostered respect and understanding among the diverse communities of our culturally rich borough, instilled pride in our neighborhoods, and stimulated the imaginations of our schoolkids. This distinguished record of service makes BAC an ideal guide to the borough's cultural scene today.

Like BAC's website, which includes an online version of this directory along with other helpful information, this reference book is a key resource for bringing the arts in Brooklyn to the attention of the world, both inside and outside the borough. So whether you live in Brooklyn or not, we hope that the 2008 *Directory of Brooklyn Arts Organizations* will reveal to you just how much there is to experience here.

Christine C. Quinn
Speaker of the New York City Council

Domenic M. Recchia, Jr
Chair, Committee on Council Cultural Affairs

DEAR READER,

At the turn of the millennium, Brooklyn saw an extraordinary upsurge in locally-based artistic activity. This created a need for a single, all-inclusive guide to the borough's arts organizations that would serve both the general public and the art-makers themselves. In response, in 2001 the Brooklyn Arts Council proudly introduced the *Directory of Brooklyn Arts Organizations*—a top-to-bottom record of a borough undergoing an exciting cultural renaissance —both in print and online.

It's no secret that Brooklyn's arts community has continued to grow at a rapid pace in the years since, and the time had come for a thorough, updated and expanded version of the original directory. In keeping with its initial mandate, BAC's new directory encompasses both nonprofit and for-profit entities, from grassroots community groups and storefront galleries to world-renowned institutions.

This print directory is matched by an online version that can be accessed on BAC's website (www.brooklynartscouncil.org). The web version is searchable, links directly to each group's website, and will be updated regularly by the groups themselves. Both versions provide mailing addresses, phone and fax numbers, e-mail addresses, website addresses, venue locations, contacts, and descriptions. With so much information accessible in one convenient place, we are confident that this new directory will become an essential resource for presenters, curators, libraries, corporate funders, elected officials, and arts professionals of all stripes, just as its predecessor did.

In addition to a searchable online version of this directory, BAC's website also features an online registry of individual artists, indexed by discipline and searchable by keyword. Arts organizations and individual artists are invited to register for these online databases free of charge. For more information, visit www.brooklynartscouncil.org.

A project of this scope isn't something BAC could have undertaken on its own. We gratefully acknowledge the support of JPMorgan Chase in making this new directory possible. As Seth Edwards, Vice President of Community Relations at JPMorgan Chase, notes:

> "JPMorgan Chase has long supported Brooklyn's cultural organizations through its regrant program, as we believe that investing in the arts strengthens our community. BAC's *Directory of Brooklyn Arts Organizations* provides a comprehensive overview of the hundreds of cultural groups that enrich Brooklyn, and we at JPMorgan Chase are proud to sponsor this valuable resource."

In addition, the New York City Department of Cultural Affairs, the New York State Council on the Arts, and the New York City Council were partners in supporting this overview of the arts in Brooklyn.

For its part, BAC, which celebrated its fortieth anniversary in 2006, looks forward to many more years of serving Brooklyn's artists and arts organizations.

Dr. Thomas F. Schutte
Chairman of the Board
Brooklyn Arts Council

Ella J. Weiss
President
Brooklyn Arts Council

TABLE OF CONTENTS

ALPHABETICAL INDEX CHART

The Alphabetical Index Chart is an alphabetical listing of every organization in the directory, presented in an easy-to-use grid format. The grid shows each organization's Primary category (indicated with a star), Secondary categories (indicated with a circle) and the page number where you can find more information about that organization.

Each organization has only one Primary category, but may have a number of Secondary categories. For example, a theater company will have as its Primary category "Theater" and may list "Literature" as a Secondary category if it commissions new plays, and "Opera and Musical Theater" if it stages musicals in addition to plays.

If you are looking for a particular organization, locate it in the Categorical Listings and find the page number where its full listing can be found. If you are interested in finding organizations that offer Arts for Children and Teens, for example, simply browse through that section of the Category Listings.

KEY
* PRIMARY CATEGORY
O SECONDARY CATEGORY

KEY
* PRIMARY CATEGORY
O SECONDARY CATEGORY

KEY
* PRIMARY CATEGORY
O SECONDARY CATEGORY

	PAGE NUMBER	ARCH. & URBAN/ENVIRON. DESIGN	ARTS FOR CHILDREN/TEENS	ARTS SERVICES	COMPUTER ARTS/NEW MEDIA	DANCE	EDUCATIONAL INSTITUTIONS	FILM/VIDEO	FOLK ARTS	GALLERIES	HISTORICAL SOCIETIES	LITERARY ARTS
AMERICAN THEATRE OF HARLEM	147					O						
ANDHOW THEATER COMPANY I, INC.	148	O										
ANNUAL GOWANUS ARTISTS STUDIO TOUR	139											
ARCHIPELAGO BOOKS	85			O								*
ARMSTRONG & ASSOCIATES	18			*								
ART 101	66									*		
ART GALLERY AT KINGSBOROUGH COMMUNITY COLLEGE, CUNY	66	O				O				*		
ART GLASS STUDIO	163			O								
ART LILLARD'S HEAVENLY BAND	114											
ART PLAZA CULTURAL CENTER	18		O	*		O						
ART WITHOUT WALLS/FREE SPACE	6		*	O								O
ARTICHOKE DANCE COMPANY	31		O			*						
ARTMOVINGPROJECTS	29				*							
ARTS ACTION RESEARCH	18			*								
ART'S HOUSE SCHOOLS, INC	6		*	O		O						
ARTSCETERA	6		*			O						
ARTWORKS FOR YOUTH	7		*									
ASIAN AMERICAN WOMEN ARTISTS ALLIANCE	164	O						O				
ATTITUDE: THE DANCERS' MAGAZINE	32					*		O				O
AUTONOMEDIA	85											*
AWAAM: ARAB WOMEN ACTIVE IN THE ARTS AND MEDIA	29				*		O					
AXELLE FINE ARTS, LTD.	18			*						O		
BAC ARTS IN EDUCATION	7		*			O		O				O

KEY
* PRIMARY CATEGORY
O SECONDARY CATEGORY

KEY
* PRIMARY CATEGORY
O SECONDARY CATEGORY

KEY
* PRIMARY CATEGORY
O SECONDARY CATEGORY

KEY
* PRIMARY CATEGORY
O SECONDARY CATEGORY

	PAGE NUMBER	ARCH. & URBAN/ENVIRON. DESIGN	ARTS FOR CHILDREN/TEENS	ARTS SERVICES	COMPUTER ARTS/NEW MEDIA	DANCE	EDUCATIONAL INSTITUTIONS	FILM/VIDEO	FOLK ARTS	GALLERIES	HISTORICAL SOCIETIES	LITERARY ARTS
BETTER BROOKLYN COMMUNITY CENTER	8	*				O						
BIG DANCE THEATER	148					O						
BILLIE HOLIDAY THEATRE	148											
BINDLESTIFF FAMILY VARIETY ARTS, INC.	149	O						O	O			
BLACK AND LATINO FILMMAKER'S COALITION	50							*				
BLACK MOON THEATRE COMPANY, INC.	92	O										
BOAST COMMUNICATIONS	19	O	*			O						
BOMB MAGAZINE	93											O
BOOKLYN ARTISTS ALLIANCE	164	O	O									O
BRAVE NEW WORLD REPERTORY THEATRE	149											
BREAKNBONES	50							*				
BREEDINGGROUND PRODUCTIONS	93					O	O	O	O			O
BRIC ARTS | MEDIA | BROOKLYN	93	O			O	O	O			O		
BRIC ROTUNDA GALLERY	164	O	O				O			O		
BRICK THEATER, INC., THE	149	O				O	O					
BRICSTUDIO	140		O			O						
BRIGHTON BALLET THEATER	32					*			O			
BRIGHTON NEIGHBORHOOD ASSOCIATION, INC.	94											
BROOKLYN ALTERNATIVE SMALL PRESS FAIR	86											*
BROOKLYN ART INCUBATOR	19	O	*				O					
BROOKLYN ARTISANS GALLERY	67									*		
BROOKLYN ARTISTS GYM	164	O	O							O		
BROOKLYN ARTS COUNCIL	20	O	*			O	O	O	O			

KEY
* PRIMARY CATEGORY
O SECONDARY CATEGORY

MULTI-DISCIPLINARY ARTS	MUSEUMS	MUSIC	OPERA/MUSIC THEATER	PERFORMANCE ART	PRESENTING ORGANIZATIONS	THEATER	VISUAL ARTS	VISUAL/PERFORMING ARTS SCHOOLS	PAGE NUMBER	
									8	BETTER BROOKLYN COMMUNITY CENTER
						*			148	BIG DANCE THEATER
					O	*			148	BILLIE HOLIDAY THEATRE
		O		O	O	*			149	BINDLESTIFF FAMILY VARIETY ARTS, INC.
									50	BLACK AND LATINO FILMMAKER'S COALITION
*					O				92	BLACK MOON THEATRE COMPANY, INC.
									19	BOAST COMMUNICATIONS
*							O		93	BOMB MAGAZINE
					O		*		164	BOOKLYN ARTISTS ALLIANCE
						*			149	BRAVE NEW WORLD REPERTORY THEATRE
									50	BREAKNBONES
*		O	O	O					93	BREEDINGGROUND PRODUCTIONS
*		O	O	O	O				93	BRIC ARTS	MEDIA	BROOKLYN
		O					*		164	BRIC ROTUNDA GALLERY
O		O	O	O	O	*			149	BRICK THEATER, INC., THE
		O		O		*	O		140	BRICSTUDIO
									32	BRIGHTON BALLET THEATER
*					O				94	BRIGHTON NEIGHBORHOOD ASSOCIATION, INC.
									86	BROOKLYN ALTERNATIVE SMALL PRESS FAIR
									19	BROOKLYN ART INCUBATOR
							O		67	BROOKLYN ARTISANS GALLERY
							*		164	BROOKLYN ARTISTS GYM
					O		O		20	BROOKLYN ARTS COUNCIL

KEY
✳ PRIMARY CATEGORY
O SECONDARY CATEGORY

	PAGE NUMBER	ARCH. & URBAN/ENVIRON. DESIGN	ARTS FOR CHILDREN/TEENS	ARTS SERVICES	COMPUTER ARTS/NEW MEDIA	DANCE	EDUCATIONAL INSTITUTIONS	FILM/VIDEO	FOLK ARTS	GALLERIES	HISTORICAL SOCIETIES	LITERARY ARTS
BROOKLYN ARTS COUNCIL INTERNATIONAL FILM FESTIVAL	50			O				✳				
BROOKLYN ARTS EXCHANGE	94		O	O		O				O		
BROOKLYN BALLET	33		O			✳						
BROOKLYN BOTANIC GARDEN	107	O										
BROOKLYN CENTER CINEMA	50							✳				
BROOKLYN CENTER FOR THE PERFORMING ARTS AT BROOKLYN COLLEGE (BCBC)	140		O			O						
BROOKLYN CENTER FOR THE URBAN ENVIRONMENT	3	✳	O									
BROOKLYN CHAMBER ORCHESTRA, THE	115											
BROOKLYN CHILDREN'S MUSEUM	107		O				O					
BROOKLYN CHILDREN'S THEATRE	8		✳									
BROOKLYN COLLEGE ART GALLERY	67									✳		
BROOKLYN COLLEGE CONSERVATORY OF MUSIC	116				O		O					
BROOKLYN COLLEGE DEPARTMENT OF FILM	51						O	✳				
BROOKLYN COLLEGE DEPARTMENT OF THEATER	150						O					
BROOKLYN COLLEGE PREPARATORY CENTER FOR THE PERFORMING ARTS	116					O						
BROOKLYN COMMUNITY CHORUS	116											
BROOKLYN CONTEMPORARY CHORUS, INC.	116											
BROOKLYN DAILY EAGLE	86			O								✳
BROOKLYN FILM & ARTS FESTIVAL	51							✳				

KEY
* PRIMARY CATEGORY
O SECONDARY CATEGORY

KEY
✳ PRIMARY CATEGORY
O SECONDARY CATEGORY

KEY
* PRIMARY CATEGORY
O SECONDARY CATEGORY

MULTI-DISCIPLINARY ARTS	MUSEUMS	MUSIC	OPERA/MUSIC THEATER	PERFORMANCE ART	PRESENTING ORGANIZATIONS	THEATER	VISUAL ARTS	VISUAL/PERFORMING ARTS SCHOOLS	PAGE NUMBER	
		*							117	BROOKLYN FOUR PLUS ONE, INC., THE
		*			O				117	BROOKLYN FRIENDS OF CHAMBER MUSIC
	O								83	BROOKLYN HISTORICAL SOCIETY
									51	BROOKLYN INTERNATIONAL FILM FESTIVAL
					*				140	BROOKLYN JEWISH FILM FESTIVAL
*				O			O		107	BROOKLYN MUSEUM
		O						*	175	BROOKLYN MUSIC SCHOOL
									20	BROOKLYN PAPER, THE
		*							117	BROOKLYN PHILHARMONIA CHORUS
O		*							117	BROOKLYN PHILHARMONIC
									86	BROOKLYN PUBLIC LIBRARY
*		O				O	O		94	BROOKLYN RAIL, THE
					*				141	BROOKLYN SOCIETY FOR ETHICAL CULTURE, THE
		*							118	BROOKLYN SYMPHONY ORCHESTRA
O					O		O		45	BROOKLYN TECHNOLOGY EXCHANGE
				O		*			150	BROOKLYN THEATRE ARTS PROJECT, INC., THE
							*		165	BROOKLYN WATERCOLOR SOCIETY
					O		*		165	BROOKLYN WATERFRONT ARTISTS COALITION
		*							118	BROOKLYN WOMEN'S CHORUS, THE

KEY
* PRIMARY CATEGORY
O SECONDARY CATEGORY

KEY
✳ PRIMARY CATEGORY
O SECONDARY CATEGORY

Multi-Disciplinary Arts	Museums	Music	Opera/Music Theater	Performance Art	Presenting Organizations	Theater	Visual Arts	Visual/Performing Arts Schools	Page Number	Organization
O		O			O				86	BROOKLYN WRITERS SPACE
									52	BROOKLYN YOUNG FILMMAKERS CENTER
		O	O						9	BROOKLYN YOUTH CHORUS ACADEMY
		✳	O		O				118	BROOKLYN-QUEENS CONSERVATORY OF MUSIC
		O							87	BROWNSTONE POETS, THE
									20	BURN BRIGHT LIFEWORKS
O		O			O	✳			150	BUSHWICK STARR, THE
✳							O		94	CABINET
									9	CARIBBEAN AMERICAN SPORTS AND CULTURAL YOUTH MOVEMENT, INC.
					O	✳			150	CARIBBEAN CULTURAL THEATRE
				✳					135	CAROLYN HULSE DANCE TROUPE
✳	O		O		O	O	O		95	CAVE
		O	O	O	✳				141	CELEBRATE BROOKLYN PERFORMING ARTS FESTIVAL
✳									95	CENTER FOR INTERNATIONAL ART IN COMMUNITY
✳							O		95	CENTER FOR THANATOLOGY RESEARCH & EDUCATION
							O		3	CENTER FOR URBAN PEDAGOGY, THE
		✳			O				118	CENTRAL BROOKLYN JAZZ CONSORTIUM
							O		68	CHASSIDIC ART INSTITUTE
✳	O								95	CHASSIDIC DISCOVERY WELCOME CENTER
		✳							119	CHELSEA STRING BAND
O		O			O				33	CHEZ BUSHWICK

KEY
* PRIMARY CATEGORY
O SECONDARY CATEGORY

	PAGE NUMBER	ARCH. & URBAN/ENVIRON. DESIGN	ARTS FOR CHILDREN/TEENS	ARTS SERVICES	COMPUTER ARTS/NEW MEDIA	DANCE	EDUCATIONAL INSTITUTIONS	FILM/VIDEO	FOLK ARTS	GALLERIES	HISTORICAL SOCIETIES	LITERARY ARTS
CH'I CONTEMPORARY FINE ART	68									*		
CHRISTIANA DRAPKIN JAZZ GROUP	119											O
CINDERS GALLERY	68									*		
CIRCUIT PRODUCTIONS	96		O	O		O						
CIRCUS AMOK	151		O					O				
CIRKULOCK, INC.	60					O		*				
CITY RELIQUARY MUSEUM & CIVIC ORGANIZATION, THE	108	O										
CLINTON HILL ART GALLERY	68			O						*		
CLINTON HILL SIMPLY ART & FRAMING GALLERY	68			O						*		
CODE FOUNDATION, THE	21			*								
COLLAPSABLE GIRAFFE	151											
COLLECTIVE OPERA COMPANY	131											
COMMUNICABLE ARTS	151											
COMMUNITY THEATRE INTERNATIONALE	136					O						
CONEY ISLAND HISTORY PROJECT	83	O									*	
CONEY ISLAND USA	136											
CONFLUX FESTIVAL	96							O				
CONJUNCTIONARTS, INC.	166			O								
CONJUNTO NUEVO MILENIO	60					O		*				
CONNECTION WORKS, INC.	9	*										
CONNI CONVERGENCE ENTERPRISES, LLC	136											
COOL CULTURE	10	*	O									
CORA, INC.	34	O				*						
CORRIDOR GALLERY	69	O								*		

KEY
* PRIMARY CATEGORY
O SECONDARY CATEGORY

KEY
* PRIMARY CATEGORY
o SECONDARY CATEGORY

KEY
* PRIMARY CATEGORY
O SECONDARY CATEGORY

KEY
✳ PRIMARY CATEGORY
○ SECONDARY CATEGORY

Organization	PAGE NUMBER	ARCH. & URBAN/ENVIRON. DESIGN	ARTS FOR CHILDREN/TEENS	ARTS SERVICES	COMPUTER ARTS/NEW MEDIA	DANCE	EDUCATIONAL INSTITUTIONS	FILM/VIDEO	FOLK ARTS	GALLERIES	HISTORICAL SOCIETIES	LITERARY ARTS
DOWNTOWN BROOKLYN PARTNERSHIP	22	○		✳								
DRAMA OF WORKS	152											
DREAMERS FILM SOCIETY, THE	53							✳				
DRUMSONG AFRICAN BALLET THEATRE, INC.	97	○				○			○			
DUMBO ARTS CENTER	166			○				○		○		
DUŠAN TÝNEK DANCE THEATRE	36					✳						
DZIECI	152	○	○									
EGRESS THEATRE COMPANY	152	○										○
EL PEQUEÑO ARTISTA	11		✳			○						
EL PUENTE	97	○										
ELDERS SHARE THE ARTS	98								○			○
ELECTRIK GODDESS CLUB ORQUESTRA	120											
ELEVENTEN GALLERY, THE	70			○						✳		○
ELSIE MANAGEMENT	22			✳	○							
ENCOMPASS NEW OPERA THEATRE	132											
ENRICO CARUSO MUSEUM OF AMERICA, THE	108						○					
ERROL GRIMES DANCE GROUP	36					✳						
ESTHERGRACE DESIGNS	4	✳										
ETGALLERIES	70			○						✳		
EVA DEAN DANCE	36			○		✳						
EVIDENCE, INC.	36					✳						
EX GALLERY	70									✳		
FALCONWORKS ARTISTS GROUP	152	○										
FAMILY TREE COLLECTIVE	142											

KEY
✳ PRIMARY CATEGORY
○ SECONDARY CATEGORY

KEY
* PRIMARY CATEGORY
O SECONDARY CATEGORY

KEY
* PRIMARY CATEGORY
O SECONDARY CATEGORY

KEY
* PRIMARY CATEGORY
O SECONDARY CATEGORY

KEY
* PRIMARY CATEGORY
O SECONDARY CATEGORY

MULTI-DISCIPLINARY ARTS	MUSEUMS	MUSIC	OPERA/MUSIC THEATER	PERFORMANCE ART	PRESENTING ORGANIZATIONS	THEATER	VISUAL ARTS	VISUAL/PERFORMING ARTS SCHOOLS	PAGE NUMBER	
O							O		71	GALLERY AT HARRIET'S ALTER EGO, THE
			O			*			153	GALLERY PLAYERS, THE
									4	GARRISON ARCHITECTS
							O		71	GEORGE WASHINGTON CARVER GALLERY
									23	GIBA IN DESIGN
							O		72	GITANA ROSA GALLERY
						*			153	GLASS CONTRAPTION, THE
							O		72	GLORIA KENNEDY GALLERY
					O				87	GOING COASTAL, INC.
							*	O	168	GOLOBOROTKO'S STUDIO
									37	GOSPEL DANCE THEATRE
				O		*		O	153	GOSSIP FACTORY, THE
									53	GOVERNESS FILMS
*				O					98	GOWANUS STUDIO SPACE, INC., THE
		O			*				142	GOWANUS WILDCATS
		*							121	GRACE & SPIRITUS CHORALE OF BROOKLYN
	*								108	GREENPOINT MONITOR MUSEUM, THE
									60	GREENWICH MORRIS MEN
	O						*		168	GREEN-WOOD HISTORIC FUND INC., THE
							O		12	GROUNDSWELL COMMUNITY MURAL PROJECT
		O							60	HALBERT BARTON AND EL BOMBAZO DE BROOKLYN
				O	O				12	HAMPTONIANS NEW YORK

KEY
* ✳ PRIMARY CATEGORY
* O SECONDARY CATEGORY

	PAGE NUMBER	ARCH. & URBAN/ENVIRON. DESIGN	ARTS FOR CHILDREN/TEENS	ARTS SERVICES	COMPUTER ARTS/NEW MEDIA	DANCE	EDUCATIONAL INSTITUTIONS	FILM/VIDEO	FOLK ARTS	GALLERIES	HISTORICAL SOCIETIES	LITERARY ARTS
HARBOR DEFENSE MUSEUM OF FORT HAMILTON	109	O										
HEART OF BROOKLYN	23	O	O	✳		O						O
HELDER DESIGN LLC	4	✳										
HENRY GREGG GALLERY	72									✳		
HIP-HOP THEATER FESTIVAL	154											
HOGAR COLLECTION, THE	72			O			O			✳		
HOLLAND TUNNEL	73									✳		
HOPES ALIVE, INC.	154											
HQ	73									✳		
I.D.E.A.S.	154	O										
IFETAYO CULTURAL ARTS	99	O	O			O						O
ILAND, INC.	37			✳								
IMAGINE PROJECT, INC.	12	✳	O			O						O
IMMIGRANTS' THEATRE PROJECT	154											
IMPACT THEATER	155											
INI NYC	99											
INTERDANCE FOUNDATION, INC.	37				O	✳		O				
INTERNATIONAL AFRICAN ARTS FESTIVAL	24			✳								
IRONDALE ENSEMBLE PROJECT	155	O										
ISSUE PROJECT ROOM	99				O	O		O		O		
ITALIAN OPERA COMPANY, INC., THE	132	O										
JAZZREACH, INC.	121											
JEWISH CHILDREN'S MUSEUM	109	O										
JEWISH FOLK CRAFTS GUILD	73									✳		

KEY
✳ PRIMARY CATEGORY
○ SECONDARY CATEGORY

MULTI-DISCIPLINARY ARTS	MUSEUMS	MUSIC	OPERA/MUSIC THEATER	PERFORMANCE ART	PRESENTING ORGANIZATIONS	THEATER	VISUAL ARTS	VISUAL/PERFORMING ARTS SCHOOLS	PAGE NUMBER	
	✳								109	HARBOR DEFENSE MUSEUM OF FORT HAMILTON
○	○	○					○		23	HEART OF BROOKLYN
									4	HELDER DESIGN LLC
							○		72	HENRY GREGG GALLERY
○						✳			154	HIP-HOP THEATER FESTIVAL
○		○					○		72	HOGAR COLLECTION, THE
							○		73	HOLLAND TUNNEL
				○		✳			154	HOPES ALIVE, INC.
							○		73	HQ
						✳			154	I.D.E.A.S.
✳	○				○				99	IFETAYO CULTURAL ARTS
○									37	ILAND, INC.
		○	○	○			○		12	IMAGINE PROJECT, INC.
						✳			154	IMMIGRANTS' THEATRE PROJECT
				○		✳			155	IMPACT THEATER
✳				○					99	INI NYC
									37	INTERDANCE FOUNDATION, INC.
○					○				24	INTERNATIONAL AFRICAN ARTS FESTIVAL
					○	✳			155	IRONDALE ENSEMBLE PROJECT
✳		○		○					99	ISSUE PROJECT ROOM
		○	✳				○		132	ITALIAN OPERA COMPANY, INC., THE
		✳							121	JAZZREACH, INC.
	✳								109	JEWISH CHILDREN'S MUSEUM
							○		73	JEWISH FOLK CRAFTS GUILD

KEY
* PRIMARY CATEGORY
o SECONDARY CATEGORY

KEY
* PRIMARY CATEGORY
O SECONDARY CATEGORY

KEY
* PRIMARY CATEGORY
O SECONDARY CATEGORY

	PAGE NUMBER	ARCH. & URBAN/ENVIRON. DESIGN	ARTS FOR CHILDREN/TEENS	ARTS SERVICES	COMPUTER ARTS/NEW MEDIA	DANCE	EDUCATIONAL INSTITUTIONS	FILM/VIDEO	FOLK ARTS	GALLERIES	HISTORICAL SOCIETIES	LITERARY ARTS
LONG ISLAND UNIVERSITY MUSIC DEPARTMENT, BROOKLYN CAMPUS	46						*					
LONG ISLAND UNIVERSITY, BROOKLYN CAMPUS	46						*					
LOOP 2.4.3	122											
LOS BOMBEROS DE BROOKLYN, INC.	61					O		*				
LOTHAR OSTERBURG STUDIO	24		*									
LOTUS PROMOTIONS	24		*									
MAGNOLIA TREE EARTH CENTER	46	O					*			O		
MANI	122		O									
MANY MOODS PRODUCTION COMPANY	123			O								
MARIE-CHRISTINE GIORDANO DANCE COMPANY	38			O		*						
MARK MORRIS DANCE GROUP	38			O		*						
MARMARA'S DANCE OF THE NILE REVUE	38					*			O			
MARQUIS STUDIOS, LTD.	100			O								
MARTIN LUTHER KING JR. CONCERT SERIES	123											
MATA FESTIVAL	123											
MBS MUSIC & ENTERTAINMENT	123											
M'CAHAYA ARTS & EDUCATION FOUNDATION	54						*					
MCCAIG-WELLES GALLERY	75		O							*		
MEANRED PRODUCTIONS	124											
MEDGAR EVERS COLLEGE PREPARATORY SCHOOL CONTEMPORARY DANCE THEATRE, THE	175					O						

KEY
* PRIMARY CATEGORY
O SECONDARY CATEGORY

MULTI-DISCIPLINARY ARTS	MUSEUMS	MUSIC	OPERA/MUSIC THEATER	PERFORMANCE ART	PRESENTING ORGANIZATIONS	THEATER	VISUAL ARTS	VISUAL/PERFORMING ARTS SCHOOLS	PAGE NUMBER	
		O							46	LONG ISLAND UNIVERSITY MUSIC DEPARTMENT, BROOKLYN CAMPUS
		O		O		O	O		46	LONG ISLAND UNIVERSITY, BROOKLYN CAMPUS
		*							122	LOOP 2.4.3
		O							61	LOS BOMBEROS DE BROOKLYN, INC.
							O		24	LOTHAR OSTERBURG STUDIO
									24	LOTUS PROMOTIONS
									46	MAGNOLIA TREE EARTH CENTER
		*							122	MANI
		*							123	MANY MOODS PRODUCTION COMPANY
									38	MARIE-CHRISTINE GIORDANO DANCE COMPANY
									38	MARK MORRIS DANCE GROUP
									38	MARMARA'S DANCE OF THE NILE REVUE
*									100	MARQUIS STUDIOS, LTD.
		*			O				123	MARTIN LUTHER KING JR. CONCERT SERIES
		*			O				123	MATA FESTIVAL
		*							123	MBS MUSIC & ENTERTAINMENT
		O							54	M'CAHAYA ARTS & EDUCATION FOUNDATION
							O		75	MCCAIG-WELLES GALLERY
		*					O		124	MEANRED PRODUCTIONS
								*	175	MEDGAR EVERS COLLEGE PREPARATORY SCHOOL CONTEMPORARY DANCE THEATRE, THE

KEY
* PRIMARY CATEGORY
o SECONDARY CATEGORY

KEY
* PRIMARY CATEGORY
O SECONDARY CATEGORY

MULTI-DISCIPLINARY ARTS	MUSEUMS	MUSIC	OPERA/MUSIC THEATER	PERFORMANCE ART	PRESENTING ORGANIZATIONS	THEATER	VISUAL ARTS	VISUAL/PERFORMING ARTS SCHOOLS	PAGE NUMBER	
O							O		75	METAPHOR CONTEMPORARY ART
		O			*				143	METROTECH BUSINESS IMPROVEMENT DISTRICT
		O	O				O	O	24	MICHAEL ALAN'S DRAW-A-THON
O	*								110	MICRO MUSEUM
							O		75	MILL BASIN DELI & FINE ART GALLERY
									39	MISNOMER DANCE THEATER
O									39	MIXED BAG & COMPANY
							O		75	MOMENTA ART
O		O	O				O	O	54	MONKEY TOWN
						*			156	MONTAUK THEATRE PRODUCTIONS
		O							61	MOUNTAIN REDBIRD MUSIC
		O	O			*	O		156	MOVING THEATER
							O		25	MUDPIT, THE
	*						O		110	MUSEUM OF CONTEMPORARY AFRICAN DIASPORAN ART
						O			13	MY VOICE THEATRE
				*		O			132	NARROWS COMMUNITY THEATER, INC.
		O			O		O		30	NAT CREOLE ONLINE
							O		76	NEIL STEVENSON FINE ART LLC
							O		76	NELSON HANCOCK GALLERY
O							*		170	NEW GENERAL CATALOG
	O								46	NEW YORK AQUARIUM
		*	O						124	NEW YORK BAROQUE

KEY
* PRIMARY CATEGORY
○ SECONDARY CATEGORY

	PAGE NUMBER	ARCH. & URBAN/ENVIRON. DESIGN	ARTS FOR CHILDREN/TEENS	ARTS SERVICES	COMPUTER ARTS/NEW MEDIA	DANCE	EDUCATIONAL INSTITUTIONS	FILM/VIDEO	FOLK ARTS	GALLERIES	HISTORICAL SOCIETIES	LITERARY ARTS
NEW YORK CIRCUS ARTS ACADEMY	176											
NEW YORK DEAF THEATRE, LTD.	156											
NEW YORK TRANSIT MUSEUM	110	○									○	
NIA THEATRICAL PRODUCTION COMPANY	156		○									
NIETZSCHE MUSIC PROJECT, THE	124											
NOEL POINTER FOUNDATION	124											
NORA STEPHENS / NORANEWDANCE	39					*	○					
NOT AN ALTERNATIVE, INC.	143											
NOT FOR PROFIT PICTURES	143		○									
NUNU GALLERIE	76		○							*		
NURTUREART	170	○	○									
NY WRITERS COALITION	88	○	○									*
OBJECT IMAGE GALLERY	76									*		
OBRUMANKOMA SANKOFA TRADITIONALS OF GHANA	39					*						
OFFICEOPS	100					○	○					
OLD AMERICAN CAN FACTORY, THE	144	○				○	○					○
OLD STONE HOUSE OF BROOKLYN	111	○										
OMNI ENSEMBLE LTD., THE	125											
ONE SIXTY GLASS	25		*							○		
ONE STORY	88											*
ONE WORLD SYMPHONY	125											
OPERA ON TAP	132		○									
ORANGE VECTOR	25		*									
PAGE 73 PRODUCTIONS	157		○									

KEY
* PRIMARY CATEGORY
O SECONDARY CATEGORY

KEY
* PRIMARY CATEGORY
O SECONDARY CATEGORY

	PAGE NUMBER	ARCH. & URBAN/ENVIRON. DESIGN	ARTS FOR CHILDREN/TEENS	ARTS SERVICES	COMPUTER ARTS/NEW MEDIA	DANCE	EDUCATIONAL INSTITUTIONS	FILM/VIDEO	FOLK ARTS	GALLERIES	HISTORICAL SOCIETIES	LITERARY ARTS
PAINT ACROSS AMERICA	170	O										
PAINTED POT, THE	26	O	*									
PANTONIC STEEL ORCHESTRA	125	O										
PARENTS AS PRIMARY TEACHERS, INC.	14	*					O					
PARIJAT DESAI DANCE COMPANY	40	O				*	O					
PARK SLOPE GALLERY	76			O						*		
PARK SLOPE SINGERS	126											
PARKER'S BOX	76									*		
PARTNERSHIP FOR PARKS	5	*										
PAUL ROBESON THEATER	157		O	O		O						
PDM PERFORMING ARTS CORPORATION	100		O			O						
PENDU PRODUCTIONS	170											
PERFORMING ARTS & SPECIAL EVENTS, KINGSBOROUGH COMMUNITY COLLEGE	144						O					
PERIPHERAL MEDIA PROJECTS, INC.	171		O					O				
PETER KYLE DANCE	40					*						
PHILIPPA KAYE COMPANY	101					O						
PIER GLASS	26			*								
PIEROGI	77								O	*		
PLACE IN HISTORY	5	*										
PLG ARTS	101		O									O
PLUTO	77								O	*		
POC DOC FILM DEVELOPMENT, INC.	54		O					*				
POLISH AMERICAN FOLK DANCE COMPANY	62					O			*			

KEY
✳ PRIMARY CATEGORY
O SECONDARY CATEGORY

KEY
* PRIMARY CATEGORY
O SECONDARY CATEGORY

	PAGE NUMBER	ARCH. & URBAN/ENVIRON. DESIGN	ARTS FOR CHILDREN/TEENS	ARTS SERVICES	COMPUTER ARTS/NEW MEDIA	DANCE	EDUCATIONAL INSTITUTIONS	FILM/VIDEO	FOLK ARTS	GALLERIES	HISTORICAL SOCIETIES	LITERARY ARTS
POLIZZI FINE ART	77									*		
POLYNESIAN DANCE FOUNDATION	62					O			*			
PORTSIDE NEWYORK	111											
POTPOURRI OF COLOR PERFORMING ARTS COMPANY	157					O						
PRATT INSTITUTE	47						*			O		
PROPEL-HER DANCE COLLECTIVE	40					*						
PROSPECT PARK & PROSPECT PARK ALLIANCE	101	O	O							O		
PROSPECT PARK AUDUBON CENTER	5	*	O						O	O		
PROTEUS GOWANUS	101						O			O		O
PROTO-TYPE THEATER, INC.	157											
PUPPETEERS COOPERATIVE, THE	158											
PUPPETRY ARTS THEATRE, INC., THE	102											
PUPPETWORKS	158		O									
PURELEMENTS: AN EVOLUTION IN DANCE	40		O	O		*						
QIIQ PRODUCTIONS	158		O									
QUEST JR. DRUM & BUGLE CORPS, INC.	126											
RABBIT HOLE ENSEMBLE	158											
RADIOHOLE	138											
RAIZES DO BRASIL CAPOEIRA BROOKLYN	62					O			*			
RAY ABRAMS BIG (17-PIECE) SWING BAND, THE	126											
REALFORM	171			O				O				O

KEY
* PRIMARY CATEGORY
O SECONDARY CATEGORY

KEY
✳ PRIMARY CATEGORY
○ SECONDARY CATEGORY

	PAGE NUMBER	ARCH. & URBAN/ENVIRON. DESIGN	ARTS FOR CHILDREN/TEENS	ARTS SERVICES	COMPUTER ARTS/NEW MEDIA	DANCE	EDUCATIONAL INSTITUTIONS	FILM/VIDEO	FOLK ARTS	GALLERIES	HISTORICAL SOCIETIES	LITERARY ARTS
RECORDING ADVENTURE WORKSHOP	126		○									
REDHAWK NATIVE AMERICAN ARTS COUNCIL	26			✳					○			
REEL SISTERS OF THE DIASPORA FILM FESTIVAL	54							✳				
REEL WORKS TEEN FILMMAKING	55		○					✳				
REGINA OPERA COMPANY	133											
RETURN OF THE SUN	41					✳						
REVELATION PERFORMING ARTS STUDIO, INC.	176		○	○		○				○		
RHYTHM VISIONS PRODUCTION COMPANY, INC.	14	✳										
RIVIERA, THE	77	○						○		✳		
ROLEY POLEY PRODUCTIONS, LLC	55							✳				
ROOFTOP FILMS	55							✳				
ROOM 58	88			○								✳
ROUGH ON RATS PRODUCTIONS	55							✳				
RUBELLE AND NORMAN SCHAFLER GALLERY AT THE PRATT INSTITUTE	78						○			✳		
RUDDER BLADE PRODUCTIONS, INC.	56							✳				
RUSH PHILANTHROPIC ARTS FOUNDATION	14	✳										
RYAN REPERTORY COMPANY	159	○										
S.E.E.D GALLERY	78									✳		
S.E.M. ENSEMBLE, INC.	127											
SABA -THE ASSOCIATION OF YEMENI AMERICANS	102	○	○									
SABOOGE THEATRE	159											

KEY
* PRIMARY CATEGORY
O SECONDARY CATEGORY

KEY
* PRIMARY CATEGORY
O SECONDARY CATEGORY

	PAGE NUMBER	ARCH. & URBAN/ENVIRON. DESIGN	ARTS FOR CHILDREN/TEENS	ARTS SERVICES	COMPUTER ARTS/NEW MEDIA	DANCE	EDUCATIONAL INSTITUTIONS	FILM/VIDEO	FOLK ARTS	GALLERIES	HISTORICAL SOCIETIES	LITERARY ARTS
SACKETT GROUP, THE	159											
SAFE-T-GALLERY	78							O		*		
SANKARANKA GALLERY	78									*		
SANKOFA ART CENTRE	78									*		
SARAH BOWEN GALLERY	78									*		
SCENARIOS USA	56		O					*				
SCHOOL FOR MUSICAL PERFORMANCE	127		O									
SEASIDE SUMMER CONCERT SERIES	127									·		
SECRET PROJECT ROBOT	172									O		
SHADOW BOX THEATRE, INC., THE	15		*	O								
SHADOW PUPPET THEATRE	159		O									
SHARON'S DANCE THEATRE	41		O			*						
SHIR CHADASH: THE BROOKLYN JEWISH COMMUNITY CHORUS	127											
SHOSTAKOVICH MUSIC, ARTS, & SPORT SCHOOL, INC.	128		O				O					
SILVER-BROWN DANCE COMPANY	41		O			*						
SLATE GALLERY	79			O						*		
SLAVIC ARTS ENSEMBLE	128											
SLOPE MUSIC	128											
SMACK MELLON	172									O		
SMUDGE STUDIO	172	O										
SOAPBOX GALLERY	172							O		O		
SOFT SKULL PRESS, INC.	88					·						*
SOL WORKS, INC.	15		*	O								
SOMETHING POSITIVE, INC.	102					O						

KEY
* PRIMARY CATEGORY
O SECONDARY CATEGORY

MULTI-DISCIPLINARY ARTS	MUSEUMS	MUSIC	OPERA/MUSIC THEATER	PERFORMANCE ART	PRESENTING ORGANIZATIONS	THEATER	VISUAL ARTS	VISUAL/PERFORMING ARTS SCHOOLS	PAGE NUMBER	
						*			159	SACKETT GROUP, THE
					O		O		78	SAFE-T-GALLERY
							O		78	SANKARANKA GALLERY
							O		78	SANKOFA ART CENTRE
							O		78	SARAH BOWEN GALLERY
O									56	SCENARIOS USA
		*						O	127	SCHOOL FOR MUSICAL PERFORMANCE
		*							127	SEASIDE SUMMER CONCERT SERIES
							*		172	SECRET PROJECT ROBOT
O		O							15	SHADOW BOX THEATRE, INC., THE
						*			159	SHADOW PUPPET THEATRE
						O			41	SHARON'S DANCE THEATRE
		*							127	SHIR CHADASH: THE BROOKLYN JEWISH COMMUNITY CHORUS
		*						O	128	SHOSTAKOVICH MUSIC, ARTS, & SPORT SCHOOL, INC.
									41	SILVER-BROWN DANCE COMPANY
					O		O		79	SLATE GALLERY
		*							128	SLAVIC ARTS ENSEMBLE
		*							128	SLOPE MUSIC
							*		172	SMACK MELLON
							*		172	SMUDGE STUDIO
							*		172	SOAPBOX GALLERY
									88	SOFT SKULL PRESS, INC.
O					O				15	SOL WORKS, INC.
*									102	SOMETHING POSITIVE, INC.

KEY
* PRIMARY CATEGORY
O SECONDARY CATEGORY

KEY
* ✶ PRIMARY CATEGORY
* ○ SECONDARY CATEGORY

KEY
* PRIMARY CATEGORY
O SECONDARY CATEGORY

	PAGE NUMBER	ARCH. & URBAN/ENVIRON. DESIGN	ARTS FOR CHILDREN/TEENS	ARTS SERVICES	COMPUTER ARTS/NEW MEDIA	DANCE	EDUCATIONAL INSTITUTIONS	FILM/VIDEO	FOLK ARTS	GALLERIES	HISTORICAL SOCIETIES	LITERARY ARTS
THEATER GARDEN, LTD.	133		O									
THELMA HILL PERFORMING ARTS CENTER	42					*						
TIFFANY MILLS COMPANY	42					*						
TILLIE'S OF BROOKLYN	173											
TONEL LAKAY DANCE THEATRE	42		O	O		*			O			
TOPIARY PRODUCTIONS, INC.	56							*				
TRIANGLE ARTS ASSOCIATION	173											
TRIPLE Z MUSIC	129											
TRISKELION ARTS	42					*	O					
TROIKA RANCH	104				O							
TUCKABERRY PRODUCTIONS	160		O									
TWW INC.	16	*	O		O							O
UGLY DUCKLING PRESSE	89											*
UNDER THE TABLE	160											
UNDERBRIDGE PICTURES	80	O								*	O	
UNION STREET DANCE	43			O		*						
UNIONDOCS	56							*				
UNITED COMMUNITY CENTERS	63	O					*					
URBAN BUSH WOMEN	43					*						
URBAN DIVERS, THE	80									*		
URBANGLASS	174									O		
VAMPIRE COWBOYS THEATRE COMPANY	160											
VERTEXLIST	30				*		O			O		
VERTICAL PLAYER REPERTORY	133											
VICTORIAN PLACE CULTURAL CENTER	104											
VISUAL ART STUDIO	57							*				
VOLCANO LOVE	43		O			*						

KEY
* PRIMARY CATEGORY
O SECONDARY CATEGORY

KEY
* PRIMARY CATEGORY
O SECONDARY CATEGORY

	PAGE NUMBER	ARCH. & URBAN/ENVIRON. DESIGN	ARTS FOR CHILDREN/TEENS	ARTS SERVICES	COMPUTER ARTS/NEW MEDIA	DANCE	EDUCATIONAL INSTITUTIONS	FILM/VIDEO	FOLK ARTS	GALLERIES	HISTORICAL SOCIETIES	LITERARY ARTS
VOX POP	104											O
WAGMAG	174			O								
WALKER INTERNATIONAL COMMUNICATIONS GROUP	104			O								
WATERFRONT MUSEUM, THE	111											
WCV, INC.	43					*						
WEEKSVILLE HERITAGE CENTER	84	O	O	O			O	O	O	O	*	
WEONE FILM PRODUCTIONS	57				O			*				
WESSEL + O'CONNOR FINE ART	80									*		
WEST INDIAN AMERICAN DAY CARNIVAL ASSOCIATION, INC.	145		O	O					O			
WHITE BIRD PRODUCTIONS	161		O									
WHITE WAVE YOUNG SOON KIM DANCE COMPANY	44		O			*						
WILLIAMSBURG ART & HISTORICAL CENTER	105											
WILLIAMSBURG ART NEXUS	146					O						
WISELEPHANT	27			*	O		O					
WITNESS	57							*				
WOMEN IN STEEL	130											
WORLD ACCORDING TO SHORTS, THE	57							*				
WORLD EATER RECORDINGS	130			O	O			O				
WRIGHT NOW! PERFORMANCEEXPERIENCE	44		O			*						
WYCKOFF FARMHOUSE MUSEUM	112									O	O	
YOUNG DANCERS IN REPERTORY	44		O			*						
YWCA BROWNSVILLE EARLY LEARNING CENTER	16		*			O						
ZION GALLERY	81			O						*		

KEY
✳ PRIMARY CATEGORY
O SECONDARY CATEGORY

MULTI-DISCIPLINARY ARTS	MUSEUMS	MUSIC	OPERA/MUSIC THEATER	PERFORMANCE ART	PRESENTING ORGANIZATIONS	THEATER	VISUAL ARTS	VISUAL/PERFORMING ARTS SCHOOLS	PAGE NUMBER	
✳									104	VOX POP
							✳		174	WAGMAG
✳									104	WALKER INTERNATIONAL COMMUNICATIONS GROUP
O	✳	O			O				111	WATERFRONT MUSEUM, THE
									43	WCV, INC.
									84	WEEKSVILLE HERITAGE CENTER
									57	WEONE FILM PRODUCTIONS
							O		80	WESSEL + O'CONNOR FINE ART
					✳				145	WEST INDIAN AMERICAN DAY CARNIVAL ASSOCIATION, INC.
						✳			161	WHITE BIRD PRODUCTIONS
				O					44	WHITE WAVE YOUNG SOON KIM DANCE COMPANY
✳	O				O				105	WILLIAMSBURG ART & HISTORICAL CENTER
O						O	✳		146	WILLIAMSBURG ART NEXUS
					O		O		27	WISELEPHANT
									57	WITNESS
	✳								130	WOMEN IN STEEL
									57	WORLD ACCORDING TO SHORTS, THE
O		✳	O		O				130	WORLD EATER RECORDINGS
				O					44	WRIGHT NOW! PERFORMANCEXPERIENCE
	✳								112	WYCKOFF FARMHOUSE MUSEUM
									44	YOUNG DANCERS IN REPERTORY
									16	YWCA BROWNSVILLE EARLY LEARNING CENTER
							O		81	ZION GALLERY

We must carry the arts to the people, not wait for the people to come to the arts.

ARTHUR MITCHELL

CATEGORICAL LISTINGS

Without an architecture of our own we have no soul of our own civilization.

FRANK LLOYD WRIGHT

ARCHITECTURE & URBAN/ ENVIRONMENTAL DESIGN

0.00156 ACRES
See Primary listing under Visual Arts

AD HOC ART
See Primary listing under Galleries

ART GALLERY AT KINGSBOROUGH COMMUNITY COLLEGE, CUNY
See Primary listing under Galleries

BROOKLYN BOTANIC GARDEN
See Primary listing under Museums

BROOKLYN CENTER FOR THE URBAN ENVIRONMENT (BCUE)
Tennis House, Prospect Park
Brooklyn, NY 11215

Tel 718-788-8500
Fax 718-499-3750
Email bcueinfo@bcue.org
Web www.bcue.org

Executive Director Sandi Franklin

Founded in 1978, the Brooklyn Center for the Urban Environment now serves over 100,000 children, youth, and adults in and across the city, encouraging exploration of both the city's history and the sustainability of its future through public tours, school programs, and community-based educational initiatives.

Secondary Categories: Arts for Children/Teens

BROOKLYN PUBLIC LIBRARY
See Primary listing under Literary Arts

THE CENTER FOR URBAN PEDAGOGY (CUP)
232 Third Street
Brooklyn, NY 11215

Tel 718-596-7721
Fax 718-596-7721
Email info@anothercupdevelopment.org
Web www.anothercupdevelopment.org

Director Rosten Woo

The Center for Urban Pedagogy (CUP) creates educational projects about places and how they change. The center's projects bring together professionals from the fields of art and design with community-based advocates and researchers, who then work with CUP staff to create projects ranging from high school curricula to educational exhibitions.

Secondary Categories: Arts for Children/Teens, Arts Services, Visual Arts

THE CITY RELIQUARY MUSEUM AND CIVIC ORGANIZATION
See Primary listing under Museums

CONEY ISLAND HISTORY PROJECT
See Primary listing under Historical Societies

DOWNTOWN BROOKLYN PARTNERSHIP
See Primary listing under Arts Services

ESTHERGRACE DESIGNS
260 Decatur Street
Brooklyn, NY 11233

Tel 718-221-5005
Email mario@esthergrace.com
Web www.esthergrace.com

Partner: Mario Moorhead

Specializing in green design and sustainable practices, EstherGrace Designs offers exhibition and interior design.

Secondary Categories: Visual Arts

FULTON MALL IMPROVEMENT ASSOCIATION
See Primary listing under Presenting Organizations

GALAPAGOS ART SPACE
See Primary listing under Multi-Disciplinary Arts

GARRISON ARCHITECTS
45 Main Street, Suite 1026
Brooklyn, NY 11201

Tel 718-596-8300
Fax 718-596-8310
Email tpeterson@garrisonarchitects.com
Web www.garrisonarchitects.com

Principal: James Garrison

Garrison Architects is a firm specializing in sustainable design, tectonics, and modular architecture. The firm makes buildings that respond to environmental contexts, employing a range of sustainability strategies from the elimination of air conditioning to the conservation of water and natural resources. Current projects include Restoration Plaza in Bedford Stuyvesant, Rivendell School in Brooklyn, and the Syracuse University School of Architecture at Syracuse University.

GITANA ROSA GALLERY
See Primary Listing under Galleries

THE GOWANUS STUDIO SPACE, INC.
See Primary listing under Multi-Disciplinary Arts

THE GREENPOINT MONITOR MUSEUM
See Primary listing under Museums

THE GREEN-WOOD HISTORIC FUND, INC.
See Primary listing under Visual Arts

HARBOR DEFENSE MUSEUM OF FORT HAMILTON
See Primary listing under Museums

HEART OF BROOKLYN
See Primary listing under Arts Services

HELDER DESIGN LLC
151 Driggs Avenue #2L
Brooklyn, NY 11222

Web www.helderdesign.com

Principal: Mark Helder

Dedicated to sustainable and green building design, Helder Design is committed to bringing energy efficient, environmentally responsible, housing to the high-end as well as the lower income and affordable housing sector. Helder Design's work has been exhibited at the AIA Center for Architecture in New York City, among other venues.

LEFFERTS HISTORIC HOUSE
See Primary listing under Museums

MAGNOLIA TREE EARTH CENTER
See Primary listing under Educational Institutions

METROTECH BUSINESS IMPROVEMENT DISTRICT
See Primary Listing under Presenting Organizations

THE OLD AMERICAN CAN FACTORY
See Primary listing under Presenting Organizations

OLD STONE HOUSE OF BROOKLYN
See Primary listing under Museums

PARTNERSHIPS FOR PARKS
The Arsenal, 830 Fifth Avenue
New York, NY 10021

Site address:
Brooklyn Borough Office
c/o Litchfield Villa, 95 Prospect Park
West, Brooklyn, NY 11215

Tel 212-360-1310
Fax 212-360-1350
Web www.partnershipsforparks.org
Director: Jason Schwartz

Partnerships for Parks is a joint program of City Parks Foundation and the New York City Department of Parks & Recreation, created in 1995 to spur greater community involvement in and support for parks. The Partnership believes that parks are essential to the life of the city, and that community involvement is essential to the life of a park.

PLACE IN HISTORY
1205 Manhattan Avenue
Brooklyn, NY 11222

Tel 917-981-5481
Email info@placeinhistory.org
Web www.placeinhistory.org

Director: Paul Parkhill

Place in History sponsors collaborative projects addressing urban history, urban planning, and the physical and social fabric of the city. Through public installations, publications, and events related to urban themes, Place in History strives to broaden public exposure to the complex histories underlying everyday urban settings.

Secondary Category: Multi-Disciplinary Arts

PROSPECT PARK & PROSPECT PARK ALLIANCE
*See Primary listing under
Multi-Disciplinary Arts*

PROSPECT PARK AUDUBON CENTER
95 Prospect Park West
Brooklyn, NY 11215

Site address:
Lincoln Road/Ocean Avenue
entrance to Prospect Park
Brooklyn, NY 11215

Tel 718-287-3400
Web www.prospectpark.org

Vice President for Education:
Maria Cobo

The Prospect Park Audubon Center is a state-of-the-art facility dedicated to wildlife preservation and natural education, located inside a historic New York City Landmark. Surrounded by nature trails in acres of restored natural habitat, the Audubon Center also houses the Park's Visitor Center, with an information desk, café, and gift shop.

*Secondary categories: Arts for
Children/Teens, Folk Arts, Galleries*

SMUDGE STUDIO
See Primary listing under Visual Arts

UNDERBRIDGE PICTURES
See Primary listing under Galleries

UNITED COMMUNITY CENTERS
See Primary listing under Folk Arts

WEEKSVILLE HERITAGE CENTER
*See Primary listing under Historical
Societies*

ARCHITECTURE & URBAN/
ENVIRONMENTAL DESIGN

ARTS FOR CHILDREN/TEENS

2 PUNKS PUPPET THEATRE
94 Wyckoff Street, #3R
Brooklyn, NY 11201

Tel 877-466-6431
Email 2punks@2punkpuppets.com
Web www.2punkpuppets.com

Performer: Gretchen E. Van Lente

2 Punks Puppet Theatre's specialty is taking myths, legends, and fables and restoring them to what the author, culture, or storyteller originally intended by making them into amazing tabletop, shadow, and hand-puppet shows.

Secondary Category: Theater

AFRICUSSION-PERCUSSION DISCUSSION
See Primary listing under Music

ANDHOWTHEATER COMPANY I, INC.
See Primary listing under Theater

ART PLAZA CULTURAL CENTER
See Primary listing under Arts Services

ART WITHOUT WALLS/FREE SPACE
165 Clinton Avenue
Brooklyn, NY 11205

Tel 914-457-5369
Email Attia@aol.com

Executive Director: Mae Jackson

Art Without Walls is dedicated to providing support services for children and families. The focus is on the collaboration of the arts and education to stimulate personal growth, respect for self and others, cultural awareness, and self-empowerment through various creative activities.

Secondary Categories: Arts Services, Literary Arts, Multi-Disciplinary Arts

ARTICHOKE DANCE COMPANY
See Primary listing under Dance

ART'S HOUSE SCHOOLS, INC. (ART'S HOUSE DANCE SCHOOL)
1627 Mermaid Avenue
Brooklyn, NY 11224

Tel 718-996-2000
Email arts_house1@yahoo.com
Web www.artshouseschools.org

Executive Director: Sophia S. Harrison

Art's House Schools, Inc. founder Sophia Harrison believes that every child who is willing should be given the opportunity to study dance, and that there are disciplines in dance that can instill positive traits in children. Classes are available in ballet, tap, and modern dance for male and female students ages 4-17.

Secondary Categories: Arts Services, Dance, Visual/Performing Arts Schools

ARTSCETERA
212 Smith Street
Brooklyn, NY 11201

Tel 718-643-6817
Fax 718-643-6817
Email info@artscetera.com
Web www.artscetera.com

Executive Director: Nanette M. De Cillis

ArtsCetera is a multi-faceted arts studio in Cobble Hill. In addition to being a leader in the field of music and art programs for children up to age six, the studio is often reconfigured for adult events, including art exhibits, rehearsals, and community meetings.

Secondary Category: Dance

ARTWORKS FOR YOUTH
226 North 5th Street
Brooklyn, NY 11211

Tel 917-376-0571
Email artworksforyouth@aol.com
Web www.artworksforyouth.org

Executive Director: John V. Lombardo

The mission of ArtWorks for Youth is to provide free after school visual arts instruction, mentoring, and academic support to underserved students in South Africa.

Secondary Category: Visual Arts

ASIAN AMERICAN WOMEN ARTISTS ALLIANCE
See Primary listing under Visual Arts

BAC ARTS IN EDUCATION
55 Washington Street, Suite 218
Brooklyn, NY 11201

Tel 718-625-0080
Email bac@brooklynartscouncil.org
Web www.brooklynartscouncil.org

President: Ella J. Weiss

BAC Arts in Education (AIE) facilitates visual, literary, performing, and digital arts programming for students, teachers, parents, and other educators, as well as senior centers and community facilities throughout New York City. Programs include short- and long-term student workshops, assembly performances, professional development, and parent involvement workshops.

Secondary Categories: Dance, Folk Arts, Literary Arts, Music, Theater, Visual Arts

BAILEY'S CAFÉ
See Primary listing under Multi-Disciplinary Arts

BAMSS THEATRE WORKS
(BY ALL MEANS SAVE SOME THEATRE WORKS)
1068 Dean Street
Brooklyn, NY 11216

Tel 718-636-5819
Email BAMSSinc@aol.com
Web www.bamsstheatreworks.org

Directors: Ben and Olive Harney

The programs at BAMSS Theatre Works develop theater skills, life skills, and build community. Through the process of exploring varied theatrical styles and materials, and preparing them for presentation, workshop participants learn skills that relate to their lives; from relationships and education to careers.

Secondary Categories: Dance, Theater

BEDFORD STUYVESANT RESTORATION CORPORATION'S CENTER FOR ARTS AND CULTURE - SKYLIGHT GALLERY
See Primary listing under Galleries

BEDFORD STUYVESANT RESTORATION CORPORATION'S CENTER FOR ARTS AND CULTURE - YOUTH ARTS ACADEMY
See Primary listing under Visual/Performing Arts Schools

BENSONHURST WEST END COMMUNITY COUNCIL
See Primary listing under Historical Societies

ARTS FOR CHILDREN/TEENS

**BETTER BROOKLYN
COMMUNITY CENTER**
900 Fulton Street, Second Floor
Brooklyn, NY 11238

Tel 718-624-1992
Fax 718-624-1833
Email info@bbccenter.org
Web www.bbccenter.org

Executive Director: Andy A. Lewis

Dedicated to improving the quality of
life for all individuals and families in
the local community, Better Brooklyn
Community Center offers ten-week
programs for young adults in Drama
& Creative Writing and Yoga & Dance.
Both programs culminate in a performance in which participants display
their newly acquired skills.

Secondary Category: Dance

BINDLESTIFF FAMILY VARIETY ARTS, INC.
See Primary listing under Theater

BLACK MOON THEATRE COMPANY, INC.
*See Primary listing under
Multi-Disciplinary Arts*

BOAST COMMUNICATIONS, INC.
See Primary listing under Arts Services

BOOKLYN ARTISTS ALLIANCE
See Primary listing under Visual Arts

BRIC ARTS | MEDIA | BROOKLYN
*See Primary listing under
Multi-Disciplinary Arts*

BRIC ROTUNDA GALLERY
See Primary listing under Galleries

THE BRICK THEATER, INC.
See Primary listing under Theater

BROOKLYN ART INCUBATOR
See Primary listing under Arts Services

BROOKLYN ARTISTS GYM
See Primary listing under Visual Arts

BROOKLYN ARTS COUNCIL
See Primary listing under Arts Services

BROOKLYN ARTS EXCHANGE
*See Primary listing under
Multi-Disciplinary Arts*

**BROOKLYN CENTER FOR THE
PERFORMING ARTS AT BROOKLYN
COLLEGE (BCBC)**
*See Primary listing under Presenting
Organizations*

**BROOKLYN CENTER FOR THE URBAN
ENVIRONMENT**
*See Primary listing under Architecture
& Urban/Environmental Design*

BROOKLYN CHILDREN'S MUSEUM
See Primary listing under Museums

BROOKLYN CHILDREN'S THEATRE
135 Prospect Park SW, #B7
Brooklyn, NY 11218

Tel 718-369-6388
Email amy@brooklynchildrenstheatre.net
Web www.brooklynchildrenstheatre.net

Executive Director: Amy White Graves

Brooklyn Children's Theatre is an
after school musical theater program
serving grades 1 through 10, with fall
and spring sessions in which the children rehearse and perform a musical
production. The children learn acting,
singing, dancing, and teamwork in
a supportive, confidence-building
environment.

*Secondary Categories: Music,
Opera/Music Theater, Theater*

BROOKLYN HISTORICAL SOCIETY
*See Primary listing under Historical
Societies*

BROOKLYN MUSEUM
See Primary listing under Museums

BROOKLYN PHILHARMONIC
See Primary listing under Music

BROOKLYN PUBLIC LIBRARY
See Primary listing under Literary Arts

BROOKLYN YOUNG FILMMAKERS CENTER
See Primary listing under Film/Video

BROOKLYN YOUTH CHORUS ACADEMY
179 Pacific Street
Brooklyn, NY 11201

Tel 718-243-9447
Fax 718-855-1371
Email info@brooklynyouthchorus.org
Web www.brooklynyouthchorus.org

Founder and Artistic Director:
Dianne Berkun

Founded in 1992 with the mission of helping children of all backgrounds realize their potential both as musicians and as individuals, the Grammy Award-winning Brooklyn Youth Chorus Academy now stands as one of the country's leading youth choruses, and the only voice-based after school music academy in New York City.

Secondary Categories: Music, Opera/Music Theater

BROOKLYN-QUEENS CONSERVATORY OF MUSIC
See Primary listing under Music

CARIBBEAN AMERICAN SPORTS AND CULTURAL YOUTH MOVEMENT, INC. (CASYM)
249 Sterling Street
Brooklyn, NY 11212

Tel 718-735-6708
Fax 718-735-5258
Email casyminfo@aol.com
Web www.casym.com

President: William T. Jones

CASYM is the acronym for the Caribbean American Sports and Cultural Youth Movement. Since its inception as a nonprofit organization in 1983, CASYM has provided academic, recreational, social, and cultural activities

for young people in the Crown Heights, Flatbush, and East Flatbush sections of Brooklyn.

CARIBBEAN CULTURAL THEATRE
See Primary listing under Theater

THE CENTER FOR URBAN PEDAGOGY
See Primary listing under Architecture & Urban/Environmental Design

CIRCUIT PRODUCTIONS, INC.
See Primary listing under Multi-Disciplinary Arts

CIRCUS AMOK
See Primary listing under Theater

CONNECTION WORKS, INC.
521 17th Street
Brooklyn, NY 11215

Tel 718-369-6931
Email robigarcia@hotmail.com
Web www.connectionworks.org

Executive Director: Robert J. Garcia

Connection Works is a 501(c)(3) nonprofit organization formed to engage the Brooklyn community with a cultural center featuring the performance, presentation, development, and education of music and art. Its programs increase awareness and appreciation for various traditional and "cutting edge" forms of music, all of which contribute to our rich Brooklyn culture. Connection Works believes in and supports the practice of creativity as a means to nourish the mind, body, and spirit.

Secondary Categories: Music, Performance Art

COOL CULTURE
80 Hanson Place, Suite 604
Brooklyn, NY 11215

Tel 718-230-4186
Fax 718-230-4556
Email info@cool-culture.org
Web www.cool-culture.org

Executive Director: Candice Anderson

Cool Culture is a city-wide nonprofit organization dedicated to facilitating low-income families access to, and participation in, the cultural life of New York City, in order to provide educational experiences for children and to strengthen the capacity of parents as their child's first educator.

Secondary Category: Arts Services

CORA, INC.
See Primary listing under Dance

CORRIDOR GALLERY
See Primary listing under Galleries

COVENANT DANCE THEATRE OF BROOKLYN
See Primary listing under Dance

CREATE!
(IL PICCOLO TEATRO DELL'OPERA)
138 Court Street
Brooklyn, NY 11201

Tel 718-643-7775
Email info@createnewyork.org
Web www.createnewyork.org

Director: Emily Schriebl Scott

CREATE! serves New York City's public schools as a leading provider of quality arts education. Tapping into the city's wealth of professional performing artists, CREATE! develops long-term partnerships between artists and educators that inspire thousands of children each year, providing opportunities for enrichment not usually available to the city's public school students.

Secondary Categories: Arts Services, Dance, Folk Arts, Multi-Disciplinary Arts,

Music, Opera/Music Theater, Theater, Visual Arts

CREATIVE OUTLET DANCE THEATRE OF BROOKLYN
See Primary listing under Dance

CREATIVE WOMEN'S NETWORK
See Primary listing under Arts Services

CYNTHIA KING DANCE STUDIO, INC.
See Primary listing under Dance

CYPRESS HILLS LOCAL DEVELOPMENT CORPORATION (CYPRESS HILLS LDC)
625 Jamaica Avenue
Brooklyn, NY 11208

Tel 718-647-2800
Fax 718-647-2805
Web www.cypresshills.org

Education Director: Amy Weber

A nonprofit community organization serving 8,000 residents annually, the Cypress Hills Local Development Corporation (CHLDC) provides a range of arts programming for youth ages 6 through 18 years. The CHLDC is the leading agency of the Cypress Hills East New York Beacon and after school programs at several local schools.

DANCES AND DRUMS OF AFRICA, INC.
See Primary listing under Dance

DANCEWAVE
See Primary listing under Dance

DE NONNO PRODUCTIONS, INC.
See Primary listing under Film/Video

DIGITAL STORY WORKSHOP
See Primary listing under Film/Video

DOLL AND TOY MUSEUM OF NYC
See Primary listing under Museums

DRUMSONG AFRICAN BALLET THEATRE, INC.
See Primary listing under
Multi-Disciplinary Arts

DZIECI
See Primary listing under Theater

EGRESS THEATRE COMPANY
See Primary listing under Theater

EL PEQUEÑO ARTISTA
372 15th Street, # 1A
Brooklyn, NY 11215
Site address:
249 20th Street
Brooklyn, NY 11215
Tel 718-965-1406
Email elpequenoartista@gmail.com
Web www.elpequenoartista.com
Director: Carolina Conde
A bilingual arts center for children,
El pequeño artista offers workshops
for children between the ages of five
months and eight years in subjects
such as drumming, salsa and ballet,
visual arts, music, and cooking. El
pequeño artista has also launched a
new language immersion program for
very young children.
Secondary Categories: Dance, Music

EL PUENTE
See Primary listing under
Multi-Disciplinary Arts

FALCONWORKS ARTISTS GROUP
See Primary listing under Theater

FILIPINO ARTS & MUSIC ENSEMBLE
See Primary listing under Music

FLATBUSH DEVELOPMENT CORPORATION (FDC)
1616 Newkirk Avenue
Brooklyn, NY 11226
Site address:
P.S. 217, 1100 Newkirk Avenue
Brooklyn, NY 11230

Tel 718-859-4595
Fax 718-859-4632
Email cevans@fdconline.org
Web www.fdconline.org
Executive Director: Robin Redmond

Flatbush Development Corporation's
(FDC) mission is to enhance the quality
of life for all segments of the Flatbush community. Its innovative youth
programs offer cultural arts activities
and community performances. FDC
also sponsors events like the Flatbush
Victorian House Tour and the Flatbush
Frolic, which showcases local performers and artists.
Secondary Category: Multi-Disciplinary Arts

FLATBUSH YMCA
See Primary listing under Arts Services

THE FLYING MACHINE THEATER, INC.
See Primary listing under Theater

FRANKLIN FURNACE ARCHIVE, INC.
See Primary listing under Visual Arts

GALAPAGOS ART SPACE
See Primary listing under
Multi-Disciplinary Arts

THE GLASS CONTRAPTION
See Primary listing under Theater

GOLOBOROTKO'S STUDIO
See Primary listing under Visual Arts

GOSPEL DANCE THEATRE
See Primary listing under Dance

THE GOWANUS STUDIO SPACE, INC.
See Primary listing under
Multi-Disciplinary Arts

ARTS FOR CHILDREN/TEENS

GROUNDSWELL COMMUNITY MURAL PROJECT
339 Douglass Street
Brooklyn, NY 11217

Tel 718-254-9782
Email info@groundswellmural.org
Web www.groundswellmural.org

Executive Director: Amy C. Sananman

A Brooklyn-based nonprofit founded in 1996, Groundswell Community Mural Project brings together artists, grass-roots organizations, and teens to create high-quality works of public art in New York City, with a special focus on Brooklyn. Through Groundswell, participants take active ownership of their futures and equip themselves with the tools necessary for social change.

Secondary Category: Visual Arts

HAMPTONIANS NEW YORK (BROOKLYN CARIBBEAN YOUTH FEST)
1562 Rockaway Parkway
Brooklyn, NY 11236

Tel 718-927-6817
Web www.caribbeanyouthfest.org

President: Maxine Alexander

Hamptonians New York (HNY) brings together Caribbean American and Caribbean immigrant youth at events highlighting their common bond. HNY's flagship event is the Brooklyn Caribbean Youth Fest, an annual day-long celebration of Caribbean culture held in Prospect Park that features reggae and soca music, dance, spoken word, and visual art.

Secondary Categories:
Folk Arts, Performance Art,
Presenting Organizations

HEART OF BROOKLYN
See Primary listing under Arts Services

I.D.E.A.S.
See Primary listing under Theater

IFETAYO CULTURAL ARTS
See Primary listing under
Multi-Disciplinary Arts

IMAGINE PROJECT, INC.
540 Ocean Parkway
Brooklyn, NY 11218

Tel 718-851-8091
Email imagineproject@aol.com
Web www.imagineproject.org

Director: Bill Bartlett

The Imagine Project, Inc. was founded in 1992 on the principle that there exists within each child a creative energy which must not lie dormant. Having worked in 130 New York City schools and other venues in the past 15 years, Imagine Project offers programs in drama, improvisation, photography, music, and art.

Secondary Categories: Arts Services,
Dance, Literary Arts, Music,
Opera/Music Theater, Performance Art,
Theater

IRONDALE ENSEMBLE PROJECT
See Primary listing under Theater

THE ITALIAN OPERA COMPANY, INC.
See Primary listing under Opera/Music
Theater

JEWISH CHILDREN'S MUSEUM
See Primary listing under Museums

K.S. J.A.M.M. DANCE TROUPE, INC.
See Primary listing under Dance

KINGS BAY YM-YWHA
See Primary listing under Presenting
Organizations

THE LADSONIAN FOUNDATION, INC.
See Primary listing under Music

THE LAUNDROMAT PROJECT
See Primary listing under Visual Arts

THE LEARNING ABOUT MULTIMEDIA PROJECT (THE LAMP)

809 Union Street, Suite 3
Brooklyn, NY 11215

Tel 917-295-6811
Email dc2@thelampnyc.org
Web www.thelampnyc.org

Executive Director: D.C. Vito

The LAMP (The Learning About Multimedia Project) is a nonprofit community-based organization dedicated to bridging the gaps that have developed between youths, their parents, and educators. Through LAMP's hands-on workshops, participants create and interact with their own media, gaining a better understanding of, and a critical perspective on, all forms of multimedia.

LEFFERTS HISTORIC HOUSE
See Primary listing under Museums

MANI
See Primary listing under Music

MARIE-CHRISTINE GIORDANO DANCE COMPANY (MCGDC)
See primary listing under Dance

MARK MORRIS DANCE GROUP
See Primary listing under Dance

MARQUIS STUDIOS, LTD.
See Primary listing under Multi-Disciplinary Arts

MIXED BAG & COMPANY, INC.
See Primary listing under Dance

THE MUDPIT
See Primary listing under Arts Services

MUSEUM OF CONTEMPORARY AFRICAN DIASPORAN ART
See Primary listing under Museums

MY VOICE THEATRE (MVT) RIDGEWOOD BUSHWICK YOUTH CENTER

1474 Gates Avenue
Brooklyn, NY 11237

Tel 718-381-9653
Fax 718-381-9650
Email myvoicetheatre@rbscc.org
Web www.rbscc.org

Director of Creative Arts Programming and Education:
Francis William Blacklock

An issues-based youth theatre company, My Voice Theatre is dedicated to developing the whole child by using educational theater programs and staged productions to build self-esteem, confidence, and a sense of community, while celebrating diversity in a supportive, non-competitive environment.

Secondary Category: Theater

NEW YORK TRANSIT MUSEUM
See Primary listing under Museums

NURTUREART
See Primary listing under Visual Arts

NY WRITERS COALITION
See Primary listing under Literary Arts

OPERA ON TAP
See Primary listing under Opera/Music Theater

PAINT ACROSS AMERICA
See Primary listing under Visual Arts

THE PAINTED POT
See Primary listing under Arts Services

PANTONIC STEEL ORCHESTRA
See Primary listing under Music

ARTS FOR CHILDREN/TEENS

PARENTS AS PRIMARY TEACHERS, INC.
198 Hancock Street
Brooklyn, NY 11216
Tel 718-857-8487
Email parentsasprimary
teachers@gmail.com
Web www.parentsasprimaryteachers.org
Executive Director: Yoidette D. Erima

Through arts education programs, Parents As Primary Teachers provides training and support to parents who are homeschooling or complementing their child's conventional classroom education.

Secondary Category: Educational Institutions

PARIJAT DESAI DANCE COMPANY
See Primary listing under Dance

PAUL ROBESON THEATER
See Primary listing under Theater

PDM PERFORMING ARTS CORPORATION
See Primary listing under Multi-Disciplinary Arts

PLG ARTS
See Primary listing under Multi-Disciplinary Arts

PROSPECT PARK & PROSPECT PARK ALLIANCE
See Primary listing under Multi-Disciplinary Arts

PROSPECT PARK AUDUBON CENTER
See Primary listing under Architecture & Urban/Environmental Design

PUPPETWORKS
See Primary listing under Theater

PURELEMENTS: AN EVOLUTION IN DANCE
See Primary listing under Dance

QIIQ PRODUCTIONS
See Primary listing under Theater

RECORDING ADVENTURE WORKSHOP
See Primary listing under Music

REEL WORKS TEEN FILMMAKING
See Primary listing under Film/Video

REVELATION PERFORMING ARTS STUDIO, INC.
See Primary listing under Visual/Performing Arts School

RHYTHM VISIONS PRODUCTION COMPANY, INC.
P.O. Box 24794
Brooklyn, NY 11202
Tel 718-350-4993
Email rhythmvisions1@aol.com
Executive Director: Renita L. Martin

Rhythm Visions Production Company, Inc. (RVPC) was founded in order to counter limited employment opportunities for artists of color and reduced public arts funding while providing professional arts programming to local communities. RVPC aids communities of color by making art accessible, employing artists of color, and empowering youth of color through arts education.

Secondary Category: Multi-Disciplinary Arts

THE RIVIERA
See Primary Listing under Galleries

RUSH PHILANTHROPIC ARTS FOUNDATION (RUSH EAST NY)
334 Grand Avenue
Brooklyn, NY 11238
Site address:
2590 Atlantic Avenue
Brooklyn, NY 11207
Tel 718-230-5002
Fax 718-638-0741
Email mmcneal@rushphilanthropic.org
Web www.rushphilanthropic.org
Director: Meridith McNeal

Rush Philanthropic Arts Foundation was conceived with the intention of broadening access to the arts, engaging youth, and nurturing new and diverse voices in a chronically underserved community. Housed in an 11,000-square-foot building, the foundation includes a gallery space, classrooms, a student gallery, artist studios, office and meeting space, and "green" educational spaces, including a rooftop garden.

Secondary Categories:
Multi-Disciplinary Arts, Visual Arts

RYAN REPERTORY COMPANY
See Primary listing under Theater

SABA -THE ASSOCIATION OF YEMENI AMERICANS
See Primary listing under
Multi-Disciplinary Arts

SCENARIOS USA
See Primary listing under Film/Video

SCHOOL FOR MUSICAL PERFORMANCE
See Primary listing under Music

THE SHADOW BOX THEATRE, INC. (SBT)
138 South Oxford Street, #2A
Brooklyn, NY 11217
Site address:
c/o The Brooklyn Music School Playhouse

126 St. Felix Street
Brooklyn, NY 11217

Tel 718-398-7772
Email shadowboxtheatre@yahoo.com
Web www.shadowboxtheatre.org

Artistic and Executive Director:
Sandra Robbins

The Shadow Box Theatre, Inc. is a musical puppet theater performing for elementary school groups and families at a resident theater, Brooklyn Music School Playhouse, and on tour. Shadow Box's arts education programs include in-school workshops, professional development, parent engagement, and the publication of storybooks and audio based on shows.

Secondary Categories:
Arts Services, Multi-Disciplinary Arts,
Opera/Music Theater

SHADOW PUPPET THEATRE
See Primary listing under Theater

SHARON'S DANCE THEATRE (SDT)
See Primary listing under Dance

SHOSTAKOVICH MUSIC, ARTS, AND SPORT SCHOOL, INC.
See Primary listing under Music

SILVER-BROWN DANCE COMPANY
See Primary listing under Dance

SOL WORKS, INC.
(FROM THE SOL, INC.)
Tel 646-319-4025
Email patrice@solworksinc.org
Web www.solworksinc.org
Founder and Executive Director:
Patrice E. Fenton

Sol Works, Inc. serves to empower and illuminate peoples of African descent and their cultures through the production of multimedia events, artist consultation services, and educational programs. At the heart of every event and educational program is the goal of increasing arts participation within the communities of the African Diaspora.

Secondary Categories: Arts Services,
Multi-Disciplinary Arts, Presenting
Organizations

SOUL TIGERS MARCHING BAND, INC.
See Primary listing under Music

SPOKE THE HUB DANCING, INC.
See Primary listing under
Multi-Disciplinary Arts

STAGES OF LEARNING
138 South Oxford Street
Brooklyn, NY 11217

Tel 718-398-2494
Email info@stagesoflearning.org
Web www.stagesoflearning.org

President and CEO: Floyd Rumohr

Stages of Learning's mission is to help children in grades 3 through 7 learn by using drama to bring curriculum content to life. Stages uses the classroom as a stage on which students can act out each class's academic material under the guidance of a qualified teaching artist.

Secondary Category: Theater

STAGG STREET CENTER FOR CHILDREN
See Primary listing under Visual/Performing Arts School

STREB LABORATORY FOR ACTION MECHANICS
See Primary listing under Multi-Disciplinary Arts

TWW INC. (TALKS WITH WOLVES)
317 Clermont Avenue
Brooklyn, NY 11205

Tel 718-230-4870
Email swilson@talkswithwolves.org
Web www.talkswithwolves.org
Founder, CEO, and President: Stephen A. Wilson, Jr.

TWW Inc. promotes cultural literacy and awareness through a hands-on approach to the visual and performing arts. Guided by a vision of a culturally diverse society with an increased understanding of other civilizations, TWW provides opportunities for creative self-expression via the influence of two specific cultures—African and Native American.

Secondary Categories: Arts Services, Dance, Literary Arts, Theater, Visual Arts

THEATER GARDEN, LTD.
See Primary listing under Opera/Music Theater

TONEL LAKAY DANCE THEATRE
See Primary listing under Dance

TUCKABERRY PRODUCTIONS, INC.
See Primary listing under Theater

VOLCANO LOVE
See Primary listing under Dance

WEEKSVILLE HERITAGE CENTER
See Primary listing under Historical Societies

WEST INDIAN AMERICAN DAY CARNIVAL ASSOCIATION, INC.
See Primary listing under Presenting Organizations

WHITE BIRD PRODUCTIONS
See Primary listing under Theater

WHITE WAVE YOUNG SOON KIM DANCE COMPANY
See Primary listing under Dance

WRIGHT NOW! PERFORMANCE EXPERIENCE
See Primary listing under Dance

YOUNG DANCERS IN REPERTORY, INC.
See Primary listing under Dance

YWCA BROWNSVILLE EARLY LEARNING CENTER
1592 East New York Avenue
Brooklyn, NY 11212

Tel 718-342-2905
Fax 718-342-2905
Email edelva@ywcanyc.org
Web www.ywcanyc.org

Director: Evelyn Delva

The YWCA Brownsville Early Learning Center focuses on the uniqueness of the individual child. The dance and other arts programs encourage children to develop skills and a love of learning.

Secondary Category: Dance

ARTS SERVICES

10 GRAND PRESS
1024 Dean Street, #3
Brooklyn, NY 11238

Email grandpress@yahoo.com
Web www.10grandpress.com

An independent print shop that specializes in fine art printing, 10 Grand Press welcomes newcomers to the medium as well as veteran printmakers. Artists work with a professional printer to create original works on paper, and are supported in their explorations by the prospect of opening up new artistic possibilities.

Secondary Category: Visual Arts

3RD WARD
See Primary listing under Multi-Disciplinary Arts

651 ARTS
See Primary listing under Presenting Organizations

AD HOC ART
See Primary listing under Galleries

AFRICUSSION-PERCUSSION DISCUSSION
See Primary listing under Music

AKILA WORKSONGS, INC.
P.O. Box 250553
Brooklyn, NY 11225

Tel 718-756-8501
Email frontdesk@akilaworksongs.com
Web www.akilaworksongs.com

Founder and President: April R. Silver

AKILA WORKSONGS, Inc. is a leading arts and activism company offering management, public relations, and consulting services. It was founded in 1993 by social entrepreneur, activist, and writer April R. Silver.

ALLIANCE OF RESIDENT THEATRES/ NEW YORK (A.R.T./NEW YORK)
138 South Oxford Street
Brooklyn, NY 11217

Tel 718-398-3078
Fax 718-398-2794
Email jhoman@art-newyork.org,
sbok@art-newyork.org
Web www.offbroadwayonline.com

Manager, South Oxford Space:
Jerry Homan
Assistant Manager, South Oxford Space: Stephanie Bok

A.R.T./New York is the leadership organization for the nonprofit theater community in New York City, providing grants, workshops, loans, and low-cost office and rehearsal space to hundreds of arts groups. South Oxford Space in Fort Greene houses 21 theater groups, and has rehearsal and event space available for rent.

Secondary Category: Theater

ARCHIPELAGO BOOKS
See Primary listing under Literary Arts

ARMSTRONG & ASSOCIATES (MADE IN BROOKLYN PARTNERS)

453 State Street
Brooklyn, NY 11217

Tel 718-330-0776
Email armmic@earthlink.net

Partner: Michael A. Armstrong

Specializing in strategic planning for Brooklyn nonprofit cultural, historical, civic, and social service organizations, Armstrong & Associates provides outreach to the world from a Brooklyn perspective, with extensive experience in marketing, special events, newsletters and other publications, and publicity.

ART GLASS STUDIO

See Primary listing under Visual Arts

ART PLAZA CULTURAL CENTER

620 62nd Street
Brooklyn, NY 11220

Tel 718-567-8800
Email admin@artplazaculturalcenter.org
Web www.artplazaculturalcenter.org

Art Plaza Cultural Center is a multilingual, community-oriented arts center providing dance and music classes for children, teens, and adults. The Center offers a varied dance program from ballroom to Chinese dance to hip hop, and a music school incorporating lessons in piano and keyboards, strings, woodwinds, brass, percussions, and voice.

*Secondary Categories:
Arts for Children/Teens, Dance,
Multi-Disciplinary Arts, Music,
Visual Arts*

ART WITHOUT WALLS/FREE SPACE

See Primary listing under Arts for Children/Teens

ARTS ACTION RESEARCH

423 Atlantic Avenue, #1E
Brooklyn, NY 11217

Tel 718-797-3661
Fax 718-797-3570
Email aaresearch@artsaction.com
Web www.artsaction.com

Director: Nello Mary McDaniel

ARTS Action Research (AAR) is an arts consulting group that works with all types of arts organizations. AAR consults on planning, leadership development and transition, board development, organizational structures and restructuring, audience development, and a full range of development, communication, and operating needs.

ART'S HOUSE SCHOOLS, INC.

See Primary listing under Arts for Children/Teens

AXELLE FINE ARTS, LTD.

312 Atlantic Avenue
Brooklyn, NY 11201

Tel 718-246-1200
Email office@axelle.com
Web www.axelle.com

Headquartered in Brooklyn, and with gallery branches in Manhattan and three other American cities, Axelle Fine Arts, Ltd. offers screenprinting and framing services, in addition to mounting regular solo exhibitions.

Secondary Category: Galleries

BAC GALLERY

See Primary listing under Galleries

BARRONARTS, L.L.C.

63 Flushing Avenue, Unit 196
Brooklyn, NY 11205

Site address:
Brooklyn Navy Yard
63 Flushing Avenue
Brooklyn, NY 11205

Tel 718-797-4260
Fax 718-246-2920
Email info@barronarts.com
Web www.barronarts.com

President: Jeffrey Barron

Barronarts, L.L.C. is a comprehensive arts service organization specializing in stretcher frames, fine art panels, floater frames, canvas and linen stretching and priming, custom pedestals, fine art packing, crating, and shipping. Barronarts also provides custom design and manufacturing of artists' materials and structures such as pedestals, wall shelves, and display cases.

BEDFORD STUYVESANT RESTORATION CORPORATION'S CENTER FOR ARTS AND CULTURE
See Primary listing under Multi-Disciplinary Arts

BEDFORD-STUYVESANT ARTISTS' ASSOCIATION (BESAA)
152 MacDonough Street
Brooklyn, NY 11216

Tel 718-919-8014
Email info@besaa.org
Web www.besaa.org

President: Fedrecia Hartley

The Bedford-Stuyvesant Artists' Association gathers visual artists of various cultures and brings them together in the local community in order to network and support one another. Members exhibit their art all over the neighborhood during an annual "Studio Strut" every October.

Secondary Category: Visual Arts

BOAST COMMUNICATIONS, INC.
37 Troy Avenue
Brooklyn, NY 11213

Email boast@boastinc.org
Web www.boastinc.org

Founder and President: Robin Gibson

An artist development agency, BOAST Communications, Inc. is driven by the firm belief that maximizing an individual's exposure to the arts stimulates the mind as well as the soul. BOAST Communications is dedicated to educating urban communities in theater, dance, and singing.

Secondary Categories: Arts for Children/Teens, Dance

BOOKLYN ARTISTS ALLIANCE
See Primary listing under Visual Arts

BRIC ROTUNDA GALLERY
See Primary listing under Galleries

BRICSTUDIO
See Primary listing under Presenting Organizations

BROOKLYN ART INCUBATOR (BAI)
141 Spencer Street, #104
Brooklyn, NY 11205

Tel 718-208-0526
Email bkartincubator@yahoo.com
Web www.brooklynartincubator.org

President and CEO: Carl M. Hixson

A nonprofit arts organization, Brooklyn Arts Incubator (BAI) works at the community level to provide arts education in classrooms, seminars, assemblies, and professional development workshops, and also provides employment opportunities for teaching artists. BAI artists are developing artistic renderings of ecologically responsible sustainable development sites across the country.

Secondary Categories: Arts for Children/Teens, Film/Video

BROOKLYN ARTISTS GYM
See Primary listing under Visual Arts

BROOKLYN ARTS COUNCIL (BAC)
55 Washington Street, Suite 218
Brooklyn, NY 11201
Tel 718-625-0080
Fax 718-625-3294
Email bac@brooklynartscouncil.org
Web www.brooklynartscouncil.org
President: Ella J. Weiss

Founded in 1966, BAC serves Brooklyn's cultural groups and artists by helping them create and present their work. Programs include the Community Arts Regrant Program, Professional Development Seminars, Arts in Education, BAC Folk Arts, Printmaker's Portfolio Project, the Brooklyn Arts Council International Film Festival, and BAC Gallery. BAC's website includes a comprehensive online Registry of Brooklyn Artists and Directory of Brooklyn Arts Organizations.

Secondary Categories:
Arts for Children/Teens, Dance, Film/Video, Folk Arts, Galleries, Presenting Organizations, Visual Arts

BROOKLYN ARTS COUNCIL INTERNATIONAL FILM FESTIVAL
See Primary listing under Film/Video

BROOKLYN ARTS EXCHANGE
See Primary listing under Multi-Disciplinary Arts

BROOKLYN BALLET
See Primary listing under Dance

BROOKLYN DAILY EAGLE
See Primary listing under Literary Arts

THE BROOKLYN PAPER (GO BROOKLYN)
55 Washington Street, Suite 624
Brooklyn, NY 11201
Tel 718-834-9350, ext. 104
Fax 718-834-9278
Email gobrooklyn@brooklynpaper.com
Web www.brooklynpaper.com

Arts Editor: Adam Rathe
The Brooklyn Paper and Go Brooklyn are providers of Brooklyn arts, culture, style, and dining listings as well as reviews and features which appear both in print and online.

Secondary Category: Literary Arts

THE BROOKLYN RAIL
See Primary listing under Multi-Disciplinary Arts

BROOKLYN TECHNOLOGY EXCHANGE
See Primary listing under Educational Institutions

BROOKLYN WRITERS SPACE
See Primary listing under Literary Arts

BURN BRIGHT LIFEWORKS
479 4th Avenue, #2L
Brooklyn, NY 11215
Tel 917-464-5609
Email burnbrightlifeworks@mail.com
Web www.burnbrightlifeworks.com
Founder: Ozioma Egwuonwu

Burn Bright Lifeworks is a full-service development company specializing in artistic and creative development. Services, seminars, and workshops are offered in a range of topics, including (but not limited to) creative expansion, personal branding, business, networking and marketing strategies, as well as all-around career coaching.

CENTER FOR INTERNATIONAL ART IN COMMUNITY
See Primary listing under Multi-Disciplinary Arts

THE CENTER FOR URBAN PEDAGOGY
See Primary listing under Architecture & Urban/Environmental Design

CHASSIDIC ART INSTITUTE
See Primary listing under Galleries

CHEZ BUSHWICK
See Primary listing under Dance

CIRCUIT PRODUCTIONS, INC.
*See Primary listing under
Multi-Disciplinary Arts*

CLINTON HILL ART GALLERY
See Primary listing under Galleries

**CLINTON HILL SIMPLY ART &
FRAMING GALLERY**
See Primary listing under Galleries

THE CODE FOUNDATION, INC.
456 Nostrand Avenue
Brooklyn, NY 11216

Tel 718-398-1766
Fax 718-623-1855

Executive Director: Dave Daniels

The Code Foundation, Inc. is a vol-
unteer-driven nonprofit organization
located in central Brooklyn whose
mission is to organize, support, and
create partnerships within community
development. The Code's three primary
project areas are music and culture,
youth development and training, and
environment and health awareness.

Secondary Categories: Music, Visual Arts

CONJUNCTIONARTS, INC.
See Primary listing under Visual Arts

COOL CULTURE
*See Primary listing under Arts for
Children/Teens*

**COURIER-LIFE PUBLISHING (CNG
COMMUNITY NEWSPAPER GROUP)**
1733 Sheepshead Bay Road
Brooklyn, NY 11235

Tel 718-615-2500
Fax 718-615-3817
Email dehnj@aol.com
Web www.courierlife.net

Publisher: Dan Holt

Courier-Life Publishing is a community newspaper and magazine
publisher based in Brooklyn, with 14
weekly newspapers covering all of the
borough's neighborhoods. In addition,

Courier-Life publishes several ethnic
newspapers and the weekly arts
guide 24/7.

COVENANT DANCE THEATRE OF BROOKLYN
See Primary listing under Dance

CREATE!
*See Primary listing under Arts for
Children/Teens*

CREATIVE WOMEN'S NETWORK (CWN)
P.O. Box 290-682
Brooklyn, NY 11229

Tel 917-881-5134
Fax 718-951-7218
Email creativwomenntwk@aol.com
Web www.creativewomensnetwork.com
or www.sonicbids.com/lisaroma

Founder and Director: Lisa Roma

Creative Women's Network (CWN)
promotes healing, education, and
empowerment through the arts—specifically by providing a range of creative
and professional development services,
such as book, magazine, newsletter,
and graphic design, printing and publishing, creative writing, performance,
other arts workshops, and much more.

*Secondary Categories:
Arts for Children/Teens, Computer
Arts/New Media, Literary Arts,
Multi-Disciplinary Arts, Music, Theater,
Visual Arts*

DANCES AND DRUMS OF AFRICA, INC.
See Primary listing under Dance

DOBBIN MILL
See Primary listing under Visual Arts

ARTS SERVICES

DOWNTOWN BROOKLYN PARTNERSHIP
15 MetroTech Center, 19th Floor
Brooklyn, NY 11201
Tel 718-403-1600
Fax 718-403-1650
Email info@dbpartnership.org
Web www.dbpartnership.org
President: Joseph F. Chan

The Downtown Brooklyn Partnership works with local elected officials, academic institutions, arts organizations, community groups, and developers to aid in the economic revitalization of downtown Brooklyn, as well as to create a vibrant, mixed-use cultural district around BAM. It also sponsors live music events and provides affordable office space to nonprofit creative organizations.

Secondary Category: Architecture & Urban/Environmental Design

DUMBO ARTS CENTER
See Primary listing under Visual Arts

DZIECI
See Primary listing under Theater

THE ELEVENTEN GALLERY
See Primary listing under Galleries

ELSIE MANAGEMENT
Brooklyn Navy Yard
Brooklyn, NY 11205
Tel 718-797-4577
Email info@elsieman.org
Web www.elsieman.org
Director: Laura Colby

Delivering live performances to communities across the globe, Elsie Management offers a broad spectrum of celebrated national and international touring artists. Its diverse roster includes theater, physical theater, special attractions, world music, and the finest in contemporary dance.

Secondary Categories: Dance, Music, Opera/Music Theater, Performance Art

ETGALLERIES
See Primary listing under Galleries

EVA DEAN DANCE
See Primary listing under Dance

FLATBUSH YMCA
1401 Flatbush Avenue
Brooklyn, NY 11210
Tel 718-469-8100
Email djourdain@ymcanyc.org
Executive Director: Dordy Jourdain

Started in 1924, the Flatbush YMCA is a community-based organization that promotes positive values through programs and services that build spirit, mind, and body. The Flatbush YMCA offers civic engagement and community service programs, after school and early childhood development programs, arts and humanities programs designed to develop artistic talents and skills, and many other services.

Secondary Categories: Arts for Children/Teens, Dance

FORTH ESTATE
19 Thames Street
Brooklyn, NY 11206
Tel 917-677-8008
Fax 917-677-8008
Email info@forthestate.com
Web www.forthestate.com
Owner: Luther Davis

Forth Estate was founded in 2005 by master printer Luther Davis and printmaker Glen Baldridge in the interest of producing editioned works by emerging artists using both traditional and technologically innovative approaches to printmaking. Forth Estate prints are in the collections of the New York Public Library, MoMA, and the Jundt Art Museum.

Secondary Category: Visual Arts

FORTY GREENE AVENUE CULTURAL CENTER
40 Greene Avenue
Brooklyn, NY 11238

Alternate address:
54 Greene Avenue, 2nd Floor
Brooklyn, NY 11238

Tel 718-783-9794
Fax 718-783-1549
Founder and Board President:
Josephine English

Forty Greene Avenue Cultural Center acts as a forum for artists and community to create, develop, and preserve artistic expressions reflecting the experiences of people of African descent. The center produces and presents critically acclaimed productions, fosters collaboration between emerging and established artists, and offers training and production opportunities in the performing arts.

Secondary Category: Performance Art, Presenting Organizations, Theater

FREE103POINT9
See Primary listing under Multi-Disciplinary Arts

GALERIA GALOU
See Primary listing under Galleries

GIBA IN DESIGN
7422 15th Avenue, #2
Brooklyn, NY 11228

Tel 347-268-1024
Email gbashour@gmail.com
Owner: Gina Bashour

GiBa in Design offers a range of services at artist-friendly prices, including video editing, analog transfers (VHS and audiocassette to DVD and CD), graphic design (logos, business cards, postcards, brochures, and other print media), videography, and photograph and slide digitizing, archiving, and retouching.

Secondary Category: Film/Video

GOLOBOROTKO'S STUDIO
See Primary listing under Visual Arts

THE GOWANUS STUDIO SPACE, INC.
See Primary listing under Multi-Disciplinary Arts

HEART OF BROOKLYN (HEART OF BROOKLYN: A CULTURAL PARTNERSHIP)
789 Washington Avenue
Brooklyn, NY 11238

Tel 718-638-7700
Fax 718-638-7740
Web www.heartofbrooklyn.org
Director: Ellen F. Salpeter

Heart of Brooklyn is a partnership of the leading cultural organizations located near Grand Army Plaza—the Brooklyn Botanical Garden, the Brooklyn Children's Museum, the Brooklyn Museum, the Brooklyn Public Library, Prospect Park, and the Prospect Park Zoo.

Secondary Categories: Architecture & Urban/Environmental Design, Arts for Children/Teens, Educational Institutions, Literary Arts, Multi-Disciplinary Arts, Museums, Music, Visual Arts

THE HOGAR COLLECTION
See Primary listing under Galleries

IFETAYO CULTURAL ARTS
See Primary listing under Multi-Disciplinary Arts

IMAGINE PROJECT, INC.
See Primary listing under Arts for Children/Teens

INTERDANCE FOUNDATION, INC.
See Primary listing under Dance

INTERNATIONAL AFRICAN ARTS
FESTIVAL (AFRICAN STREET FESTIVAL)
P.O. Box 47-1730
Brooklyn, NY 11247
Site address:
1360 Fulton Street
Brooklyn, NY 11216
Tel 718-638-6700
Fax 718-638-3707
Email info@iaafestival.org
Web www.iaafestival.org

Chairman: Basir Mchawi

The International African Arts Festival plays a central role in Brooklyn's African arts community. The Festival's dance, music, and spoken word programs consist of a range of traditions, from Yoruba to Rastafarian, art forms from steel bands to gospel choirs, genres from jazz to reggae, and nationalities from Senegalese to Garifuna.

Secondary Categories: Multi-Disciplinary Arts, Presenting Organizations

K.S. J.A.M.M. DANCE TROUPE, INC.
See Primary listing under Dance

KINGS BAY YM-YWHA
See Primary listing under Presenting Organizations

KLEZMER PLUS
See Primary listing under Music

LEWIS GALLERY
See Primary listing under Galleries

LIKE THE SPICE
See Primary listing under Galleries

LMAKPROJECTS
See Primary listing under Galleries

LOTHAR OSTERBURG STUDIO
232 3rd Street, #B-303
Brooklyn, NY 11215
Tel 212-627-0002
Email lotharosterburg@earthlink.net
Web www.lotharosterburg
photogravure.com

Master Printer: Lothar Osterburg

Lothar Osterburg Studio specializes in collaborative photogravure plate-making and printing. It also offers collaborative projects in etching, weekend and week-long workshops for those who want to learn the process, and a reasonably-priced rental studio with intaglio plate-making and editioning capabilities.

Secondary Category: Visual Arts

LOTUS PROMOTIONS
Tel 917-415-7439
Email info@lotuspromotions.com
Web www.lotuspromotions.com

President: Yvette M. Pennacchia

Lotus Promotions brings beauty into the world by showcasing original fine art to industry experts such as designers, architects, and other corporate buyers and private collectors. By visiting the Lotus Promotions online gallery, clients have the opportunity to view works by national and international painters, sculptors, photographers, and multimedia visual artists.

MANY MOODS PRODUCTION COMPANY
See Primary listing under Music

MCCAIG-WELLES GALLERY
See Primary listing under Galleries

MICHAEL ALAN'S DRAW-A-THON
68 Jay Street, #909
Brooklyn, NY 11201
Email artisticrevolution@gmail.com
Web www.michaelalanart.com

Founder: Michael Alan

Michael Alan's Draw-A-Thon is a figure drawing and performance art marathon that offers an alternative to conventional figure drawing by adding narrative, theatrical, and musical components in a public space where artists create and form community. The event is presented in DUMBO and draws 40 to 60 artists of all ages and skill levels every week.

Secondary Categories: Film/Video, Galleries, Music, Performance Art, Theater, Visual Arts

MILL BASIN DELI AND FINE ART GALLERY
See Primary listing under Galleries

THE MUDPIT
228 Manhattan Avenue
Brooklyn, NY 11206

Tel 718-218-9424
Email mudpitnyc@aol.com
Web www.mudpitnyc.com

Owner: Cindy Gatto

The Mudpit is a full-service clay facility, providing classes in wheel-throwing, handbuilding, tilemaking, and moldmaking, as well as selling ceramic supplies and renting space. The Mudpit has 12 wheels, an extruder, slabroller, tile press, slipcasting table, 4 electric kilns, a raku kiln, saggar kiln, and a Cone 10 reduction kiln.

Secondary Categories: Arts for Children/Teens, Galleries, Visual Arts

MUSEUM OF CONTEMPORARY AFRICAN DIASPORAN ART
See Primary listing under Museums

NIA THEATRICAL PRODUCTION COMPANY, INC.
See Primary listing under Theater

NOT FOR PROFIT PICTURES
See Primary listing under Presenting Organizations

NUNU GALLERIE
See Primary listing under Galleries

NURTUREART
See Primary listing under Visual Arts

NY WRITERS COALITION
See Primary listing under Literary Arts

ONE SIXTY GLASS
160 Berry Street
Brooklyn, NY 11211

Tel 718-486-9620
Fax 718-486-9615
Email info@onesixtyglass.com
Web www.onesixtyglass.com

Owner: Michiko Sakano

One Sixty Glass is a glassblowing studio in Williamsburg. Open to the public, One Sixty Glass offers glassblowing classes for beginners, rentals, and items for sale. Its facility is capable of everything from creating large-scale sculptures to hosting events, and services range from commissioned glass work to antique repairs.

Secondary Category: Galleries

ORANGE VECTOR
372 2nd Street, #4C
Brooklyn, NY 11215

Tel 917-374-11215
Email orangevector@gmail.com
Web www.orangevector.com

Co-Directors: Jamie E. Kruse and Stephen Nguyen

ORANGE VECTOR is a collaboration between artists Jamie E. Kruse and Stephen Nguyen, who support their art practices through freelance graphic and web design, among other activities. ORANGE VECTOR specializes in creative online portfolios as well as the supporting print materials needed for exhibition and individual artist promotion.

Secondary Category: Visual Arts

PAGE 73 PRODUCTIONS
See Primary listing under Theater

ARTS SERVICES

THE PAINTED POT
339 Smith Street
Brooklyn, NY 11231

Tel 718-222-0334
Fax 718-222-0335
Email mail@paintedpot.com
Web www.paintedpot.com

Director: Lisa M. Meyer

The Painted Pot is a "paint your own" pottery studio as well as a full working pottery studio with classes for adults and children. The Painted Pot's studio offers classes for beginning and advanced students, and also has nine potter's wheels, a slab roller, extruder, and a back yard for all students to enjoy.

Secondary Categories: Arts for Children/Teens, Visual Arts

PARK SLOPE GALLERY
See Primary listing under Galleries

PAUL ROBESON THEATER
See Primary listing under Theater

PERIPHERAL MEDIA PROJECTS, INC.
See Primary listing under Visual Arts

PIER GLASS (MARY ELLEN BUXTON AND KEVIN KUTCH)
499 Van Brunt Street, Suite 2A
Brooklyn, NY 11231

Tel 718-237-2073
Fax 718-237-0894
Email buxtonkutch@msn.com
Web www.pierglass.net

Partner: Kevin W. Kutch

Pier Glass is an artisan glass studio and shop located at the Beard Street Warehouse in Red Hook. The studio offers the handblown designs of its founders/artists, including thick-walled, multi-colored, multiple-bubbled functional glass sculpture such as bowls and vases, and decorative perfume bottles.

Secondary Category: Visual Arts

POC DOC FILM DEVELOPMENT, INC.
See Primary listing under Film/Video

PURELEMENTS: AN EVOLUTION IN DANCE
See Primary listing under Dance

REALFORM
See Primary listing under Visual Arts

REDHAWK NATIVE AMERICAN ARTS COUNCIL
726 42nd Street
Brooklyn, NY 11232

Tel 718-686-9297
Email redhawkarts@mindspring.com
Web www.redhawkcouncil.org

Director: Cliff Matias

A Native American arts and cultural organization, the Redhawk Native American Arts Council supports and serves First Nations artists by presenting educational programs and hosting festivals and Native celebrations throughout the New York City area.

Secondary Category: Folk Arts

REVELATION PERFORMING ARTS STUDIO, INC.
See Primary listing under Visual/Performing Arts School

ROOM 58
See Primary listing under Literary Arts

SABA - THE ASSOCIATION OF YEMENI AMERICANS
See Primary listing under Multi-Disciplinary Arts

THE SHADOW BOX THEATRE, INC.
See Primary listing under Arts for Children/Teens

SLATE GALLERY
See Primary listing under Galleries

SOL WORKS, INC.
See Primary listing under Arts for Children/Teens

SPOKE THE HUB DANCING, INC.
See Primary listing under
Multi-Disciplinary Arts

STACY STEWART SMITH GALLERY
See Primary listing under Visual Arts

TONEL LAKAY DANCE THEATRE
See Primary listing under Dance

TWW INC.
See Primary listing under Arts for
Children/Teens

UNION STREET DANCE
See Primary listing under Dance

WAGMAG
See Primary listing under Visual Arts

WALKER INTERNATIONAL
COMMUNICATIONS GROUP, INC.
See Primary listing under
Multi-Disciplinary Arts

WEEKSVILLE HERITAGE CENTER
See Primary listing under Historical
Societies

WEST INDIAN AMERICAN DAY
CARNIVAL ASSOCIATION, INC.
See Primary listing under Presenting
Organizations

WISELEPHANT
45 Main Street
Brooklyn, NY 11201

Tel 347-417-7690
Email info@wiselephant.com
Web www.wiselephant.com
**Managing Partner and Channel
Director, Art and Design:**
Jason Moriber

Wiselephant is dedicated to launch-
ing and sustaining any artist's creative
ventures. To that end, Wiselephant has
assembled a management team with
broad, diverse experience across many
fields to counsel artists and support,
market, and manage the business
aspects of their careers.

Secondary Categories: Computer
Arts/New Media, Film/Video,
Performance Art, Visual Arts

WORLD EATER RECORDINGS, NYC
See Primary listing under Music

ZION GALLERY
See Primary listing under Galleries

ARTS SERVICES

I'm not sure a bad person can write a good book. If art doesn't make us better, then what on earth is it for?

ALICE WALKER

COMPUTER ARTS/ NEW MEDIA

0.00156 ACRES
See Primary listing under Visual Arts

ART GALLERY AT KINGSBOROUGH
COMMUNITY COLLEGE, CUNY
See Primary listing under Galleries

ARTMOVINGPROJECTS
166 North 12th Street
Brooklyn, NY 11211

Tel 917-301-6680 / 917-301-0306
Email info@artmovingprojects.com
Web www.artmovingprojects.com

Co-Directors: Aron Namenwirth and
Nancy Horowitz

Open since 1995, Williamsburg's
artMovingProjects specializes in
conceptual, political, new media, and
performance art.

*Secondary Categories: Performance Art,
Visual Arts*

AWAAM: ARAB WOMEN ACTIVE IN
THE ARTS AND MEDIA
464 3rd Avenue
Brooklyn, NY 11215

Tel 718-399-9851
Web www.awaam.org

Founding Director: Mona K. Eldahry

AWAAM's goal is to empower a generation of young women and girls with the
necessary community-organizing and
media skills to act as leaders within
their communities, which have endured
increasing hardship in recent years.
As Arab and Muslim women, AWAAM
endeavors to position themselves as
producers, rather than objects, of
mass media.

Secondary Category: Film/Video

BCAT/ BROOKLYN COMMUNITY
ACCESS TELEVISION
See Primary listing under Film/Video

BRIC ARTS | MEDIA | BROOKLYN
*See Primary listing under
Multi-Disciplinary Arts*

BROOKLYN COLLEGE CONSERVATORY
OF MUSIC
See Primary listing under Music

BROOKLYN TECHNOLOGY EXCHANGE
*See Primary listing under Educational
Institutions*

CHEZ BUSHWICK
See Primary listing under Dance

COMMUNITY THEATRE INTERNATIONALE
See Primary listing under Performance Art

CREATIVE WOMEN'S NETWORK
See Primary listing under Arts Services

DARMSTADT
See Primary listing under Music

DIGITAL STORY WORKSHOP
See Primary listing under Film/Video

FREE103POINT9
*See Primary listing under
Multi-Disciplinary Arts*

GALAPAGOS ART SPACE
*See Primary listing under
Multi-Disciplinary Arts*

THE GOWANUS STUDIO SPACE, INC.
See Primary listing under
Multi-Disciplinary Arts

ISSUE PROJECT ROOM
See Primary listing under
Multi-Disciplinary Arts

KINGS BAY YM-YWHA
See Primary listing under Presenting
Organizations

LIKE THE SPICE
See Primary listing under Galleries

LMAKPROJECTS
See Primary listing under Galleries

**LONG ISLAND UNIVERSITY MEDIA
ARTS DEPARTMENT, BROOKLYN
CAMPUS**
See Primary listing under Educational
Institutions

MONKEY TOWN
See Primary listing under Film/Video

NAT CREOLE ONLINE
164 133rd Street, #3
New York, NY 10030

Tel 646-644-5179
Email ph@natcreole.com
Web www.natcreole.com

Founder and Editor: Phillip Harvey

Site address:
47 Duffield Street #3
Brooklyn, NY 11201

Nat Creole is an online magazine dedicated to offering an entertaining yet
informed perspective on the literature,
politics, art, and music of contemporary global culture, and to broadening
the conversation on the arts and their
role in an increasingly interconnected
world. *Nat Creole* also provides opportunities to artists and authors who
don't have the support structures necessary to build their careers effectively.

*Secondary Categories: Dance, Literary
Arts, Music, Presenting Organizations,
Visual Arts*

TABLA RASA GALLERY
See Primary listing under Galleries

TROIKA RANCH
See Primary listing under
Multi-Disciplinary Arts

VERTEXLIST
138 Bayard Street
Brooklyn, NY 11222

Tel 646-258-3792
Email info@vertexlist.net
Web www.vertexlist.net

Director: Marcin Ramocki

An artist-run space in Williamsburg,
vertexList was founded in 2003 with
the mission of supporting emerging
media artists. vertexList seeks artwork
conceptually involved in exposing the
codes of post-capitalist culture, via
both new and traditional media.

*Secondary Categories: Film/Video,
Galleries, Multi-Disciplinary Arts,
Visual Arts*

WEONE FILM PRODUCTIONS
See Primary listing under Film/Video

WISELEPHANT
See Primary listing under Arts Services

WORLD EATER RECORDINGS, NYC
See Primary listing under Music

DANCE

651 ARTS
See Primary listing under Presenting Organizations

ADRIENNECELESTEFADJO DANCE (ACF DANCE, INC.)
Tel 347-645-7068
Email info@acfdance.com
Web www.acfdance.com
Artistic and Executive Director: Adrienne C. Fadjo

Under the artistic direction of Adrienne Celeste Fadjo, ACF Dance, Inc. performs pieces of "psychological complexity and depth" (The Brooklyn Rail) that range in both movement style and choreographic approach. Fadjo's work—primarily rooted in, but not limited to, modern dance—is strongly based in music, and always explores the human condition.

Secondary Category: Performance Art

ALLEN|BODY GROUP
See Primary listing under Multi-Disciplinary Arts

AMERICAN CREATIVE DANCE
70 Fourth Place
Brooklyn, NY 11231
Tel 917-301-6084
Email nvn@americancreativedance.org
Web www.americancreativedance.org
Director: Nancy Vining Van Ness

American Creative Dance produces new works of music, theater, and dance using a unique form of collaborative composition that allows artists to create in performance.

Secondary Category: Music

AMERICAN THEATRE OF HARLEM
See Primary listing under Theater

ART PLAZA CULTURAL CENTER
See Primary listing under Arts Services

ARTICHOKE DANCE COMPANY
121 Sterling Place
Brooklyn, NY 11217
Tel 917-627-8770
Email artichokedance@artichoke dance.org
Web www.artichokedance.org
Artistic and Executive Director: Lynn Neuman

Artichoke Dance Company's daring partnering and passion-filled movement depict human relationships in action. The company collaborates with artists in various media in presenting original movement-based works. Believers in art's power to effect positive change, Artichoke offers a range of educational programs appropriate for a wide variety of populations.

Secondary Categories: Arts for Children/Teens, Multi-Disciplinary Arts, Performance Art

ART'S HOUSE SCHOOLS, INC.
See Primary listing under Arts for Children/Teens

ARTSCETERA
See Primary listing under Arts for Children/Teens

DANCE

ATTITUDE: THE DANCERS' MAGAZINE
93 Montague Street, Suite 303
Brooklyn, NY 11201
Email dancegiantsteps@hotmail.com
Web www.geocities.com/dance
attitude

Editor-in-Chief: Bernadine Jennings

Attitude: *The Dancers' Magazine* was launched in 1982 as an artist-initiated trade journal and audience development tool. Attitude profiles diverse dance artists from both the New York region and the global community, and also publishes features, reviews, research news, ads, and announcements.

Secondary Categories: Folk Arts, Literary Arts, Multi-Disciplinary Arts, Music, Theater

BAC ARTS IN EDUCATION
See Primary listing under Arts for Children/Teens

BAC FOLK ARTS
See Primary listing under Folk Arts

BAHIA KAO
See Primary listing under Music

BAM
See Primary listing under Multi-Disciplinary Arts

BAMSS THEATRE WORKS
See Primary listing under Arts for Children/Teens

BEDFORD STUYVESANT RESTORATION CORPORATION'S CENTER FOR ARTS AND CULTURE -YOUTH ARTS ACADEMY
See Primary listing under Visual/Performing Arts School

BETTER BROOKLYN COMMUNITY CENTER
See Primary listing under Arts for Children/Teens

BIG DANCE THEATER
See Primary listing under Theater

BOAST COMMUNICATIONS, INC.
See Primary listing under Arts Services

BREEDINGGROUND PRODUCTIONS
See Primary listing under Multi-Disciplinary Arts

BRIC ARTS | MEDIA | BROOKLYN
See Primary listing under Multi-Disciplinary Arts

THE BRICK THEATER, INC.
See Primary listing under Theater

BRICSTUDIO
See Primary listing under Presenting Organizations

BRIGHTON BALLET THEATER (BBT/ SCHOOL OF RUSSIAN BALLET)
2001 Oriental Boulevard
Building T7, 2nd Floor, Room 7211
Brooklyn, NY 11235

Tel 718-769-9161
Email bbt@onebox.com
Web www.brightonballet.org

Founder and Executive Director: Irina Roizin

A nonprofit professional school of Russian ballet and folk dance, Brighton Ballet Theatre (BBT) is dedicated to providing the highest quality dance education for children ages 2-19. Established in 1987, BBT sits in the heart of New York's Russian cultural district (Brighton Beach/Manhattan Beach), on the campus of Kingsborough Community College.

Secondary Category: Folk Arts

BROOKLYN ARTS COUNCIL
See Primary listing under Arts Services

BROOKLYN ARTS EXCHANGE
See Primary listing under Multi-Disciplinary Arts

BROOKLYN BALLET
145 Hicks Street
Brooklyn, NY 11201
Site address:
154 Hicks Street, #A-54
Brooklyn, NY 11201
Tel 718-246-0146
Fax 718-624-5198
Email brooklynballet@earthlink.net
Web www.brooklynballet.org

Artistic Director: Lynn F. Parkerson

The Brooklyn Ballet is a contemporary ballet company dedicated to artistic excellence and education. The company has a professional dance school presenting a season of performances, and serves the diverse community through educational outreach projects.

Secondary Category: Arts Services

BROOKLYN CENTER FOR THE PERFORMING ARTS AT BROOKLYN COLLEGE (BCBC)
See Primary listing under Presenting Organizations

BROOKLYN COLLEGE PREPARATORY CENTER FOR THE PERFORMING ARTS
See Primary listing under Music

BROOKLYN MUSIC SCHOOL
See Primary listing under Visual/Performing Arts School

BROOKLYN PHILHARMONIC
See Primary listing under Music

BROOKLYN PUBLIC LIBRARY
See Primary listing under Literary Arts

THE BROOKLYN RAIL
See Primary listing under Multi-Disciplinary Arts

THE BUSHWICK STARR
See Primary listing under Theater

CAROLYN HULSE DANCE TROUPE
See Primary listing under Performance Art

CAVE
See Primary listing under Multi-Disciplinary Arts

CELEBRATE BROOKLYN PERFORMING ARTS FESTIVAL
See Primary listing under Presenting Organizations

CHEZ BUSHWICK
304 Boerum Street, #23
Brooklyn, NY 11206
Tel 718-418-4405
Fax 718-418-4405
Email info@chezbushwick.net
Web www.chezbushwick.net

Founder: Jonah Bokaer

Chez Bushwick is an artist-run organization dedicated to interdisciplinary art and performance, with a strong focus on experimental dance. Since its inception in 2002, the organization has offered a $5 subsidy for rehearsal space, thereby fostering the creation of new work. Chez Bushwick also sponsors monthly performance programs that encourage creative risk-taking.

Secondary Categories: Arts Services, Computer Arts/New Media, Film/Video, Multi-Disciplinary Arts, Music, Performance Art

CIRCUIT PRODUCTIONS, INC.
See Primary listing under Multi-Disciplinary Arts

CIRKULOCK, INC.
See Primary listing under Folk Arts

CONJUNTO NUEVO MILENIO
See Primary listing under Folk Arts

DANCE

CORA, INC.
(SHANNON HUMMEL/CORA DANCE)
117 4th Place, Suite 3A
Brooklyn, NY 11231

Tel 718-858-2520
Email shummel@coradance.org
Web www.coradance.org

Artistic Director: Shannon L. Hummel

Cora, Inc. is a contemporary company performing the collaborative choreographic works of Shannon Hummel. Sophisticated and inventive, these works are vivid explorations of the human condition and brought to life by an outstanding ensemble of performers. As well as work for the formal stage, the company is dedicated to bringing dance to underserved communities, particularly those in isolated rural areas.

Secondary Category: Arts for Children/Teens

COVENANT DANCE THEATRE OF BROOKLYN (CDT)
1600 Sheepshead Bay Road
Brooklyn, NY 11235

Tel 718-891-6199
Fax 718-891-0259
Email covdance@aol.com
Web www.covenantdance.com

Artistic Director: Marla A. Hirokawa

Covenant Dance Theatre (CDT) seeks to serve, inspire, and refresh through dance, and to promote esteem for the arts. Novice and professional artists collaborate in original story dance works, and CDT also offers two arts in education programs that provide performances and workshops linked with school curricula.

Secondary Categories: Arts for Children/Teens, Arts Services, Multi-Disciplinary Arts, Music

CPR - CENTER FOR PERFORMANCE RESEARCH
140 Second Avenue, #501
New York, NY 10003

Site address:
361 Manhattan Avenue
Brooklyn, NY 11211

Email info@johnjasperse.org

Founders: John Jasperse and Jonah Bokaer

CPR's founders, John Jasperse and Jonah Bokaer, envision a vital center for research, education, and presentation of contemporary dance and performance in Williamsburg, owned and operated by two organizations: John Jasperse Company/Thin Man Dance, Inc., and Jonah Bokaer/Chez Bushwick, Inc.

CREATE!
See Primary listing under Arts for Children/Teens

CREATIVE OUTLET DANCE THEATRE OF BROOKLYN (CO)
80 Hanson Place, Suite 303
Brooklyn, NY 11217

Tel 718-636-9312
Fax 718-857-4997
Email info@creativeoutlet.org
Web www.creativeoutlet.org

Artistic Director: Jamel Gaines

Creative Outlet Dance Theatre of Brooklyn was founded in 1994 to provide an environment that nurtures artists' spiritual, mental, and physical well-being. Creative Outlet's mission is to supply the means for artists to develop and perfect their craft through dance, theater, spoken word, film, and live music.

Secondary Category: Arts for Children/Teens

CYNTHIA KING DANCE STUDIO, INC.

1256 Prospect Avenue
Brooklyn, NY 11218

Tel 718-437-0101
Email cynthiakingdance@aol.com
Web www.cynthiakingdance.com

Director: Cynthia King

Cynthia King Dance Studio, Inc. is dedicated to providing a fertile training ground for dancers and a place for teachers/choreographers to present new and original works. Cynthia King's own innovative curriculum embraces traditional to emerging styles, inspiring dancers to strive for both technical excellence and meaningful artistry.

Secondary Category: Arts for Children/Teens

DANCE GIANT STEPS, INC.
See Primary listing under Multi-Disciplinary Arts

DANCE THEATRE ETCETERA
See Primary listing under Multi-Disciplinary Arts

DANCES AND DRUMS OF AFRICA, INC. (CHARLES MOORE DANCE THEATRE)

397 Bridge Street
Brooklyn, NY 11201

Tel 718-254-0670
Artistic Director: Ella T. Moore

One of the oldest nonprofit African American arts organizations in Brooklyn, Dances and Drums of Africa, Inc., aka the Charles Moore Dance Theatre, was founded in 1974 by Charles and Ella Moore to demonstrate the beauty and variety of African, Caribbean, and African American culture.

Secondary Categories: Arts for Children/Teens, Arts Services, Multi-Disciplinary Arts, Music, Theater

DANCEWAVE

422 Greenwood Avenue
Brooklyn, NY 11218

Tel 718-522-4696
Email dwavebklyn@yahoo.com
Web www.dancewave.org

Executive and Artistic Director: Diane Jacobowitz

Dancewave, a premiere arts and education organization, offers young people unique exposure to a world-class level of performing arts study through programs which include arts education in New York City public schools, unique pre-professional companies of young people performing the work of world-renowned choreographers, and comprehensive training that offers young people the opportunity to study a wide range of dance disciplines.

Secondary Category: Arts for Children/Teens

DARRAH CARR DANCE

445 Grand Street
Brooklyn, NY 11211

Tel 917-975-9152
Email darrah@darrahcarrdance.com
Web www.darrahcarrdance.com

Artistic Director: Darrah Carr

Darrah Carr Dance specializes in ModERIN, a unique blend of traditional Irish step and contemporary modern dance, and offers workshops for children and adults at the ModERIN Club in Williamsburg. The club is also the home of DCWee, a junior company featuring young performers ages 8-14 years.

Secondary Category: Folk Arts

DRUMSONG AFRICAN BALLET THEATRE, INC.
See Primary listing under Multi-Disciplinary Arts

DANCE

DUŠAN TÝNEK DANCE THEATRE
415 9th Street, #54
Brooklyn, NY 11215
Tel 718-249-7708
Email dwayne@dusantynek.org
Web www.dusantynek.org
President: Dwayne Linville

Dušan Týnek Dance Theatre is an eight-member modern dance performance group named one of New York's "top five dance companies of 2006" by the *New York Times*. Since 2003, the company has held home seasons at The Kitchen, Dance Theater Workshop, Ailey Citigroup Theater, and Joyce SoHo.

Secondary Category: Theater

EL PEQUEÑO ARTISTA
See Primary listing under Arts for Children/Teens

ELSIE MANAGEMENT
See Primary listing under Arts Services

ERROL GRIMES DANCE GROUP
P.O. Box 05026, Pratt Station
Brooklyn, NY 11205
Site address:
50 Taaffe Place
Brooklyn, NY 11205
Tel 718-596-0560
Email info@egdance.org
Web www.egdance.org
Artistic Director: Errol Grimes

The Errol Grimes Dance Group seeks to explore, through contemporary dance, themes that are informed by an American as well as Afro West Indian perspective. The Errol Grimes Dance Group also conducts residencies, workshops, lectures, and symposia in the communities in which it performs.

EVA DEAN DANCE
725 Union Street
Brooklyn, NY 11215
Tel 718-857-8368
Fax 718-857-8368
Email studio@evadeandance.org
Web www.evadeandance.org
Artistic Director: Eva Dean

The mission of Eva Dean Dance is to strengthen dance as a performing art in New York City—by developing and reaching diverse audiences, by supporting the work of other choreographers and dancers, by creating and performing the choreography of Eva Dean, and by teaching Eva Dean Dance technique and repertory.

Secondary Category: Arts Services

EVIDENCE, INC.
(EVIDENCE, A DANCE COMPANY)
80 Hanson Place, Suite 605
Brooklyn, NY 11217
Tel 718-230-4633
Fax 718-230-4641
Email info@evidencedance.com
Web www.evidencedance.com
Artistic Director: Ronald K. Brown

Brooklyn native and choreographer Ronald K. Brown founded Evidence, Inc. in 1985 with the mission of promoting understanding of the human experience in the African Diaspora through dance and storytelling. The company is committed to engaging dance enthusiasts of all ages through its various educational programs, outreach activities, and public performances.

FILIPINO ARTS & MUSIC ENSEMBLE
See Primary listing under Music

FLATBUSH YMCA
See Primary listing under Arts Services

GALAPAGOS ART SPACE
See Primary listing under
Multi-Disciplinary Arts

**GOSPEL DANCE THEATRE
(SUTRANA DANCE THEATRE)**
861 East 45th Street
Brooklyn, NY 11203

Tel 718-583-0020

Artistic and Financial Director:
A. Cecilia Carrington

Gospel Dance Theatre aims to provide both the discipline and joy of dance to young and old via its professional dance company. It offers dance workshops in its "Dance To Go" program for community organizations, dances of worship and praise, available to church groups and other organizations, and apprentice dancers trained by GDT.

*Secondary Category: Arts for
Children/Teens*

THE GOSSIP FACTORY
See Primary listing under Theater

GREENWICH MORRIS MEN
See Primary listing under Folk Arts

**HALBERT BARTON AND EL BOMBAZO
DE BROOKLYN**
See Primary listing under Folk Arts

IFETAYO CULTURAL ARTS
*See Primary listing under
Multi-Disciplinary Arts*

ILAND, INC. (BIRDBRAIN DANCE)
Email info@ilandart.org
Web www.ilandart.org

Artistic Director: Jennifer Monson

iLAND, Inc. (Interdisciplinary Laboratory for Art, Nature and Dance) investigates the power of dance to illuminate a kinetic understanding of the world. Incorporated in 2004, with a fundamental commitment to environmental sustainability in art and the urban context, iLAND cultivates cross-disciplin-

ary research among artists, environmentalists, scientists, urban designers, and other fields.

Secondary Category: Multi-Disciplinary Arts

IMAGINE PROJECT, INC.
*See Primary listing under Arts for
Children/Teens*

INTERDANCE FOUNDATION, INC.
459 State Street
Brooklyn, NY 11217

Tel 718-237-0567
Email gdunaif@i-dance.org
Web www.i-dance.org

Executive Director: Gwendolyn Dunaif

InterDance Foundation, Inc. is dedicated to preserving and promoting traditional dances from around the world. Through its i-Dance awards program, the Foundation offers scholarships and grants to individuals and companies in the field of traditional dance.

*Secondary Categories: Arts Services,
Folk Arts*

ISSUE PROJECT ROOM
*See Primary listing under
Multi-Disciplinary Arts*

DANCE

K.S. J.A.M.M. DANCE TROUPE, INC.
229 Rogers Avenue
Brooklyn, NY 11225
Tel 718-221-2136
Fax 718-221-2137
Email info@ksjammdancetroupe.com
Web www.ksjammdancetroupe.com
Executive Director, Artistic Director, and Choreographer: Kashani Stokley

K.S. J.A.M.M. Dance Troupe, Inc. provides youth and young adults from economically disadvantaged backgrounds with a means of self-expression and self-development through exceptional dance, choreography, and costuming. Students learn modern, jazz, tap, African, and hip hop dance. The culmination of the year's work is presented in an annual June recital.

Secondary Categories: Arts for Children/Teens, Arts Services

KINGS BAY YM-YWHA
See Primary listing under Presenting Organizations

LA TROUPE MAKANDAL, INC.
See Primary listing under Folk Arts

LA TROUPE ZETWAL
See Primary listing under Folk Arts

LOS BOMBEROS DE BROOKLYN, INC.
See Primary listing under Folk Arts

MARIE-CHRISTINE GIORDANO DANCE COMPANY (MCGDC)
220 25th Street
Brooklyn, NY 11232
Tel 718-369-6459
Email info@mcgiordanodance.org
Web www.mcgiordanodance.org
Artistic and Executive Director: Marie-Christine Giordano

The Marie-Christine Giordano Dance Company (MCGDC) embraces both artistic expression and education. In its artistic endeavors, MCGDC presents thoughtful, moving pieces that explore the differing facets of dance and the complex landscape of the human heart. In its educational programs, MCGDC uses dance to convey positive messages of hope, accomplishment, and community.

Secondary Category: Arts for Children/Teens

MARK MORRIS DANCE GROUP (MMDG)
3 Lafayette Avenue
Brooklyn, NY 11217
Tel 718-624-8400
Fax 718-624-8900
Email info@mmdg.org
Web www.mmdg.org
Executive Director: Nancy Umanoff

MMDG's mission is to develop, promote, and sustain dance, music, and opera productions by Mark Morris, and to serve as a cultural resource for the community. In addition to performances, programs include classes for ages 4 to adult, Parkinson's patients, school groups, and rehearsal space rentals (including subsidized rates for the dance community).

Secondary Category: Arts for Children/Teens

MARMARA'S DANCE OF THE NILE REVUE
355 President Street
Brooklyn, NY 11231
Tel 718-852-0521
Director: Marmara Gacovino

Marmara's Dance of the Nile Revue is a Middle Eastern dance performance group that also teaches and offers both public and private demonstrations.

Secondary Category: Folk Arts

**MISNOMER DANCE THEATER
(CHRIS ELAM)**
588 10th Street, Suite 4
Brooklyn, NY 11215
Tel 917-602-0478
Web www.misnomer.org
Artistic Director: Chris Elam

Founded in 1998 by choreographer
Chris Elam, Misnomer Dance Theater
is a modern dance company that finds
hope, humor, and absurdity in people's
efforts to relate to one another. Elam
devises exchanges—whether between
adolescent sisters, estranged lovers, or
animalistic creatures—that alternately
produce moments of poignant tender-
ness or dismal misunderstandings.

MIXED BAG & COMPANY, INC.
P.O. Box 022235
Brooklyn, NY 11202
Site address:
123 Smith Street
Brooklyn, NY 11201
Tel 718-243-0875
Artistic Director: Niambi Keyes

Mixed Bag & Company, Inc. was formed
in 1985 as a performing arts nonprofit
organization under the direction of
Niambi Keyes. The organization preserves traditional and contemporary
styles of music, dance, and drama
through performances, training, and
an educational component. Today, the
company continues to make these art
forms more accessible to surrounding
communities.
*Secondary Categories: Arts for
Children/Teens, Multi-Disciplinary Arts*

MOVING THEATER
See Primary listing under Theater

NARROWS COMMUNITY THEATER, INC.
*See Primary listing under Opera/Music
Theater*

NAT CREOLE ONLINE
*See Primary listing under Computer
Arts/New Media*

NORA STEPHENS / NORANEWDANCE
100 Monroe Street, #1
Brooklyn, NY 11216
Email info@noranewdance.com
Web www.noranewdance.com
Founder: Nora S. Stephens

Nora Stephens / noranewdance
specializes in experimental dance and
inter-disciplinary performance and
video work.
*Secondary Categories: Film/Video,
Multi-Disciplinary Arts, Performance Art*

**OBRUMANKOMA SANKOFA
TRADITIONALS OF GHANA
(KUSUM AGORO GROUP)**
572 Prospect Place
Brooklyn, NY 11238
Tel 718-230-4997
Web www.drumghana.tripod.com/
multiculturalstudies
Artistic Director: Okyerema K.
Prekese-Akyeampong

Obrumankoma Sankofa Traditionals
of Ghana is a performing arts group
dedicated to the arts and culture of
Ghana, West Africa. The Obrumankoma
Sankofa Traditionals presents authentic Ghanaian percussion, singing, and
dancing for audiences of all ages, and
its members have extensive experience
with some of the best groups in Ghana.
*Secondary Categories: Multi-Disciplinary
Arts, Music*

OFFICEOPS
*See Primary listing under
Multi-Disciplinary Arts*

THE OLD AMERICAN CAN FACTORY
*See Primary listing under Presenting
Organizations*

DANCE

PARIJAT DESAI DANCE COMPANY
Tel 646-645-1178
Email info@parijatdesai.org
Web www.parijatdesai.org

Artistic Director: Parijat Desai

Parijat Desai Dance Company performs a dynamic blend of Indian classical and modern dance, as well as yoga and martial art. Choreographer Parijat Desai reconstructs form and rhythm, finding unexpected, organic connections between movement forms. She also reframes the theatrical and storytelling aspect of bharatha natyam, using text—and a little humor—to connect with audiences more directly.

Secondary Categories:
Arts for Children/Teens, Folk Arts, Multi-Disciplinary Arts

PAUL ROBESON THEATER
See Primary listing under Theater

PDM PERFORMING ARTS CORPORATION
See Primary listing under Multi-Disciplinary Arts

PETER KYLE DANCE
963 Lorimer Street, #1
Brooklyn, NY 11222

Tel 347-218-1820
Email info@peterkyledance.org
Web www.peterkyledance.org

Artistic Director: Peter Kyle

Peter Kyle Dance is a contemporary dance company dedicated to interdisciplinary collaboration and to expanding the reach and vitality of all the arts. Through innovative performances and outreach programs, the company celebrates a fundamental belief in the power of the imagination and the human figure in motion.

Secondary Category: Theater

PHILIPPA KAYE COMPANY
See Primary listing under Multi-Disciplinary Arts

POLISH AMERICAN FOLK DANCE COMPANY
See Primary listing under Folk Arts

POLYNESIAN DANCE FOUNDATION
See Primary listing under Folk Arts

POTPOURRI OF COLOR PERFORMING ARTS COMPANY
See Primary listing under Theater

PROPEL-HER DANCE COLLECTIVE
725 4th Avenue, #G5
Brooklyn, NY 11232

Web www.propelherdance.com

Co-Founder: Betsy Miller

Propel-her Dance Collective provides emerging female choreographers with opportunities to present new works. A unique resource for both artistic and administrative support, the Collective provides the foundation necessary for generating and presenting choreographic works through resource- and idea-sharing, collaborative fundraising and marketing efforts, and mentor relationships with established artists.

PURELEMENTS: AN EVOLUTION IN DANCE
1417 Prospect Place, Suite A4
Brooklyn, NY 11213

Tel 718-362-1721
Fax 718-362-1721
Email info@purelements.org
Web www.purelements.org

Co-Executive Artistic Director:
Kevin A. Joseph

Purelements strives to inspire its audiences, supporters, and students to enjoy the liberation of harnessing their own personal creativity. The company prides itself on effectively reaching diverse populations within the cultural and fine arts communities. Purelements offers multi-faceted performing arts/

education programs and encourages its students to think "outside the box."

Secondary Categories: Arts for Children/Teens, Arts Services

RAIZES DO BRASIL CAPOEIRA BROOKLYN
See Primary listing under Folk Arts

RETURN OF THE SUN
33 Seeley Street
Brooklyn, NY 11218

Tel 718-855-2080
Email info@returnofthesun.org
Web www.returnofthesun.org

Artistic Director: Rina Rinkewich

Return of the Sun is a modern dance company dedicated to bringing the work of artistic director Rina Rinkewich and its company members to the public. Additionally, it offers modern dance classes and workshops to adults and children of all ages and levels of experience.

REVELATION PERFORMING ARTS STUDIO, INC.
See Primary listing under Visual/Performing Arts School

SHARON'S DANCE THEATRE (SDT)
1061 Atlantic Avenue
Brooklyn, NY 11238

Tel 718-399-6865

Director: Sharon E. Farmer

Sharon's Dance Theatre (SDT) offers ballet, tap, and jazz classes for ages 3 years and up, with lyrical, modern, and hip hop also included. The professional teaching staff helps students master complex dance forms, and students learn teamwork, develop creative thinking skills, and goal-setting. SDT has a national, multi-award winning dance competition team.

Secondary Categories: Arts for Children/Teens, Theater

SILVER-BROWN DANCE COMPANY (SBD)
11 Sterling Place, Suite 5C
Brooklyn, NY 11217

Tel 917-482-8404
Email silverbrowndance@aol.com
Web www.silverbrowndance.org

Artistic Director: Eva Bordeaux Silverstein

A nonprofit foundation founded in 1998, the Silver-Brown Dance Company (SBD), has appeared before audiences across the globe and maintains a year-round schedule of performance, education, and outreach activity for audiences of all ages and backgrounds. Born in Brooklyn, Artistic Director Eva Silverstein has been hailed as "a true-blue Brooklyn treasure," creating work that celebrates the human spirit.

Secondary Category: Arts for Children/Teens

SOMETHING POSITIVE, INC.
See Primary listing under Multi-Disciplinary Arts

SOULFELT EXPRESSION, LLC
757 Jefferson Avenue
Brooklyn, NY 11221

Tel 917-696-4903
Email info@soulfeltexpression.com
Web www.soulfeltexpression.com

Founder: Catherine M. Miller

SoulFelt Expression, LLC, a gospel dance group, combines modern dance technique with a spiritual theme. By working through various levels of choreography, SoulFelt's sessions allow dancers to tap into their own expressive movements, and develop their individual gifts, in order to spread the gospel. Their rehearsals are preparation for community outreach through dance.

DANCE

SPOKE THE HUB DANCING, INC.
See Primary listing under
Multi-Disciplinary Arts

ST. JOSEPH'S COLLEGE, NY
See Primary listing under Educational
Institutions

STREB LABORATORY FOR ACTION
MECHANICS
See Primary listing under
Multi-Disciplinary Arts

TWW INC.
See Primary listing under Arts for
Children/Teens

THELMA HILL PERFORMING ARTS
CENTER (THPAC)
900 Fulton Street
Brooklyn, NY 11238

Tel 718-875-9710
Email thelmahill@msn.com
Web www.thelmahill.com

Executive Chairman: Alex Smith, Jr.

The Thelma Hill Performing Arts Center
(THPAC) builds bridges of understanding through the presentation of
choreographic works by artists of color.
THPAC is deeply committed to educating the community about dance, and
expresses this commitment through
performances, workshops, seminars,
and community projects.

Secondary Categories: Performance Art,
Presenting Organizations, Theater

TIFFANY MILLS COMPANY
(MIND TO MOVE, INC.)
129 Columbia Heights, #45
Brooklyn, NY 11201

Email info@tiffanymillscompany.org
Web www.tiffanymillscompany.org

Artistic Director: Tiffany J. Mills

Tiffany Mills Company presents live
performances of contemporary dance
(with choreography by Tiffany Mills)
and engages in a range of residency
and community activities. The com-

pany collaborates with artists from
various disciplines not only to stimulate audiences viscerally, aesthetically,
and intellectually, but also to expand
the form and increase its visibility.

Secondary Category: Multi-Disciplinary Arts

TONEL LAKAY DANCE THEATRE
1128 East 43rd Street
Brooklyn, NY 11210
Site address:
47 Sterling Place
Brooklyn, NY 11217

Tel 718-377-6738
Email doune007@aol.com
Web www.tonellakay.org

President: Marie Edith Jean

Tonel Lakay Dance Theatre offers
lessons in both Haitian dance and
Haitian drumming. Members are also
exposed to Haitian traditional songs,
practices, poetry, art, and history. In
addition, Tonel Lokay provides members with an opportunity to explore
their own interests and share them
with the group.

Secondary Categories: Arts for
Children/Teens, Arts Services, Folk Arts,
Music, Theater

TRISKELION ARTS (ABBY BENDER
SCHMANTZE THEATRE & CIRQUE THIS!)
118 North 11th Street
Brooklyn, NY 11211

Tel 718-599-3577
Fax 718-599-3577
Email info@triskelionarts.org
Web www.triskelionarts.org

Co-Founder: Abby Bender

Triskelion Arts is a nonprofit dance
and theater space comprised of two
rehearsal studios, one of which con-
verts to a beautiful black box theater.
Triskelion's mission is to provide
affordable quality space to performing artists and to foster the work of

its resident companies, Abby Bender Schmantze Theatre and Cirque This!

Secondary Categories: Film/Video, Multi-Disciplinary Arts, Performance Art, Presenting Organizations, Theater

UNION STREET DANCE
725 Union Street
Brooklyn, NY 11215

Tel 718-857-8368
Email studio@evadeandance.org
Web www.evadeandance.org

Director: Eva Dean

Eva Dean Dance opened Union Street Dance in Park Slope in 2000. The studio provides subsidized rehearsal space rental to over 120 dance companies annually, and also offers professional-level open classes on a weekly basis, as well as an annual repertoire work-shop featuring Eva Dean Dance and guest artists.

Secondary Category: Arts Services

URBAN BUSH WOMEN
138 South Oxford Street
Brooklyn, NY 11217

Tel 718-398-4537
Email info@urbanbushwomen.org
Web www.urbanbushwomen.org

Artistic Director: Jawole Willa Jo Zollar

Urban Bush Women seeks to bring the untold, under-told histories and stories of disenfranchised people to light through dance. The group does this from a woman-centered perspective, as members of the African Diaspora community, in order to create a more equitable balance of power in the dance world and beyond.

VOLCANO LOVE (LAVA)
524 Bergen Street
Brooklyn, NY 11217

Tel 718-399-3161
Email info@lavalove.org
Web www.lavalove.org

Artistic Director: Sarah E. Johnson

LAVA's original performances integrate dance and acrobatics with various themes connected to natural and social environments. The troupe also teaches, both in its Brooklyn studio and throughout New York City and the U.S. Classes teach the physical disciplines of dance and acrobatics in addition to addressing the social, political, and creative aspects of LAVA's work.

Secondary Categories: Arts for Children/Teens, Theater

WCV, INC. (WALLY CARDONA QUARTET)
Email us@wcvismorphing.org
Web www.wcvismorphing.org

Choreographer: Wally Cardona

WCV, Inc. is a nonprofit corporation under the artistic direction of chore-ographer Wally Cardona. Formed in 1997, the company's primary goal has been to introduce audiences to new forms and ways of viewing movement, through experimentation, cross-disciplinary collaboration, and the creation of new work.

DANCE

WHITE WAVE YOUNG SOON KIM DANCE COMPANY

25 Jay Street
Brooklyn, NY 11201

Tel 718-855-8822
Fax 718-855-8822
Email info@whitewavedance.com
Web www.whitewavedance.com

Artistic Director: Young Soon Kim

WHITE WAVE acts as a potent stimulus for change and expansion of the dance and arts worlds, through dance concerts, the creation of new dance works, and education through dance classes. The company's John Ryan Theater showcases emerging and established choreographers and companies, notably in its annual Festivals Project.

Secondary Categories: Arts for Children/Teens, Presenting Organizations

WILLIAMSBURG ART NEXUS, INC.

See Primary listing under Presenting Organizations

WRIGHT NOW! PERFORMANCEXPERIENCE

48 South Oxford Street
Brooklyn, NY 11217

Tel 718-923-1851
Fax 718-923-1851
Email christalyn@wrightnowpx.org
Web www.wrightnowpx.org

Artistic Director: Christalyn E. Wright

Founded in 2001, the Wright Now! PerformanceXperience has performed in New York, West Virginia, Michigan, and Minnesota. Key mission components include working with at-risk youth, teaching Afrohopatazz (a combination of West African, hip hop, and modern jazz) and other dance forms, and providing the best dance theater possible for the community at large.

Secondary Categories: Arts for Children/Teens, Theater

YOUNG DANCERS IN REPERTORY, INC. (YDR)

P.O. Box 205037, Sunset Station
Brooklyn, NY 11220

Site address:
231 60th Street
Brooklyn, NY 11220

Tel 718-567-9620
Fax 718-567-7048
Email ydr@youngdancersinrep.org
Web www.youngdancersinrep.org

Executive Director: Craig Gabrian

Young Dancers in Repertory, Inc. provides both professional training and creative educational arts programming and performances for children, youth, and the general public. YDR has developed a nurturing yet rigorous dance program for novice through professional-level students, with classes in classical modern dance, ballet, tap, theater dance, hip hop, and international/folkloric dance.

Secondary Category: Arts for Children/Teens

YWCA BROWNSVILLE EARLY LEARNING CENTER

See Primary listing under Arts for Children/Teens

EDUCATIONAL INSTITUTIONS

BROOKLYN CHILDREN'S MUSEUM
See Primary listing under Museums

BROOKLYN COLLEGE CONSERVATORY OF MUSIC
See Primary listing under Music

BROOKLYN COLLEGE DEPARTMENT OF FILM
See Primary listing under Film/Video

BROOKLYN COLLEGE DEPARTMENT OF THEATER
See Primary listing under Theater

BROOKLYN PUBLIC LIBRARY
See Primary listing under Literary Arts

BROOKLYN TECHNOLOGY EXCHANGE
P.O. Box 521, Adelphi Station
Brooklyn, NY 11238

Web www.brooklyntech.com

Founder and Director: Marilyn Nance

Brooklyn Technology Exchange teaches creative individuals how to use technology to present their work with confidence. The Exchange conducts workshops, consults, mentors, and creates engaging public programs that promote cultural, social, and visual literacy. Workshops include Creating an Online Identity, Creating an Online Portfolio, Blogging, Google Tools, and Community Brainstorming.

Secondary Categories: Arts Services, Computer Arts/New Media, Film/Video, Multi-Disciplinary Arts, Presenting Organizations, Visual Arts

HEART OF BROOKLYN
See Primary listing under Arts Services

KUMBLE THEATER FOR THE PERFORMING ARTS, LONG ISLAND UNIVERSITY BROOKLYN CAMPUS
See Primary listing under Theater

LONG ISLAND UNIVERSITY MEDIA ARTS DEPARTMENT, BROOKLYN CAMPUS
1 University Plaza
Brooklyn, NY 11201

Tel 718-488-1052
Fax 718-780-4578
Email mediaarts@brooklyn.liu.edu
Web www.brooklyn.liu.edu/depts/mediarts

Chairman: Larry L. Banks

The Media Arts Department at Long Island University's Brooklyn campus aims to provide a comprehensive Media Arts education that integrates media arts history and theory with media arts practices, specializations, and technologies in order to prepare students for fulfilling professional and academic careers in the field.

*Secondary Categories:
Computer Arts/New Media, Film/Video*

EDUCATIONAL INSTITUTIONS

LONG ISLAND UNIVERSITY MUSIC DEPARTMENT, BROOKLYN CAMPUS
1 University Plaza
Brooklyn, NY 11201
Tel 718-488-1668
Fax 718-488-1372
Email robert.aquino@liu.edu
Web www.liu.edu/brooklyn/music
Chairman: Robert J. Aquino

The Music Department at Long Island University's Brooklyn campus offers a B.F.A. degree in Jazz Studies and a B.A. degree in Applied Music. The Jazz Clinic/Performance series offers eight free presentations each year, featuring top names in jazz. Auditions to the L.I.U. Chorus are open to the local community.

Secondary Category: Music

LONG ISLAND UNIVERSITY, BROOKLYN CAMPUS (LIU)
1 University Plaza
Brooklyn, NY 11201
Tel 718-488-1000
Web www.liu.edu
Provost: Gale Stevens Haynes

For over 80 years, Long Island University has been providing access to the American dream for generations of New Yorkers through excellence in higher education. As a traditional liberal arts institution, the University also provides its neighbors with access to educational and artistic events, many in the new Kumble Theater for the Performing Arts.

Secondary Categories: Music, Performance Art, Theater, Visual Arts

MAGNOLIA TREE EARTH CENTER
677 Lafayette Avenue
Brooklyn, NY 11216
Tel 718-387-2116
Fax 718-387-6133
Email magnoliatreectr@aol.com
President: David M. Greaves

A cultural and environmental institution listed on the National Register of Historic Places, the Magnolia Tree Earth Center develops the skills and attitudes among Bedford-Stuyvesant residents of all ages that will foster urban beautification and environmental awareness, in addition to developing human potential.

Secondary Categories: Architecture & Urban/Environmental Design, Galleries

THE MEDGAR EVERS COLLEGE PREPARATORY SCHOOL CONTEMPORARY DANCE THEATRE
See Primary listing under Visual/Performing Arts School

NEW YORK AQUARIUM
Surf Avenue and West 8th Street
Brooklyn, NY 11224
Tel 718-265-FISH
Web www.nyaquarium.com
Vice-President, Wildlife Health Services, Wildlife Conservation Society: Dr. Robert Cook

A 14-acre park where penguins, walruses, sharks and many other animals live, the New York Aquarium raises public awareness about issues facing the ocean and its inhabitants through special exhibits, public events, and research. The Aquarium offers programs year-round, for people of all ages.

Secondary Category: Museums

PARENTS AS PRIMARY TEACHERS, INC.
See Primary listing under Arts for Children/Teens

PERFORMING ARTS & SPECIAL EVENTS, KINGSBOROUGH COMMUNITY COLLEGE
See Primary listing under Presenting Organizations

PRATT INSTITUTE
200 Willoughby Avenue
Brooklyn, NY 11205

Tel 718-636-3600
Email info@pratt.edu
Web www.pratt.edu

President: Thomas F. Schutte

Founded in 1887, Pratt Institute is one of the largest independent colleges of art and design in the United States, offering undergraduate and graduate degree programs in the schools of architecture, art and design, information and library science, and liberal arts and sciences. Pratt is located on 25 landscaped acres in Clinton Hill and also has a Manhattan campus on West 14th Street.

Secondary Category: Galleries

RUBELLE AND NORMAN SCHAFLER GALLERY AT THE PRATT INSTITUTE
See Primary listing under Galleries

SHOSTAKOVICH MUSIC, ARTS, AND SPORT SCHOOL, INC.
See Primary listing under Music

ST. FRANCIS COLLEGE
180 Remsen Street
Brooklyn, NY 11201

Tel 718-522-2300
Web www.stfranciscollege.edu

President: Dr. Frank J. Macchiarola

Located in Brooklyn Heights, St. Francis College is a private, independent co-educational college that welcomes students from all walks of life. St. Francis publishes the *Arthur Miller Journal* twice a year and hosts scholarly and cultural events open to the public throughout the school year

Secondary Category: Presenting Organizations

ST. JOSEPH'S COLLEGE, NY
245 Clinton Avenue
Brooklyn, NY 11205

Tel 718-636-6800
Fax 718-636-6830
Email mbanach@sjcny.edu
Web www.sjcny.edu

President: Elizabeth Hill, CSJ

St. Joseph's College is a private, independent, co-educational liberal arts institution with a School of Arts and Sciences and a School of Professional and Graduate Studies. The college's Council for the Arts offers a season of performing arts programs and visual arts exhibitions open to the public.

Secondary Categories: Dance, Film/Video, Galleries, Literary Arts, Music, Presenting Organizations, Theater, Visual Arts

WEEKSVILLE HERITAGE CENTER
See Primary listing under Historical Societies

EDUCATIONAL INSTITUTIONS

I think that it is very important that films make people look at what they've forgotten.

SPIKE LEE

FILM/VIDEO

0.00156 ACRES
See Primary listing under Visual Arts

ACTNOW FOUNDATION (ANF)
138 South Oxford Street, Suite 1C
Brooklyn, NY 11217

Tel 347-274-0563
Email info@actnowproduction.org
Web www.actnowproduction.org

Executive Director: Aaron R. Ingram

ActNow Foundation is a film and theater company that delves into stories about race, love, family, cultural differences, and self-empowerment. ANF sponsors the "ANF Short Film Collective," a monthly short film series at NY Perks, and the "Monologue Monorail Jam," a monologue slam held twice a year at BRICstudio.

Secondary Category: Theater

AD HOC ART
See Primary listing under Galleries

AWAAM: ARAB WOMEN ACTIVE IN THE ARTS AND MEDIA
See Primary listing under Computer Arts/New Media

BAC FOLK ARTS
See Primary listing under Folk Arts

BAM
See Primary listing under Multi-Disciplinary Arts

BAM ROSE CINEMAS
30 Lafayette Avenue
Brooklyn, NY 11217

Tel 718-636-4100
Email info@bam.org
Web www.bam.org

President: Karen Brooks Hopkins

BAM Rose Cinemas features new, independent film releases and BAM-cinématek—a curated, daily repertory film program. BAMcinématek presents classics, retrospectives, festivals, premieres, and rare screenings, with special guest appearances by directors, actors, and screenwriters.

BCAT/ BROOKLYN COMMUNITY ACCESS TELEVISION
647 Fulton Street
Brooklyn, NY 11217

Tel 718-935-1122
Fax 718-935-1123
Email bcat@briconline.org
Web www.briconline.org

Executive Producer: Greg Sutton

BCAT, a program of BRIC Arts | Media | Brooklyn, operates Brooklyn's four public access channels, a media education center, Brooklyn Free Speech TV (which supplies Brooklynites with the tools to create their own programs), and Brooklyn Independent Television, which produces original Brooklyn-centric programming.

Secondary Category: Computer Arts/New Media

BINDLESTIFF FAMILY VARIETY ARTS, INC.
See Primary listing under Theater

BLACK AND LATINO FILMMAKER'S COALITION (BLFC)
473 Herikimer Street
Brooklyn, NY 11213
Email info@theblfc.org
Web www.theblfc.org

The Black and Latino Filmmaker's Coalition (BLFC) was created in order to empower, promote, nurture, and mentor Black and Latino independent filmmakers in the motion picture industry. The BLFC runs two programs: The Brooklyn Indie House, an intimate movie theater showcasing filmmakers outside the Hollywood machine, and Film Assist, assistance given to BLFC members for completing their projects.

BREAKNBONES
2202 Linden Boulevard
Brooklyn, NY 11207
Tel 212-380-8764
Email breaknbones1@yahoo.com

CEO and Founder: Joseph Maurice Springfield

An independent film production company, BreaknBones is currently developing a children's comedy, Water Works, among other projects.

BREEDINGGROUND PRODUCTIONS
See Primary listing under Multi-Disciplinary Arts

BRIC ARTS | MEDIA | BROOKLYN
See Primary listing under Multi-Disciplinary Arts

BRIC ROTUNDA GALLERY
See Primary listing under Visual Arts

THE BRICK THEATER, INC.
See Primary listing under Theater

BROOKLYN ART INCUBATOR
See Primary listing under Arts Services

BROOKLYN ARTS COUNCIL
See Primary listing under Arts Services

BROOKLYN ARTS COUNCIL INTERNATIONAL FILM FESTIVAL
55 Washington Street, Suite 218
Brooklyn, NY 11201
Tel 718-625-0080
Fax 718-625-3294
Email filmfest@brooklynartscouncil.org
Web www.brooklynartscouncil.org
President: Ella J. Weiss

The Brooklyn Arts Council International Film Festival has served independent film and video artists for over 40 years. The Festival features work by three groups which include independent, college student, and youth (K-12) in the following categories: narrative, experimental, documentary, animation, video installation, Brooklyn filmmakers, and films by women of African descent.

Secondary Category: Arts Services

BROOKLYN CENTER CINEMA
Tel 718-951-4600, ext. 18
Fax 718-951-4343
Email angel@brooklyncentercinema.com
Web www.brooklyncenter.com/cinema/index.htm

Cinema Director: Frank Angel

Brooklyn Center Cinema is a unique and integral component of the Brooklyn Center for the Performing Arts (BCBC). The Cinema presents retrospective, alternative, and independent films, as well as sneak previews and special CinEvents in Brooklyn's largest single-screen theater (2,500 seats), on a giant screen and in breathtaking Total Surround MegaSound. Many screenings are free.

BROOKLYN COLLEGE DEPARTMENT OF FILM

2900 Bedford Avenue
201 West End Building (WEB)
Brooklyn, NY 11210

Tel 718-951-5664
Fax 718-951-4733
Email film@brooklyn.cuny.edu
Web www.bcflix.net

Chairperson: Daniel Gurskis

The Department of Film at Brooklyn College offers two programs of undergraduate study. Students may earn a B.A. in film with a concentration in screenwriting, film production, film studies, or film marketing. Students who wish to focus exclusively on filmmaking may take a two-year Certificate Program in film with a concentration in film production or screenwriting.

Secondary Category: Educational Institution

BROOKLYN FILM & ARTS FESTIVAL

P.O. Box 491, Murray Hill Station
New York, NY 10156

Email brooklynfa@yahoo.com
Web www.filmbrooklyn.org

Director: A. Rahman

The Brooklyn Film & Arts Festival project is designed to reflect the dynamic social and cultural history, as well as the present reality of Brooklyn through many diverse perspectives and creative works focused primarily on the borough and its people. The Festival invites filmmakers to submit short documentaries and films for its screenings.

Secondary Category: Visual Arts

BROOKLYN INTERNATIONAL FILM FESTIVAL (BROOKLYNFEST)

180 South 4th Street
Brooklyn, NY 11211

Tel 718-388-4306
Fax 718-599-5039
Email festival@wbff.org
Web www.brooklynfest.org

Executive Director: Marco Ursino

The Brooklyn International Film Festival (BiFF) is dedicated to discovering and promoting independent filmmakers and their work. BiFF is also committed to expanding the rich cultural resources that are and will become the heritage of Brooklyn citizens. BiFF receives over 2,000 film submissions from 100 countries annually, and selects 150 films for its competition.

BROOKLYN JEWISH FILM FESTIVAL
See Primary listing under Presenting Organizations

BROOKLYN MUSEUM
See Primary listing under Museums

BROOKLYN PUBLIC LIBRARY
See Primary listing under Literary Arts

THE BROOKLYN RAIL
See Primary listing under Multi-Disciplinary Arts

BROOKLYN TECHNOLOGY EXCHANGE
See Primary listing under Educational Institution

BROOKLYN WRITERS SPACE
See Primary listing under Literary Arts

FILM/VIDEO

BROOKLYN YOUNG FILMMAKERS CENTER (BYFC)
149 North Oxford Walk
Brooklyn, NY 11205
Tel 718-935-0490
Email info@wearebyfc.org
Web www.wearebyfc.org
Director: Trayce A. Gardner

Brooklyn Young Filmmakers Center provides introductory education on film careers and film literacy to adults and teens. Its long-term goal is to open up a career guidance and networking center. It currently offers two foundational core courses as well as workshops throughout the year on specific careers in film and a free email newsletter.

Secondary Category: Arts for Children/Teens

THE BUSHWICK STARR
See Primary listing under Theater

CARIBBEAN CULTURAL THEATRE
See Primary listing under Theater

CAVE
See Primary listing under Multi-Disciplinary Arts

CELEBRATE BROOKLYN PERFORMING ARTS FESTIVAL
See Primary listing under Presenting Organizations

CHEZ BUSHWICK
See Primary listing under Dance

CONFLUX FESTIVAL
See Primary listing under Multi-Disciplinary Arts

CRUCIAL ARTS PRODUCTIONS, INC.
See Primary listing under Multi-Disciplinary Arts

CTS
See Primary listing under Galleries

DAM, STUHLTRAGER GALLERY
See Primary listing under Galleries

DARMSTADT
See Primary listing under Music

DE NONNO PRODUCTIONS, INC. (TONY DE NONNO PRODUCTIONS)
Email info@denonnoproductions.com
President and Filmmaker:
Tony De Nonno

De Nonno Productions, Inc., is a full-service television, film, and musical theater production and distribution company shepherded by Tony De Nonno, who is the writer, director, and producer of more than fifty documentary films.

Secondary Categories: Art for Children/Teens, Folk Arts, Music, Theater

DIGITAL STORY WORKSHOP
5 Delevan Street, #2U
Brooklyn, NY 11231
Tel 347-564-0213
Fax 718-398-3991
Email kristin@digitalstoryworkshop.org
Web www.digitalstoryworkshop.org
Director: Kristin S. Brenneman Eno

The goals of Digital Story Workshop are to empower young children by highlighting their spontaneous imaginative play, to provide media education to children ages 3 through 8, to facilitate meaningful artistic collaborations between adults and children, to contribute curricular material to city classrooms, and to foster creative dialogue among children from different backgrounds.

Secondary Categories: Arts for Children/Teens, Computer Arts/New Media, Multi-Disciplinary Arts, Visual Arts

THE DREAMERS FILM SOCIETY
236 Decatur Street, #4
Brooklyn, NY 11233
Tel 646-338-4298
Email patrina@cfscs.org
Web www.cfscs.org
Director of Operations and Programs:
Patrina K. Huff

The Dreamers Film Society is a collaborative of film enthusiasts, educators, filmmakers, and theorists who use film to promote dialogue to increase and challenge thinking on topics related to our diverse social, cultural, and historical experiences and perspectives. The group encourages dialogue through analysis of the visual, narrative, and technical construct of the film medium. Beyond screenings, the collaborative supports film-related projects proposed by its members.

DUMBO ARTS CENTER
See Primary listing under Visual Arts

THE ENRICO CARUSO MUSEUM OF AMERICA
See Primary listing under Museums

GALAPAGOS ART SPACE
See Primary listing under Multi-Disciplinary Arts

GIBA IN DESIGN
See Primary listing under Arts Services

GITANA ROSA GALLERY
See Primary listing under Galleries

THE GOSSIP FACTORY
See Primary listing under Theater

GOVERNESS FILMS
125 Ryerson Street
Brooklyn, NY 11205
Tel 917-554-4126
Web www.governessfilms.com
Director and Producer: Lisa Y. Russell

Governess Films is a collective and production company made up of female filmmakers who specialize in both narrative and documentary film.

THE GOWANUS STUDIO SPACE, INC.
See Primary Listing under Multi-Disciplinary Arts

THE HOGAR COLLECTION
See Primary listing under Galleries

ISSUE PROJECT ROOM
See Primary listing under Multi-Disciplinary Arts

LMAKPROJECTS
See Primary listing under Galleries

LONG ISLAND UNIVERSITY MEDIA ARTS DEPARTMENT, BROOKLYN CAMPUS
See Primary listing under Educational Institutions

FILM/VIDEO

M'CAHAYA ARTS & EDUCATION FOUNDATION
1340 Carroll Street
Brooklyn, NY 11213

Email yfree19158@aol.com
Web www.asacredproof.com

Director: Yehuda H. Freeman

The mission of M'Cahaya Arts & Education Foundation, a family-based organization, is to produce creative projects with Jewish themes, in a variety of media.

Secondary Category: Music

METAPHOR CONTEMPORARY ART
See Primary listing under Galleries

MICHAEL ALAN'S DRAW-A-THON
See Primary listing under Arts Services

MONKEY TOWN
58 North 3rd Street
Brooklyn, NY 11211

Tel 718-384-1369
Email monkeytownhq@aol.com
Web www.monkeytownhq.com

Director: Montgomery A. Knott

Monkey Town is a performance space and restaurant, with four walls of projection and 6.1 surround-sound, that hosts live music and performances, in addition to screening video art, short films, and other media.

Secondary Categories: Computer Arts/ New Media, Multi-Disciplinary Arts, Music, Performance Art, Theater, Visual Arts

MUSEUM OF CONTEMPORARY AFRICAN DIASPORAN ART
See Primary listing under Museums

NORA STEPHENS / NORANEWDANCE
See Primary listing under Dance

OFFICEOPS
See Primary listing under Multi-Disciplinary Arts

THE OLD AMERICAN CAN FACTORY
See Primary listing under Presenting Organizations

PERIPHERAL MEDIA PROJECTS, INC.
See Primary listing under Visual Arts

PIEROGI
See Primary listing under Galleries

PLUTO
See Primary listing under Galleries

POC DOC FILM DEVELOPMENT, INC.
Tel 917-776-5022
Email pocdocinstitute@yahoo.com

CEO: Shay Sellars

POC Doc Film Development, Inc. is an independent film development company committed to supporting, producing, and distributing theatrical documentaries and narrative films made by filmmakers of color. POC Doc assists filmmakers by providing professional consulting on development and production, marketing strategy, investor prospect research, and by securing resources.

Secondary Category: Arts Services

PROTEUS GOWANUS
See Primary listing under Multi-Disciplinary Arts

REALFORM
See Primary listing under Visual Arts

REEL SISTERS OF THE DIASPORA FILM FESTIVAL
Long Island University
Media Arts Department
1 University Plaza
Brooklyn, NY 11201

Tel 212-865-2982
Email reelsisters@yahoo.com
Web www.reelsisters.org

Writer and Publisher:
Carolyn A. Butts-Schmalenberger

Reel Sisters of the Diaspora Film Festival cultivates and spotlights the unique talent and struggle of women of color in the film industry, showcasing women's experiences from a global perspective. Reel Sisters provides access to leading professionals by presenting panels and workshops on topics from screenwriting to producing, and its festival includes documentary, narrative, experimental, and animation works.

REEL WORKS TEEN FILMMAKING
357 Ninth Street, 7th Floor
Brooklyn, NY 11215

Tel 718-768-7100, ext. 139
Fax 718-499-0425
Email thelab@reelworks.org
Web www.reelworks.org

Executive Director: John Williams

Founded in 2001 at the Prospect Park YMCA, Reel Works Teen Filmaking is a full-time nonprofit arts organization that serves over 150 teens each year through four core programs that allow young people to gain self-esteem, master state-of-the-art technology, and transform themselves from passive consumers to active creators of media.

Secondary Category: Arts for Children/Teens

ROLEY POLEY PRODUCTIONS, LLC
597 President Street, #3
Brooklyn, NY 11215

Fax 718-228-3626
Web www.roleypoley.com

Roley Poley Productions, LLC produces short films, documentaries, features, and corporate videos, and has a broad range of clients and resources. Roley Poley accepts large and small jobs alike.

ROOFTOP FILMS
285 Fifth Avenue, PMB 401
Brooklyn, NY 11215
Site address:
232 Third Street
Brooklyn, NY 11215

Tel 718-417-7362
Email info@rooftopfilms.com
Web www.rooftopfilms.com

Artistic Director: Mark E. Rosenberg

Bringing the underground outdoors, Rooftop Films is a nonprofit film festival and production collective that supports, creates, promotes, and shows daring short films worldwide in a weekly summer rooftop film festival. More than a film festival, Rooftop Films is a community—a collective collaboration between filmmakers and festivals, between audiences and artists, between venues and neighborhoods.

Secondary Category: Music

ROUGH ON RATS PRODUCTIONS (ROR)
315 Clinton Street
Brooklyn, NY 11231

Tel 718-875-9254
Email roughonrats@msn.com

Producer: Allison S. Prete

Rough on Rats is the documentary film production company created by Allison Prete. RoR Productions focuses on creating works that look at the physical environment and how we shape it. Previous productions include the award-winning documentary Lavender Lake: Brooklyn's Gowanus Canal.

FILM/VIDEO

**RUDDER BLADE PRODUCTIONS, INC.
(ANCHOR STUDIOS, INC.)**
123 7th Avenue, Suite 208
Brooklyn, NY 11215

Tel 347-678-2376
Fax 866-367-7123
Email contact@anchorblade.com
Web www.anchorblade.com

President: Ernest Bhabor

Rudder Blade Productions, Inc. promotes filmmaking in the public interest
by developing online and offline media
projects for the both the African and
Latino communities as well as the
general public. Rudder Blade serves as
an informational and public awareness resource on the art, history, and
culture of Africa and Latin America.

Secondary Category: Multi-Disciplinary Arts

SAFE-T-GALLERY
See Primary listing under Galleries

SCENARIOS USA
80 Hanson Place, Suite 305
Brooklyn, NY 11217

Tel 718-230-5125
Fax 718-230-4381
Email info@scenariosusa.org
Web www.scenariosusa.org

Co-Executive Director: Maura Minsky

Scenarios USA is a nonprofit organization that fosters youth leadership,
advocacy, and self-expression through
writing and filmmaking. Scenarios USA
asks participating teens to write about
issues that shape their lives for an
annual writing contest. Winning writers
are then partnered with Hollywood
filmmakers to transform their stories
into short films.

*Secondary Categories: Arts for
Children/Teens, Multi-Disciplinary Arts*

SECRET PROJECT ROBOT
See Primary listing under Visual Arts

SOAPBOX GALLERY
See Primary listing under Visual Arts

ST. JOSEPH'S COLLEGE, NY
*See Primary listing under Educational
Institutions*

TABLA RASA GALLERY
See Primary listing under Galleries

TOPIARY PRODUCTIONS, INC.
22 Verandah Place
Brooklyn, NY 11201

Tel 718-624-0946
Fax 718-246-7994
Email info@topiaryproductions.com
Web www.topiaryproductions.com

President: Ben D. Wolf

Topiary Productions, Inc. is a boutique
film and video production company.
Topiary works in fiction, documentary,
and commercial production, and
takes projects from the script to the
final edit.

TRISKELION ARTS
See Primary listing under Dance

UNIONDOCS
322 Union Avenue
Brooklyn, NY 11211

Tel 347-227-7005
Email info@uniondocs.org
Web www.uniondocs.org

Founder: Christopher J. Allen

A nonprofit documentary arts collaborative and presentation space,
UnionDocs works in video, sound, text,
live performance, music, and photography, both independently and col-
laboratively. Though its work reaches
beyond what can easily be called
"documentary," UnionDocs uses the
term because it implies an engagement
with the subject of reality.

Secondary Category: Multi-Disciplinary Arts

VERTEXLIST
See Primary listing under Computer Arts/New Media

VISUAL ART STUDIO
410 Ocean Parkway
Brooklyn, NY 11218

Tel 718-374-4241
Web www.visualartco.com

Director: Radek S.

A fully-integrated film and television production company, Visual Art Studio works with its clients from concept to production to create dynamic, powerful visuals. Its portfolio ranges from architectural films, commercials, music videos, concerts, news segments, clay animation, and fine art to documentaries, corporate films and photography.

Secondary Category: Visual Arts

WEEKSVILLE HERITAGE CENTER
See Primary listing under Historical Societies

**WEONE FILM PRODUCTIONS
(AL SANTANA PRODUCTIONS)**
P.O. Box 521
Brooklyn, NY 11238

Site address:
136 Cambridge Place
Brooklyn, NY 11238

Tel 718-636-9747
Email al@alsantana.com
Web www.alsantana.com

Principal: Alfred J. Santana

WeOne Film Productions is a film and video production company that produces independent documentaries, narrative films, and industrials. WeOne's goal is to collaborate with creative media artists—writers, editors, cinematographers, and directors—to produce quality films that entertain while addressing social, cultural, and political themes.

Secondary Category: Computer Arts/New Media

WISELEPHANT
See Primary listing under Arts Services

WITNESS
80 Hanson Place
Brooklyn, NY 11217

Tel 718-783-2000
Web www.witness.org

Executive Director: Gillian Caldwell

WITNESS uses video and online technologies to open the eyes of the world to human rights violations. WITNESS empowers people to transform personal stories of abuse into powerful tools for justice, promoting public engagement and policy change.

THE WORLD ACCORDING TO SHORTS, INC.
Web www.worldaccordingtoshorts.com

Director: Jonathan Howell

The World According to Shorts, Inc. is dedicated to promoting cultural exchange, understanding, and appreciation through the exhibition and distribution of high-quality, non-commercial foreign short films made by independent filmmakers.

WORLD EATER RECORDINGS, NYC
See Primary listing under Music

FILM/VIDEO

Any form of art is a form of power; it has impact, it can affect change—it can not only move us, it makes us move.

OSSIE DAVIS

FOLK ARTS

AFRICUSSION-PERCUSSION DISCUSSION
See Primary listing under Music

AFRO HERITAGE VENTURE
See Primary listing under Multi-Disciplinary Arts

ALLIANCE OF AFRICAN AMERICAN ARTISTS & ART FORMS (A5)
Tel 718-670-3360
Email ahgatnet@hotmail.com
President: Asantewaa Harris

The Alliance of African American Artists & Art Forms is committed to advocacy, coalition-building, and information, and resource-sharing among African American artists.

ASIAN AMERICAN WOMEN ARTISTS ALLIANCE
See Primary listing under Visual Arts

ATTITUDE: THE DANCERS' MAGAZINE
See Primary listing under Dance

BAC ARTS IN EDUCATION
See Primary listing under Arts for Children/Teens

BAC FOLK ARTS
55 Washington Street, Suite 218
Brooklyn, NY 11201
Tel 718-625-0080
Fax 718-625-3294
Email folkarts@brooklynartscouncil.org
Web www.brooklynartscouncil.org
President: Ella J. Weiss

BAC Folk Arts works with Brooklyn-based folk and traditional artists and their communities to preserve and present arts that express the borough's diverse living heritage. Music, dance, visual and material arts, and occupational and religious traditions all find wider audiences through BAC's public presentations, from the annual Folk Feet traditional dance showcase to Folk Feet Dance Workshops to the Brooklyn Maqam Arab Music Festival.

Secondary Categories: Dance, Film/Video, Music

BINDLESTIFF FAMILY VARIETY ARTS, INC.
See Primary listing under Theater

BREEDINGGROUND PRODUCTIONS
See Primary listing under Multi-Disciplinary Arts

BRIGHTON BALLET THEATER
See Primary listing under Dance

BROOKLYN ARTS COUNCIL
See Primary listing under Arts Services

CARIBBEAN CULTURAL THEATRE
See Primary listing under Theater

CENTER FOR THANATOLOGY RESEARCH AND EDUCATION, INC.
See Primary listing under Multi-Disciplinary Arts

CHELSEA STRING BAND
See Primary listing under Music

CIRCUS AMOK
See Primary listing under Theater

CIRKULOCK, INC.
(THE STREET DANCE CIRCUS)
Email info@cirkulock.com
Web www.cirkulock.com

The first street dance circus, Cirkulock's mission is to be the premier street dance circus in New York City by focusing on one-of-a-kind, cirque-style street dancers and radical circus performers for collaborative productions. Cirkulock employs acrobats, bonebreakers, dancing clowns, mutants, and others for its performance roster. More information is available at www.cirkulock.com.

Secondary Categories: Dance, Performance Art

CONJUNTO NUEVO MILENIO
126 Herkimer Street, Suite 12
Brooklyn, NY 11216

Tel 347-350-5893
Email contactus@conjuntonuevo
milenio.com
Web www.conjuntonuevomilenio.com

Executive Director: Alberto Gonzalez

Conjunto Nuevo Milenio, the New Millenium Panamanian Performing Arts Company, is a group of dedicated, professional dancers with a passion and love for Panamanian tradition and the mission to educate the public about the beauty, diversity, and richness of its culture. The company's motto, "Panama is more than a canal," fuels its desire to showcase the people, folklore, and customs through dance performances, workshops, and lectures.

Secondary Category: Dance

CREATE!
See Primary listing under Arts for Children/Teens

DARRAH CARR DANCE
See Primary listing under Dance

DE NONNO PRODUCTIONS, INCORPORATED
See Primary listing under Film/Video

DRUMSONG AFRICAN BALLET THEATRE, INC.
See Primary listing under Multi-Disciplinary Arts

ELDERS SHARE THE ARTS
See Primary listing under Multi-Disciplinary Arts

FILIPINO ARTS & MUSIC ENSEMBLE
See Primary listing under Music

GREENWICH MORRIS MEN
440 Fifth Street
Brooklyn, NY 11215

Tel 718-965-4074
Email alanfriend_music@hotmail.com
Web www.cdny.org/gmm.html

Artistic Director: Alan Friend

The Greenwich Morris Men perform ancient ritual morris dances and long-sword dances from England, in costumes that include bells around the legs for morris dances and sashes around the waist for long-sword dances. The group's energetic, colorful dances are accompanied by live music on fiddle and concertina.

Secondary Category: Dance

HALBERT BARTON AND EL BOMBAZO DE BROOKLYN
85 South Oxford Street
Brooklyn, NY 11217

Tel 718-812-2920
Email halbert.barton@gmail.com
Web www.myspace.com/elbombazo
debrooklyn

Founder, Director, and Lead Instructor: Dr. Halbert E. Barton

El Bombazo de Brooklyn was formerly with Los Bomberos de Brooklyn, founded as an interactive performance workshop in 1999. El Bombazo's purpose is to provide opportunities for Puerto Rican and African Diasporic cultural education in a community-building learn-by-doing format that incorporates music, dance, and singing.

Secondary Categories: Dance, Music

HAMPTONIANS NEW YORK
See Primary listing under Arts for Children/Teens

INTERDANCE FOUNDATION, INC.
See Primary listing under Dance

THE KURDISH HERITAGE FOUNDATION OF AMERICA
See Primary listing under Multi-Disciplinary Arts

LA TROUPE MAKANDAL, INC.
621 Rutland Road, #4C
Brooklyn, NY 11203

Tel 718-953-6638
Email makandal@earthlink.net
Web www.makandal.org

Executive Director: Lois E. Wilcken

La Troupe Makandal, Inc. channels the power of traditional Afro Haitian music and dance to represent Haiti's history and culture in theaters and schools, serving the public with performances, recordings, and instruction. Directed by NEA Heritage Fellow Frisner Augustin, Makandal creates dynamic music and dance experiences that audiences don't soon forget.

Secondary Categories: Dance, Music

LA TROUPE ZETWAL (ZETWAL DANCERS)
Tel 347-274-4468
Email admin@zetwaldancers.com
Web www.zetwaldancers.com

Group Leader: Sherley St. Fort

La Troupe Zetwal is a professional dance group specializing in traditional Haitian folklore, Soukous, and Zouk dance. Their goal is both to preserve and promote the richness of Haitian culture that isn't widely seen, and to educate audiences on the importance of tradition and culture.

Secondary Category: Dance

LEFFERTS HISTORIC HOUSE
See Primary listing under Museums

LOS BOMBEROS DE BROOKLYN, INC.
Tel 917-757-3207
Email los_sures@yahoo.com

Director and Lead Organizer: Melinda Gonzalez

The infectious rhythms and inspired dancing of Los Bomberos de Brooklyn, Inc. make the Afro Puerto Rican bomba tradition accessible and enjoyable to all through audience participation at presentations and bombazos (community celebrations). Los Bomberos also hold "Dance and Drum" classes at the Williamsburg Community Center twice a week.

Secondary Categories: Dance, Music

MARMARA'S DANCE OF THE NILE REVUE
See Primary listing under Dance

MOUNTAIN REDBIRD MUSIC (PARK SLOPE BLUEGRASS & OLD-TIME JAMBOREE)
565 9th Street
Brooklyn, NY 11215

Email info@jamesreams.com
Web www.jamesreams.com/jamboree.html

Director: James Reams

The Park Slope Bluegrass & Old-Time Jamboree is an annual event that celebrates the music of the southern Appalachian Mountains with workshops, jamming, and concerts.

Secondary Category: Music

PARIJAT DESAI DANCE COMPANY
See Primary listing under Dance

POLISH AMERICAN FOLK DANCE COMPANY (PAFDC)
261 Driggs Avenue
Brooklyn, NY 11222
Tel 718-907-6199
Email director@pafdc.org
Web www.pafdc.org

Executive Director:
Margaret Pawelkiewicz

The Polish American Folk Dance Company of Brooklyn (PAFDC) has been proud to present authentic, energetic performances to Polish and American communities since 1938. PAFDC's strength lies in the community of people who lend their talents to help achieve its goal of preserving and perpetuating the spirited songs and dances of Poland in the melting pot of America.

Secondary Categories: Dance

POLYNESIAN DANCE FOUNDATION (PDP)
Email polynesiandp@gmail.com
Web www.polynesiandp.blogspot.com

Co-Owner and Dancer: May Cacal

Originally from Hawaii and recently relocated to New York City, the Polynesian Dance Foundation presents exciting dances from Hawaii, New Zealand, Samoa, and Tahiti, with authentic handmade costumes and an emphasis on audience participation. The troupe performs professionally for various occasions ranging from backyard luaus to corporate parties and celebrity events.

Secondary Category: Dance

PROSPECT PARK AUDUBON CENTER
See Primary listing under Architecture & Urban/Environmental Design

RAIZES DO BRASIL CAPOEIRA BROOKLYN (CAPOEIRA BROOKLYN)
347 Flatbush Avenue, 2nd Floor
Brooklyn, NY 11238
Tel 646-492-4221
Email info@capoeirabrooklyn.com
Web www.capoeirabrooklyn.com

Directors: Ana and Andre Costa

Brooklyn's only full-time Capoeira studio, Raizes do Brasil Capoeira offers classes to children and adults in Capoeira, an Afro Brazilian art form that combines martial arts, acrobatics, dance, and music. Beginners are welcome to a month-long introductory course that meets twice a week. Portuguese language, samba, and music workshops are also offered. Visit our website for more details. Bem vindo!

Secondary Categories: Dance, Multi-Disciplinary Arts, Music

REDHAWK NATIVE AMERICAN ARTS COUNCIL
See Primary listing under Arts Services

THE RIVIERA
See Primary listing under Galleries

STORYCORPS
See Primary listing under Multi-Disciplinary Arts

TONEL LAKAY DANCE THEATRE
See Primary listing under Dance

UNITED COMMUNITY CENTERS (UCC)
613 New Lots Avenue
Brooklyn, NY 11207

Email jessicadias@hotmail.com
Web www.eastnewyorkfarms.org

Executive Director: Ana Aguirre

United Community Centers has been bringing arts and cultural education to the community of East New York since 1954. UCC also hosts the East New York Farms! Project, which organizes the East New York Farmers Markets, featuring annual folk arts performances for the general public.

Secondary Category: Architecture & Urban/Environmental Design

WEEKSVILLE HERITAGE CENTER
See Primary listing under Historical Societies

WEST INDIAN AMERICAN DAY CARNIVAL ASSOCIATION, INC.
See Primary listing under Presenting Organizations

WYCKOFF FARMHOUSE MUSEUM
See Primary listing under Museums

Without art the
crudeness of reality
would make the world
unbearable.

GEORGE BERNARD SHAW

GALLERIES

0.00156 ACRES
See Primary listing under Visual Arts

440 GALLERY
440 Sixth Avenue
Brooklyn, NY 11215

Tel 718-499-3844
Email info@440gallery.com
Web www.440gallery.com

Founders: Shanee Epstein and
Nancy Lunsford

440 Gallery is a collective whose members' work includes painting, drawing, photography, sculpture, and installation appropriate for both institutional and private collections. The gallery also invites outside artists and curators to participate in seasonal group shows. Its goal is to promote a lively dialogue within both the neighborhood and the larger artistic community.

Secondary Categories: Literary Arts, Music, Visual Arts

5+5 GALLERY
111 Front Street
Brooklyn, NY 11201

Tel 718-488-8383
Email gallery1@fodde.com
Web www.5plus5gallery.com

Director: Raphael Foddé

5 + 5 gallery specializes in works on paper by established and emerging artists, and encourages artists to experiment in printmaking.

Secondary Category: Visual Arts

A SPACE GALLERY
1138 Broadway
Brooklyn, NY 11221

Tel 917-776-0772
Email lisang@aspacegallery.com
Web www.aspacegallery.com

Director: Lisang Lisang

Located on the border of Bushwick and Bedford Stuyvesant, A Space Gallery exhibits visual arts in various media such as painting, photography, drawing, et cetera.

Secondary Category: Visual Arts

A.M. RICHARD FINE ART
328 Berry Street
Brooklyn, NY 11211

Tel 917-570-1476
Fax 212-717-7158
Email gallery@amrichardfineart.com
Web www.amrichardfineart.com

Director: A.M. Richard

A.M. Richard Fine Art presents contemporary art in all media, with an emphasis on emerging artists.

Secondary Category: Visual Arts

AD HOC ART (AHA)
49 Bogart Street, Unit 1G, Buzzer 22
Brooklyn, NY 11206

Tel 718-366-2466
Fax 866-599-7270
Email info@adhocart.org
Web www.adhocart.org

Co-Founder: Ray B. Cross

Ad Hoc Art (AHA) is a community-based gallery and creative center dedicated to work that is often marginalized by the larger New York art scene. AHA's focus is primarily print, drawing, and work on paper, as well as street art and the larger history of underground art, activism, and graffiti.

Secondary Categories: Architecture & Urban/Environmental Design, Arts Services, Film/Video, Music, Performance Art, Visual Arts

AG GALLERY (ABOUT GLAMOUR)
103 North 3rd Street
Brooklyn, NY 11211

Tel 718-599-3044
Web www.aboutglamour.net

President: Tomoko Ashikawa

About Glamour is a unique retail space that encompasses an art gallery, shop, and hair salon. About Glamour's mission is to provide a platform in which emerging creativities from all over the world can exhibit and promote their work, whether in the fields of art, fashion, music, or design.

Secondary Category: Visual Arts

ART 101
101 Grand Street
Brooklyn, NY 11211

Tel 718-302-2242
Email info@art101brooklyn.com
Web www.art101brooklyn.com

President and Director: Ellen E. Rand

A Williamsburg gallery with a scope beyond its modest size, ART 101 is

rooted in the community. Exhibiting artists are residents of Brooklyn, as well as other areas and countries, representing all ages and stages of careers and media. The gallery encourages visitors to stay for a while, to look, ask, and converse.

Secondary Category: Visual Arts

ART GALLERY AT KINGSBOROUGH COMMUNITY COLLEGE, CUNY
2001 Oriental Boulevard
Brooklyn, NY 11235

Tel 718-368-5449
Fax 718-368-4872
Email kccgallery@gmail.com
Web www.kingsborough.edu/
academicDepartments/art/gallery/
index.htm

Gallery Director: Peter Malone

The Art Gallery at Kingsborough Community College is dedicated to providing students, faculty, and the Brooklyn public with exhibitions presenting art of regional, national, and international standing that reflects the values and standards inherent in the curriculum of the Art Department. Exhibitions are free and open to the public.

Secondary Categories: Architecture & Urban/Environmental Design, Computer Arts/New Media, Multi-Disciplinary Arts, Visual Arts

AXELLE FINE ARTS, LTD.
See Primary listing under Arts Services

BAC GALLERY
55 Washington Street, Suite 218
Brooklyn, NY 11201

Tel 718-625-0080
Fax 718-625-3294
Email gallery@brooklynartscouncil.org
Web www.brooklynartscouncil.org

President: Ella J. Weiss

BAC Gallery is located in the heart of the vibrant DUMBO arts district and offers Brooklyn-based artists an opportunity to show their art in an environment frequented by a host of arts enthusiasts and professionals—from collectors, artists, and administrators to gallerists and community organizers.

Secondary Categories: Arts Services, Visual Arts

BAM
See Primary listing under Multi-Disciplinary Arts

BEDFORD STUYVESANT RESTORATION CORPORATION'S CENTER FOR ARTS AND CULTURE - SKYLIGHT GALLERY
1368 Fulton Street
Brooklyn, NY 11216

Tel 718-636-6949
Fax 718-636-0511
Email artws@restorationplaza.org
Web www.restorationplaza.org

President: Colvin Grannum

Sloped ceilings, skylights, and expansive windows make the 2,000-square-foot Skylight Gallery the only exhibition space of its kind in Brooklyn. Featuring contemporary artists of African descent, the Gallery serves as a valuable cultural link by providing a professional forum for artistic expression and the presentation of a variety of artistic styles.

Secondary Categories: Arts for Children/Teens, Visual Arts

BELANTHI
See Primary listing under Music

BREEDINGGROUND PRODUCTIONS
See Primary listing under Multi-Disciplinary Arts

BRIC ARTS | MEDIA | BROOKLYN
See Primary listing under Multi-Disciplinary Arts

BRIC ROTUNDA GALLERY
See Primary listing under Visual Arts

BROOKLYN ARTISANS GALLERY
221-A Court Street
Brooklyn, NY 11201

Tel 718-330-0343
Email may1clay@verizon.net
Web www.brooklynartisans.com

The Brooklyn Artisans Gallery is a co-op gallery that sells members' artwork and handmade objects, from earrings to prints, created within Brooklyn and the nearby tri-state region.

Secondary Category: Visual Arts

BROOKLYN ARTISTS GYM
See Primary listing under Visual Arts

BROOKLYN ARTS COUNCIL
See Primary listing under Arts Services

BROOKLYN ARTS EXCHANGE
See Primary listing under Multi-Disciplinary Arts

BROOKLYN COLLEGE ART GALLERY
LaGuardia Library,
2900 Bedford Avenue
Brooklyn, NY 11210-2889

Tel 718-951-5181
Email arand@brooklyn.cuny.edu

Director: Maria Catalano-Rand

The Brooklyn College Art Gallery's mission is to display work of both community and educational interest on- and off-campus.

Secondary Category: Visual Arts

BROOKLYN HISTORICAL SOCIETY
See Primary listing under Historical Societies

BROOKLYN PUBLIC LIBRARY
See Primary listing under Literary Arts

BROOKLYN WATERFRONT ARTISTS COALITION
See Primary listing under Visual Arts

GALLERIES

CAVE
See Primary listing under
Multi-Disciplinary Arts

CHASSIDIC ART INSTITUTE (CHAI)
375 Kingston Avenue
Brooklyn, NY 11213

Tel 718-774-9149
President: James J. Plesser

The Chassidic Art Institute (CHAI) was founded in 1977 to encourage the development of Chassidic art, which has its roots in Eastern European Jewish traditions. The only organization of its kind in the world, the institute houses a gallery, organizes traveling exhibitions, and hosts performances from its headquarters in the Crown Heights neighborhood.

Secondary Categories: Arts Services, Visual Arts

CHASSIDIC DISCOVERY WELCOME CENTER
See Primary listing under
Multi-Disciplinary Arts

CH'I CONTEMPORARY FINE ART
293 Grand Street
Brooklyn, NY 11211

Tel 718-218-8939
Fax 718-218-9347
Email tracy@chicontemporaryfineart.com
Web www.chicontemporaryfineart.com

Owner and Director:
Tracy A. Causey Jeffery

Ch'i Contemporary Fine Art is dedicated to presenting living artists—both emerging and mid-career—focusing on work in either an abstract, textural or a fragmented, figurative style. Ch'i hosts nine to ten exhibitions annually, in addition to artist demonstrations, studio tours, and school group visits throughout the year.

Secondary Category: Visual Arts

CINDERS GALLERY
103 Havemeyer Street
Brooklyn, NY 11211

Tel 718-388-2311
Email info@cindersgallery.com
Web www.cindersgallery.com

Co-Director: Kelie Bowman

Cinders Gallery is an artist-run space in Williamsburg that focuses on the underground art community locally and internationally by hosting monthly exhibitions and events. The Gallery's store section features artist books, zines, shirts, and handmade goodies.

Secondary Category: Visual Arts

CLINTON HILL ART GALLERY
P.O. Box 050200
Brooklyn, NY 11205

Site address:
154-A Vanderbilt Avenue
Brooklyn, NY 11205

Tel 718-852-0227
Fax 718-624-5041
Email framinglady@verizon.net

Gallery Director: L. B. Brown

The Clinton Hill Art Gallery specializes in Brooklyn-based painters and sculptors. The Gallery promotes original art for urban spaces and mounts group exhibits and solo shows for collectors' viewings and acquisitions.

Secondary Categories: Arts Services, Visual Arts

CLINTON HILL SIMPLY ART & FRAMING GALLERY
P.O. Box 050200
Brooklyn, NY 11205

Site address:
583 Myrtle Avenue
Brooklyn, NY 11205

Tel 718-857-0074
Fax 718-624-5041
Email framinglady@verizon.net

President and Gallery Director:
L .B. Brown

The Clinton Hill Simply Art & Framing Gallery specializes in art on paper, fine art reproductions, posters, offset lithographs, and original prints featuring Caribbean, Native American, African American, and Hispanic art. The Gallery provides custom picture framing services for the home and workspace as well as archival picture framing services.

Secondary Categories: Arts Services, Visual Arts

CORRIDOR GALLERY

334 Grand Avenue
Brooklyn, NY 11238

Tel 718-230-5002
Fax 718-638-0741
Email mmcneal@rushphilanthropic.org
Web www.rushphilanthropic.org

Director: Meridith McNeal

Corridor Gallery, founded and operated by artist Danny Simmons, is a community-based gallery serving Brooklyn residents and artists, with a primary focus on artist and audience development. The gallery presents five exhibitions per year with frequent public programs, and also serves as the base for the Rush Philanthropic Arts Foundation's education programs.

Secondary Categories: Arts for Children/Teens, Visual Arts

CTS (CREATIVE THRIFTSHOP)

635 Humboldt Street
Brooklyn , NY 11222

Tel 917-826-5550
Email info@creativethriftshop.com
Web www.creativethriftshop.com

Director: Lynn del Sol

CTS is quality art on the move. Championing provocative content-driven work by local and international mid-career and emerging artists in all media, CTS creates opportunities that foster its artists' growth, enabling them to broaden their reach by not only participating in museum and gallery exhibitions but also art fairs, charitable benefits, residencies, lectures, and biennales around the world.

Secondary Categories: Film/Video, Visual Arts

DABORA GALLERY

1080 Manhattan Avenue
Brooklyn, NY 11222

Tel 718-609-9629
Web www.daboragallery.com

Director: Lynda Mahan

Located in Greenpoint, Dabora is a self-described "Victorian salon art gallery."

Secondary category: Visual Arts

DAM, STUHLTRAGER GALLERY

38 Marcy Avenue
Brooklyn, NY 11211

Tel 718-387-9818
Email info@damstuhltrager.com
Web www.damstuhltrager.com

Director: Leah H. Stuhltrager

Founded in 1998, Dam, Stuhltrager Gallery is a contemporary art gallery located in Williamsburg. The gallery's mission is to emphasize the importance of art, promote artists professionally, and build financial support for the arts. Exhibited artwork is driven conceptually, not commercially.

Secondary Categories: Film/Video, Music, Performance Art, Visual Arts

DUMBO ARTS CENTER

See Primary listing under Visual Arts

THE ELEVENTEN GALLERY

1110 Fulton Street
Brooklyn, NY 11238

Tel 718-857-5696
Email eleventengallery@aol.com
Web www.myspace.com/1110gallery

Director and Curator:
D. Lammie-Hanson

A project of the South Of the Navy Yard Artists (SONYA) collective, The ElevenTen Gallery is an artist-run nonprofit gallery whose mission is to recognize, support, and celebrate the visual art and artists of its community. The ElevenTen's exhibitions feature community outreach programs such as artist talks, workshops, and discussion groups.

Secondary Categories: Arts Services, Literary Arts, Multi-Disciplinary Arts, Music, Performance Art, Visual Arts

ETGALLERIES

3026 Brighton 14 Street, Suite F7
Brooklyn, NY 11235

Tel 718-891-0677
Email admin@etgalleries.com
Web www.etgalleries.com

President and Founder:
Edward Tarashchansky

Founded by Edward Tarashchansky in 2003, ETGalleries represents and promotes unique, talented, surreal, figurative, and abstract artists from all over the world. As of 2007, ETGalleries is in the process of opening its first gallery space in SoHo New York, with branches planned for other American cities.

Secondary Categories: Arts Services, Visual Arts

EX GALLERY

872 Kent Avenue, Storefront
Brooklyn, NY 11205-2701

Tel 718-783-0060
Fax 718-399-1577
Email rasuph@aol.com

President: Suellen A. Levy

The Ex Gallery, located in the Fort Greene section of Brooklyn, hosts innovative shows by local and area artists.

Secondary Category: Visual Arts

FIVEMYLES

558 St. Johns Place
Brooklyn, NY 11238

Tel 718-783-4438
Fax 212-982-2328
Email hannetw@gmail
Web www.fivemyles.org

Director: Hanne Tierney

An exhibition and performance space, FiveMyles shows strong experimental work, with special emphasis given to emerging African American artists. FiveMyles also sponsors several annual community events, and in 2000 received an OBIE Award for "presenting magnificent contemporary works that fully engage the folks in the neighborhood."

Secondary Categories: Multi-Disciplinary Arts, Presenting Organizations, Visual Arts

FLAVORS OF HAITI FINE ARTS & CRAFTS GALLERY

111 Front Street, Gallery 228
Brooklyn, NY 11201

Tel 718-243-2292
Fax 718-243-2005
Email info@flavorsofhaiti.com
Web www.flavorsofhaiti.com

Director: Louis-Marc Lazarre

The only Haitian art gallery in the New York metropolitan area, Flavors of Haiti exhibits not only painting and sculpture, but also clothes, ceramics, and masks as well.

Secondary Category: Visual Arts

FRONT ROOM GALLERY
147 Roebling Street
Brooklyn, NY 11211

Tel 718-782-2556
Email info@frontroom.org
Web www.frontroom.org

Director: Daniel Aycock

Since 1999, the Front Room Gallery has been dedicated to exhibiting artwork by emerging and mid-career artists, with a concentration on photography, conceptual art, video, audio art, and installation. The Front Room shows works that are at times ephemeral, conceptual, or noncommercial in nature.

Secondary Category: Visual Arts

GALAPAGOS ART SPACE
See Primary listing under Multi-Disciplinary Arts

GALERIA GALOU
Email patcazorla@gmail.com
Web www.galeriagalou.com

An exhibition space created in 2003, Galeria Galou supports emerging artists, both locally and internationally. Multiculturalism and attention to diverse media are quintessential elements in the work exhibited by the Galeria Galou artists.

Secondary Categories: Arts Services, Visual Arts

GALERIA JANET KURNATOWSKI
205 Norman Avenue
Brooklyn, NY 11222

Tel 718-383-9380
Web www.galeriajanet.com

Gallery Director: Janet Kurnatowski

Founded in November 2004, Galeria Janet Kurnatowski hosts ten shows per year of emerging, mid-career, and established artists, with an emphasis on abstract painting. Visitors can always expect to see something new

and exciting on the gallery's walls.

Secondary Category: Visual Arts

GALLERIES AT LONG ISLAND UNIVERSITY BROOKLYN CAMPUS
1 University Plaza
Brooklyn, NY 11201

Tel 718-488-1198

Gallery Director: Nancy Grove

The Humanities, Salena, and Resnick Galleries of Long Island University's Brooklyn Campus host new art exhibitions of work by emerging and established artists every month throughout the school year.

Secondary Category: Visual Arts

THE GALLERY AT HARRIET'S ALTER EGO
293 Flatbush Avenue
Brooklyn, NY 11217

Tel 718-783-2074
Email info@harrietsalteregoonline.com
Web www.harrietsalteregoonline.com

Co-Owner and Curator: Ngozi Odita

Opened in the spring of 2006 in Prospect Heights, the Gallery at Harriet's Alter Ego focuses on showcasing the work of emerging artists, and has become an important resource and support vehicle for Brooklyn-based artists. The Gallery and all of its programming are free and open to the public.

Secondary Categories: Multi-Disciplinary Arts, Visual Arts

GEORGE WASHINGTON CARVER GALLERY
677 Lafayette Avenue
Brooklyn, NY 11216

Tel 718-387-2116
Fax 718-387-6133
Email info@magnoliatreeearthcenter.org
Web www.magnoliatreeearthcenter.org

President: David M. Greaves

George Washington Carver Gallery is approximately 900 square feet of space located in Bedford Stuyvesant. The gallery was created as a venue for community artists to exhibit their work, and invites local and international, non-professional and professional artists, to connect, educate, engage, inform, and inspire the community through the arts.

Secondary Category: Visual Arts

GITANA ROSA GALLERY
19 Hope Street, 1st Floor, #7
Brooklyn, NY 11211

Tel 718-387-0115
Email info@gitanarosa.com
Web www.gitanarosa.com

Founder and Director: Vanessa Liberati

Williamsburg's first "green" gallery, Gitana Rosa Gallery is dedicated to promoting emerging talents who make bold statements through artistic expression, to promoting eco-sustainable lifestyles, and to stimulating new methods of thinking. Moreover, the gallery owner and artist both contribute a portion of their sales to a revolving list of local and national environmental nonprofits.

Secondary Categories:
Architecture & Urban Development
Film/Video, Visual Arts,

GLORIA KENNEDY GALLERY
111 Front Street, Gallery 222
Brooklyn, NY 11201

Tel 718-858-5254
Email gloria@gkart.com
Web www.gkart.com/

Owner: Gloria M. Kennedy

Located in the DUMBO gallery area, the Gloria Kennedy Gallery presents contemporary art by both emerging and known artists in diverse, spectacular exhibitions that define the art space in a new vernacular. All media

are exhibited, with a special emphasis on three-dimensional works.

Secondary Category: Visual Arts

GOLOBOROTKO'S STUDIO
See Primary listing under Visual Arts

THE GOWANUS STUDIO SPACE, INC.
See Primary listing under
Multi-Disciplinary Arts

HENRY GREGG GALLERY
111 Front Street, #226
Brooklyn, NY 11201

Tel 718-408-1090
Email art@henrygregg.gallery.com
Web www.henrygregggallery.com

President: Henry M. Reed

The Henry Gregg Gallery is located in Brooklyn's vibrant DUMBO section, home to a burgeoning art scene. The Henry Gregg Gallery takes pride in both representing the work of today's nationally and internationally celebrated artists and in creating unique, innovative shows.

Secondary Category: Visual Arts

THE HOGAR COLLECTION
362 Grand Street
Brooklyn, NY 11211

Tel 718 388-5022
Email info@hogarcollection.com
Web www.hogarcollection.com

Director: Todd Rosenbaum

The Hogar Collection is a contemporary art gallery in the flourishing arts community of Williamsburg that represents local and international artists working in all media, including painting, sculpture, photography, installation, video, and sound. The gallery is dedicated to the promotion of new art, dialogues, and perspectives, and strives to reflect the diversity of our ever-changing world.

Secondary Categories: Arts Services, Film/Video, Multi-Disciplinary Arts, Music, Visual Arts

HOLLAND TUNNEL
61 South 3rd Street
Brooklyn, NY 11211

Tel 718-384-5738
Fax 718-384-5738
Email hollandtunnelart@yahoo.com
Web www.hollandtunnelart.net

Director: Paulien Lethen

A unique Williamsburg art space with a sister branch on the island of Paros, Greece, the Holland Tunnel features special exhibitions by international and local artists at select times of the year.

Secondary Category: Visual Arts

HQ
236 Grand Street
Brooklyn, NY 11211

Tel 718-418-7182
Email jaxonmcdade@ehteam.ca
Web www.hqbrooklyn.com

President: Jackson McDade

HQ is a commercial gallery with a focus on sculpture, architecture, and process-based work.

Secondary Category: Visual Arts

ISSUE PROJECT ROOM
See Primary listng under Multi-Disciplinary Arts

JEWISH FOLK CRAFTS GUILD (JFCGI)
P.O. Box 297191
Brooklyn, NY 11229

Site address:
3495 Nostrand Avenue
Brooklyn, NY 11229

Tel 646-321-5220
Email jfcgi@yahoo.com
Web www.jfcgi.org

President: Ilya Nathanson

The mission of the Jewish Folk Crafts Guild is to preserve and develop traditional Jewish visual arts and crafts. Since 2000, the Guild has presented dozens of exhibitions and other displays as well as helped to bring the work of more than 60 artists and artisans before the public.

Secondary Category: Visual Arts

KENTLER INTERNATIONAL DRAWING SPACE
353 Van Brunt Street
Brooklyn, NY 11231

Tel 718-875-2098
Email info@kentlergallery.org
Web www.kentlergallery.org

Director: Florence Neal

Founded by two artists in 1990, the Kentler International Drawing Space presents contemporary drawings and works on paper by local, national, and international artists as part of the cultural fabric of the community. Open to the public by appointment, the Kentler Flatfiles consist of drawings and works on paper by over 100 artists.

Secondary Category: Visual Arts

KLAUS VON NICHTSSAGEND GALLERY
438 Union Avenue
Brooklyn, NY 11211

Tel 718-383-7309
Email info@klausgallery.com
Web www.klausgallery.com

Co-Director: Sam Wilson

Klaus von Nichtssagend Gallery is a contemporary art gallery focused on solo exhibitions of international emerging artists.

Secondary Category: Visual Arts

KLOMPCHING LLC
111 Front Street, Suite 206
Brooklyn, NY 11201

Tel 212-796-2070
Email info@klompching.com
Web www.klompching.com

Klompching Gallery features the work of emerging talent alongside under-recognized work by established photographers. The gallery showcases photography that demonstrates creative integrity and intent, originality, narrative and aesthetic challenges, and a high level of craftsmanship. Klompching offers an itinerary of events, including book launches and signings, gallery talks, and presentations.

Secondary Category: Visual Arts

LAND GALLERY AND STUDIO (LEAGUE ARTISTS NATURAL DESIGN)
67 Front Street
Brooklyn, NY 11201

Tel 718-643-5300
Fax 718-643-5300
Email info@leaguetreatment.org
Web www.leaguetreatment.org

CEO: Hannah Achtenberg Kinn

LAND, League Artists Natural Design, is a unique studio and gallery that features work of adult artists living with disabilities. LAND is designed to help these artists develop their skills in a nurturing environment and market their art to the community in a vibrant and inclusive manner.

Secondary Category: Visual Arts

LEFFERTS HISTORIC HOUSE
See Primary listing under Museums

LEWIS GALLERY
411 Lewis Avenue (at Decatur Street)
Brooklyn, NY 11233

Tel 718-624-8372
Email lewisgallery525@aol.com
Web www.lewisgallery525.com
CEO: Gwen Lewis

Located in downtown Brooklyn, the Lewis Gallery showcases original works and limited/open edition prints by a variety of artists from both the neighborhood and around the United States. Among other services, the Gallery also provides custom framing and classes in life drawing, quilt-making, doll creation, and art for young adults.

Secondary Categories: Arts Services, Visual Arts

LIKE THE SPICE
224 Roebling Street
Brooklyn, NY 11211

Tel 718-388-5388
Fax 718-388-5488
Email info@likethespice.com
Web www.likethespice.com

Owner and Director: Marisa I. Sage

A new contemporary gallery and art instructional epicenter as committed to community as it is to art, Like the Spice reaches out to its Williamsburg neighbors with classes in graphics programs, digital photography, video, and drawing. Like the Spice also hosts monthly live performances, lectures, and workshops.

Secondary Categories: Arts Services, Computer Arts/New Media, Multi-Disciplinary Arts, Performance Art, Visual Arts

LMAKPROJECTS
526 West 26th Street, #310
New York, NY 10001

Site address:
60 North 6th Street
Brooklyn, NY 11211

Tel 718-599-0089
Email info@lmakprojects.com
Web www.lmakprojects.com

Gallery Director: Louky Keijsers

LMAKprojects, founded in 2004, is dedicated to supporting and developing artists' careers, focusing on inter-disciplinary practices, interactive situations, and collaborative ventures. Best known for showing film and video art, LMAKprojects also presents works in drawing, painting, photography, and sculpture by artists from all over the world.

Secondary Categories: Arts Services, Computer Arts/New Media, Film/Video, Performance Art, Visual Arts

MAGNOLIA TREE EARTH CENTER
See Primary listing under Educational Institutions

MCCAIG-WELLES GALLERY
129 Roebling Street
Brooklyn, NY 11211

Tel 718-384-8729
Web www.mccaigwelles.com

Director: Melissa K. McCaig-Welles

The McCaig-Welles Gallery officially opened its doors in March 2001, on the south side of Williamsburg. Several years later and a few blocks further north, the gallery continues to champion street, underground, and outsider artists. Most of McCaig-Welles' artists live and work in New York, with careers ranging from mid- to well-established.

Secondary Categories: Arts Services, Visual Arts

METAPHOR CONTEMPORARY ART
382 Atlantic Avenue
Brooklyn, NY 11217

Tel 718-254-9126
Web www.metaphorcontemporary art.com

Co-Director: Julian Jackson

metaphor contemporary art exhibits exceptional work in painting, sculpture, works on paper, and new media by emerging and mid-career artists in seven to ten exhibitions a year. metaphor also hosts readings, film and video showings, artist talks, and panel discussions.

Secondary Categories: Film/Video, Literary Arts, Multi-Disciplinary Arts, Visual Arts

MICHAEL ALAN'S DRAW-A-THON
See Primary listing under Arts Services

MILL BASIN DELI AND FINE ART GALLERY
Web www.nymuseum.com

Owner: Mark Schachner

The Mill Basin Deli and Fine Art Gallery is a restaurant specializing in kosher cusine that also happens to have a major collection of artwork decorating its walls. The collection includes works by renowned artists such as Erte, Roy Lichtenstien, James Rizzi, Marc Chagall, Alphonse Mucha, and others.

Secondary Categories: Arts Services, Visual Arts

MOMENTA ART
359 Bedford Avenue
Brooklyn, NY 11211

Tel 718-218-8058
Fax 347-448-8268
Email info@momentaart.org
Web www.momentaart.org

Director: Eric Heist

Momenta Art is an artist-run charitable institution that promotes emerging and underrepresented artists by showing work that isn't well-represented in commercial galleries because of its form or content. Momenta Art supports artists of all ages, races, and ethnicities.

Secondary Category: Visual Arts

THE MUDPIT
See Primary listing under Arts Services

NEIL STEVENSON FINE ART LLC
114 South First Street
Brooklyn, NY 11211
Email neil@stevensonfineart.com

Owner: Neil W. Stevenson

Representing contemporary artists since 1998, Neil Stevenson Fine Art LLC is a gallery dedicated to presenting the finest in contemporary art in the heart of Williamsburg.

Secondary Category: Visual Arts

NELSON HANCOCK GALLERY
111 Front Street, #204
Brooklyn, NY 11201

Tel 718-408-1190
Email info@nelsonhancockgallery.com
Web www.nelsonhancockgallery.com

Director: Nelson Hancock

Located in DUMBO's gallery district, the Nelson Hancock Gallery specializes in contemporary fine art photography.

Secondary Category: Visual Arts

NUNU GALLERIE
847-A Union Street
Brooklyn, NY 11215

Tel 718-623-8917
Web www.nunugallery.com

Owner: Vadim V. Kokhnovitch

Located in the center of Park Slope, NuNu Gallerie offers a range of services, including gallery space, quality supplies and frames, show preparation, packing, crating, and shipping for artists, as well as conservation custom framing, matting, and glazing for individuals and organizations.

Secondary Categories: Arts Services, Visual Arts

OBJECT IMAGE GALLERY
91 Fifth Avenue
Brooklyn, NY 11217

Tel 718-623-2434
Email objectimagegallery@earthlink.net

Web www.objectimagegallery.com
Owner and Director: Bob Weiss

A consignment gallery in Park Slope, the Object Image Gallery exhibits and sells contemporary paintings, prints, and drawings. While many Object Image artists are from Brooklyn, and the gallery specializes in Brooklyn scenes, Object Image also represents artists from across the country and around the world.

Secondary Category: Visual Arts

ONE SIXTY GLASS
See Primary listing under Arts Services

PARK SLOPE GALLERY
Tel 718-768-4883
Fax 718-965-4199
Email parkslopegallery@mindspring.com
Web www.parkslopegallery.com

Director: Phyllis Wrynn

Park Slope Gallery specializes in the art of the WPA Federal Art Project and American mid-century art and design, in addition to representing several gifted contemporary artists. Conveniently located in a 19th-century brownstone, and open by appointment only, the gallery also offers complete custom archival framing services.

Secondary Categories: Arts Services. Visual Arts

PARKER'S BOX
193 Grand Street
Brooklyn, NY 11211

Tel 718-388-2882
Web www.parkersbox.com

Director: Alun Williams

Based in Williamsburg, Parker's Box is committed to championing the work of both American and overseas artists whose practice and attitudes are innovative and also curious about both the mechanisms of the contemporary world and the mechanisms that operate within a work of art.

Secondary Category: Visual Arts

PIEROGI (PIEROGI 2000)
177 North 9th Street
Brooklyn, NY 11211

Tel 718-599-2144
Fax 718-599-2144
Email joe@pierogi2000.com
Web www.pierogi2000.com

Director: Joe Amrhein

An artist-run gallery in Williamsburg, Pierogi has monthly solo shows featuring emerging and mid-career artists in an eclectic range of media and styles. The Pierogi "flat files," housing the portfolios of more than 700 artists, began with the idea of making artwork available to a larger audience.

Secondary Categories: Film/Video, Performance Art, Visual Arts

PLUTO
730 Classon Avenue
Brooklyn, NY 11238

Tel 646-894-7777
Email mollybradford@plutonyc.com
Web www.plutonyc.com

President: Molly Bradford Pace

Situated at the outskirts of Prospect Heights and a short walk from the Brooklyn Museum, pluto exhibits Brooklyn artists who have the ability to draw as a foundation of their work. pluto also features curations by established Brooklyn artists and archival documentary films about the work and artists shown.

Secondary Categories: Film/Video, Visual Arts

POLIZZI FINE ART
7813 Third Avenue
Brooklyn, NY 11209

Email jerry@polizzifineart.com

Web www.polizzifineart.com

Director: Jerry Polizzi

In business in New York City for almost thirty years, Polizzi Fine Art specializes in twentieth-century and contemporary American and European art.

Secondary Category: Visual Arts

PRATT INSTITUTE
See Primary listing under Educational Institutions

PROSPECT PARK & PROSPECT PARK ALLIANCE
See Primary listing under Multi-Disciplinary Arts

PROSPECT PARK AUDUBON CENTER
See Primary listing under Architecture & Urban/Environmental Design

PROTEUS GOWANUS
See Primary listing under Multi-Disciplinary Arts

REVELATION PERFORMING ARTS STUDIO, INC.
See Primary listing under Visual/Performing Arts Schools

THE RIVIERA
103 Metropolitan Avenue
Brooklyn, NY 11211

Tel 718-599-5589
Email info@seeyouattheriviera.com
Web www.seeyouattheriviera.com

Managing Director: Chloé A. Derderian

Located near the Williamsburg waterfront, the Riviera Gallery has made a name for itself nationally and internationally as an alternative art space. As an artist-run gallery, the Riviera specializes in exhibiting gifted young artists whose work and careers don't conform to any established art world orthodoxy.

Secondary Categories: Arts for Children/Teens, Folk Arts, Visual Arts

GALLERIES

RUBELLE AND NORMAN SCHAFLER GALLERY AT THE PRATT INSTITUTE
200 Willoughby Avenue
Brooklyn, NY 11205

Tel 718-636-3517
Email exhibits@pratt.edu
Web www.pratt.edu/exhibitions

Director of Exhibitions: Nick Battis

The Rubelle and Norman Schafler Gallery exhibits art and design work by students and faculty of the Pratt Institute year-round.

Secondary Categories: Educational Institutions, Visual Arts

S.E.E.D GALLERY
111 Front Street, Suite 224
Brooklyn, NY 11201

Tel 917-622-8761
Email s.e.e.dgallery@gmail.com
Web www.seedgallerynewyork.com

Director: nya' matingo

s.e.e.d gallery's avowed mission is to show paintings that stimulate the soul, awaken the spirit, and elevate viewers' minds to new horizons where impossibilities melt away, and the power of faith reigns.

Secondary Category: Visual Arts

SAFE-T-GALLERY
111 Front Street
Brooklyn, NY 11201

Tel 718-782-5920
Fax 718-782-5938
Email info@safetgallery.com
Web www.safetgallery.com

Director: Don Burmeister

Safe-T-Gallery features works by contemporary artists for adventurous collectors. Safe-T exhibits photography, works on paper, painting, and installation art and specializes in topographical, serial, obsessive, and delusional art.

Secondary Categories: Film/Video, Performance Art, Visual Arts

SANKARANKA GALLERY
111 Front Street Suite 230-206
Brooklyn, NY 11201

Tel 718-666-3636
Email info@sankarankagallery.com
Web www.sankarankagallery.com

Gallery Director: Saihou Saidy

Sankaranka Gallery is founded on the belief that present-day African artists—professionals who produce top-quality artworks—should be given a chance to show their works to a much wider audience. Sankaranka Gallery focuses on ceramicists, painters, and sculptors from across the continent, in individual and group shows.

Secondary Category: Visual Arts

SANKOFA ART CENTRE
501 Washington Avenue
Brooklyn, NY 11238

Tel 718-399-3557
Email hramsaran@gmail.com

Director: Helen Evans Ramsaran

Established as a nonprofit in 1997, Sankofa Art Centre is a community art school dedicated to teaching art to adults who have little or no experience working in the visual arts. Located in Fort Greene, in a 900-square-foot loft space, Sankofa offers ceramics classes to adults and hosts student exhibitions with an open invitation to the entire arts community.

Secondary Category: Visual Arts

SARAH BOWEN GALLERY
210 North 6th Street
Brooklyn, NY 11211

Tel 718-302-4517
Email info@sarahbowengallery.com
Web www.sarahbowengallery.com

President Director: Sarah Bowen

sarah bowen gallery features artists who create progressive contemporary art in all media. The gallery is pleased to be part of the thriving Williamsburg art community.

Secondary Category: Visual Arts

SLATE GALLERY
136 Wythe Avenue
Brooklyn, NY 11211

Tel 718-387-3921
Email kim@slategallery.com
Web www.slategallery.com

Director: Kim Vaadia

Fitting into the spirit of the Williamsburg art scene, Slate Gallery features projects and exhibitions by emerging and established artists who are free to exhibit using traditional and non-traditional means. An equally important aspect of Slate's activities is consulting in the resale art market, specializing in both modern and contemporary art.

Secondary Categories: Arts Services, Performance Art, Visual Arts

SMACK MELLON
See Primary listing under Visual Arts

SOAPBOX GALLERY
See Primary listing under Visual Arts

SOUTH OF THE NAVY YARD ARTISTS
See Primary listing under Visual Arts

SOUTHFIRST: ART
60 North 6th Street
Brooklyn, NY 11211

Tel 718-599-4884
Email info@southfirst.org
Web www.southfirst.org

Co-Founders: Florian Altenburg and Maika Pollack

Southfirst: Art specializes in exhibitions of contemporary artists and artist-curated group shows. Run by co-founders Florian Altenburg and Maika Pollack, the space has been called "one of the best young galleries in Brooklyn" by the New York Times. It is named for the street in Williamsburg where the gallery was started in 2001.

Secondary Categories: Multi-Disciplinary Arts, Visual Arts

SPOKE THE HUB DANCING, INC.
See Primary listing under Multi-Disciplinary Arts

SPRING
126-A Front Street
Brooklyn, NY 11201

Tel 718-222-1054
Email info@spring3d.net
Web www.spring3d.net

Director: Anna Cosentino

Spring is an exhibition space and store promoting design and art through curated shows and highlighted products.

Secondary Category: Visual Arts

ST. JOSEPH'S COLLEGE, NY
See Primary listing under Educational Institutions

STACY STEWART SMITH GALLERY
See Primary listing under Visual Arts

STRIPEMAN GALLERY LTD.
101 North 3rd Street
Brooklyn, NY 11211

Tel 718-782-1552
Email stripemangallery@aol.com
Web www.stripemangallery.com

Director: Edward Schoenberg

Located in Williamsburg, the Stripeman Gallery specializes in selling works of contemporary artists.

Secondary Category: Visual Arts

GALLERIES

STUDIO 354, INC. (354 EXHIBITIONS)
354 Degraw Street
Brooklyn, NY 11231
Tel 718-625-3839
Email exhibit354@earthlink.net
President: Ron Meisner

Studio 354, Inc. is a gallery, private art dealer, and graphic design/artist's studio based in Cobble Hill.

Secondary Category: Visual Arts

TABLA RASA GALLERY
224 48th Street
Brooklyn, NY 11220
Tel 718-833-9100
Fax 718-833-9118
Email info@tablarasagallery.com
Web www.tablarasagallery.com
Director: Audrey Anastasi

Located in a turn-of-the-century carriage house in industrial Sunset Park, Tabla Rasa presents solo and group exhibitions in various styles, themes, and media, by both emerging and established artists. Tabla Rasa also hosts films, panels, presentations, book signings, and catered events.

Secondary Categories: Computer Arts/New Media, Film/Video, Multi-Disciplinary Arts, Visual Arts

UNDERBRIDGE PICTURES
111 Front Street
Brooklyn, NY 11201
Tel 718-596-0390
Email stjamesworkshop@rcn.com
Web www.underbridgepictures.com
Director: David J. Sokosh

Underbridge Pictures is a fine art gallery located in DUMBO, focusing on architectural images, with an interest in traditional and historic photographic processes, and an emphasis on images of Brooklyn and Manhattan.

Secondary Categories: Architecture & Urban/Environmental Design, Historical Societies, Visual Arts

THE URBAN DIVERS (UDEC ENVIRO MEDIA)
c/o UDEC
89 Pioneer Street
Brooklyn, NY 11231
Tel 718-802-9874
Email theurbandivers@yahoo.com
Web www.geocities.com/submerge festival
Executive Director: Ludger K. Balan

Traveling to various indoor and outdoor venues around New York Harbor, the Urban Divers' annual "Submerge" Art and Environment Festival showcases films, videos, photography, and environmental remediation exhibits by local and international artists that raise public awareness of our fragile aquatic environments, and the environmental, social, and political issues that challenge them.

Secondary Categories: Presenting Organizations, Visual Arts

URBANGLASS
See Primary listing under Visual Arts

VERTEXLIST
See Primary listing under Computer Arts/New Media

WEEKSVILLE HERITAGE CENTER
See Primary listing under Historical Societies

WESSEL + O'CONNOR FINE ART (WESSEL + O'CONNOR GALLERY)
111 Front Street
Brooklyn, NY 11201
Web www.wesseloconnor.com
Owner: William C. O'Connor

Wessel + O'Connor Fine Art is a photography gallery located in DUMBO. Recent exhibits have featured the

photographs of Eadweard Muybridge
and Andy Warhol, among others.

Secondary Category: Visual Arts

ZION GALLERY
152 McDonough Street
Brooklyn, NY 11216

Tel 718-919-8014
Email fmhartley@aol.com
Web www.ziongallerybedstuy.com

Director: Fedrecia Hartley

Located in a 19th-century brownstone
in the historic landmark district of
Bedford Stuyvesant, Zion Gallery car-
ries functional and fine art by emerging
and established artists. Zion Gallery's
mission is to enrich the community
artistically by providing exhibitions,
receptions, workshops, seminars, and
art classes.

Secondary Categories: Arts Services,
Visual Arts

The artist's job is to be
a witness to his time
in history.

ROBERT RAUSCHENBERG

HISTORICAL SOCIETIES

BAY RIDGE HISTORICAL SOCIETY
P.O. Box 090-483, Fort Hamilton
Station, Brooklyn, NY 11209
Tel 718-836-0544
President: Peter J. Scarpa

The Bay Ridge Historical Society offers
slideshows, lectures, bus trips, and
books on the south Brooklyn neighborhood of Bay Ridge.

**BENSONHURST WEST END
COMMUNITY COUNCIL (BWECC)**
2483 West 16th Street, #7H
Brooklyn, NY 11214
Tel 718-946-6667
Fax 718-975-0307
Email diegovega@aol.com
President: Carmine C. Santa Maria

The Bensonhurst West End Community Council acts as a guardian of the
community, to protect and improve the
quality of life for residents, merchants,
and children. BWECC holds monthly
meetings, open to the public, and
sponsors an art show for community
artists on the first Sunday in June of
each year.

*Secondary Category: Arts for
Children/Teens*

BROOKLYN HISTORICAL SOCIETY (BHS)
128 Pierrepont Street
Brooklyn, NY 11201
Tel 718-222-4111
Fax 718-222-3794
Web www.brooklynhistory.org
President: Deborah F. Schwartz

Founded in 1863, the Brooklyn
Historical Society is a museum, library,
and educational center dedicated to
preserving and encouraging the study
of Brooklyn's rich past, present, and
future.

*Secondary Categories: Arts for
Children/Teens, Galleries, Museums*

BROOKLYN PUBLIC LIBRARY
See Primary listing under Literary Arts

**THE BROOKLYN SOCIETY FOR
ETHICAL CULTURE**
*See Primary listing under Presenting
Organizations*

CONEY ISLAND HISTORY PROJECT
Web www.coneyislandhistory.org
President: Dan Pisark

Founded in 2004, the nonprofit Coney
Island History Project aims to increase
awareness of Coney Island's legendary and colorful past and to encourage
appreciation of the Coney Island neighborhood of today. The Project's mission is to create an oral history of the
area, sponsor educational exhibits and
events, and provide access to historical
artifacts and documentary material.

*Secondary Category: Architecture
& Urban/Environmental Design*

LEFFERTS HISTORIC HOUSE
See Primary listing under Museums

NEW YORK TRANSIT MUSEUM
See Primary listing under Museums

UNDERBRIDGE PICTURES
See Primary listing under Galleries

WEEKSVILLE HERITAGE CENTER
(SOCIETY FOR THE PRESERVATION
OF WEEKSVILLE AND BEDFORD
STUYVESANT HISTORY)
P.O. Box 130120, St. John's Station
Brooklyn, NY 11213

Site address:
1698 Bergen Street
Brooklyn, NY 11213

Tel 718-756-5250
Fax 718-756-6277
Email info@weeksvillesociety.org
Web www.weeksvillesociety.org

Executive Director: Pamela Green

Weeksville Heritage Center is the site
of three restored historic houses open
Tuesdays through Saturdays for public
tours and educational programming.
Weeksville's mission is to document,
preserve, and interpret the history of
free African American communities
in Weeksville, Brooklyn and beyond,
and to create and inspire innovative
contemporary uses of African American
history through its free public programs, performances, and arts events.

*Secondary Categories: Architecture
& Urban/Environmental Design, Arts
for Children/Teens, Arts Services,
Educational Institutions, Film/Video,
Folk Arts, Galleries*

WYCKOFF FARMHOUSE MUSEUM
See Primary listing under Museums

LITERARY ARTS

440 GALLERY
See Primary listing under Galleries

AFRO HERITAGE VENTURE
*See Primary listing under
Multi-Disciplinary Arts*

AKASHIC BOOKS
232 Third Street, Room B404
Brooklyn, NY 11215

Tel 718-643-9193
Fax 718-643-9195
Email info@akashicbooks.com
Web www.akashicbooks.com

Publisher and Editor-in-Chief:
Johnny Temple

Akashic Books is a Brooklyn-based
independent company dedicated to
publishing urban literary fiction and
political nonfiction by authors who are
either ignored by the mainstream or
who have no interest in working within
the ever-consolidating ranks of the
major corporate publishers.

ARCHIPELAGO BOOKS
232 Third Street
Brooklyn, NY 11215

Tel 718-852-6134
Fax 718-852-6135
Email info@archipelagobooks.org
Web www.archipelagobooks.org

Publisher: Jill A. Schoolman

Archipelago Books is committed to
bringing international works of classic
and contemporary literature to the
United States. Motivated by the need
to expose American audiences to
under-represented literary and cultural

traditions from diverse corners of the
world, Archipelago has published 28
titles of fiction and poetry, translated
from over a dozen languages, in its first
four years.

Secondary Category: Arts Services

ART WITHOUT WALLS/FREE SPACE
*See Primary listing under Arts for
Children/Teens*

ATTITUDE: THE DANCERS' MAGAZINE
See Primary listing under Dance

AUTONOMEDIA
P.O. Box 568, Williamsburgh Station
Brooklyn, NY 11211

Site address:
55 South Eleventh Street
Brooklyn, NY 11211

Tel 718-963-2603
Fax 718-963-2603
Email jim@autonomedia.org
Web www.autonomedia.org

Editor and Publisher: Jim Fleming

An autonomous zone for arts radicals
in both old and new media, Autonomedia publishes books on radical media,
politics, and the arts that seek to tran-
scend party lines, bottom lines, and
straight lines. Autonomedia also maintains the Interactivist Info Exchange,
an online forum for debate on themes
relevant to the books it publishes.

BAC ARTS IN EDUCATION
*See Primary listing under Arts for
Children/Teens*

BAM
*See Primary listing under
Multi-Disciplinary Arts*

BAMCAFÉ LIVE
See Primary listing under Music

BOMB MAGAZINE
*See Primary listing under
Multi-Disciplinary Arts*

BOOKLYN ARTISTS ALLIANCE
See Primary listing under Visual Arts

BREEDINGGROUND PRODUCTIONS
*See Primary listing under
Multi-Disciplinary Art*

**BROOKLYN ALTERNATIVE SMALL
PRESS FAIR**
266 12th Street, #10
Brooklyn, NY 11215

Tel 718-832-2310
Fax 718-832-2310
Email emilyholiday@gmail.com
Web www.geocities.com/emily
brooklyn/smallpressfair

Founder and Coordinator: Emily Brown

A six-hour annual event, the Brooklyn
Alternative Small Press Fair provides
a marketplace for local small presses,
poets, and writers, increases public
awareness of the quality and diversity
of contemporary small press publishing
and self-publishing, and provides
an opportunity for networking with
the public and within the literary
community.

BROOKLYN DAILY EAGLE
30 Henry Street
Brooklyn, NY 11201

Tel 718-422-7400
Email brooklyneagle@att.net
Web www.brooklyneagle.com

Publisher: Dozier Hasty

The *Brooklyn Daily Eagle* publishes a
five-day-a-week newspaper of the
same name covering local news, the
arts, sports, real estate, and the
courts. The *Daily Eagle* also publishes
the *Brooklyn Heights Press*, which
covers Brooklyn Heights, and a weekly
Bay Ridge Eagle.

Secondary Category: Arts Services

THE BROOKLYN PAPER
See Primary listing under Arts Services

BROOKLYN PUBLIC LIBRARY (BPL)
Grand Army Plaza
Brooklyn, NY 11238

Tel 718-230-2100
Web www.brooklynpubliclibrary.org

Executive Director:
Dionne Mack-Harvin

An independent library system for
the 2.5 million residents of Brooklyn,
the Brooklyn Public Library is the fifth
largest library system in the United
States, with 60 neighborhood libraries
offering free programs and services for
all ages and stages of life, including a
huge selection of books in more than
30 languages.

*Secondary Categories: Architecture
& Urban/Environmental Design,
Arts for Children/Teens, Dance,
Educational Institutions, Film/Video,
Galleries, Historical Societies*

THE BROOKLYN RAIL
*See Primary listing under
Multi-Disciplinary Arts*

BROOKLYN WRITERS SPACE
58 Garfield Place
Brooklyn, NY 11215

Tel 718-788-2697
Web www.brooklynwriters.com

Manager: Scott Adkins

A shared creative space for writers,
Brooklyn Writers Space gives its members 24/7 access to a 2000-square-
foot facility with 22 partitioned desks,
a kitchenette lounge, a roof deck, two

bathrooms, and wi-fi. Applications are available at the organization's website.

Secondary Categories: Arts Services, Film/Video, Multi-Disciplinary Arts, Opera/Music Theater, Theater

THE BROWNSTONE POETS
Fifth Avenue Restaurant
432 5th Avenue
Brooklyn, NY 11215

Tel 718-832-8131
Web www.patricia.carragon.home.att.net

Curator, Editor, and Hostess:
Patricia Carragon

The Brownstone Poets is a Brooklyn-based poetry reading series held on the first Saturday of each month, as well as the additional third Saturday every other month. Two poets are featured per reading, and an open mic precedes and follows the featured readers. The Brownstone Poets also publishes an annual anthology.

Secondary Category: Music

CABINET
See Primary listing under Multi-Disciplinary Arts

CARIBBEAN CULTURAL THEATRE
See Primary listing under Theater

CENTER FOR THANATOLOGY RESEARCH AND EDUCATION, INC.
See Primary listing under Multi-Disciplinary Arts

CHRISTIANA DRAPKIN JAZZ GROUP
See Primary listing under Music

CREATIVE WOMEN'S NETWORK
See Primary listing under Arts Services

CRUCIAL ARTS PRODUCTIONS, INC.
See Primary listing under Multi-Disciplinary Arts

DANCE GIANT STEPS, INC.
See Primary listing under Multi-Disciplinary Arts

EGRESS THEATRE COMPANY
See Primary listing under Theater

ELDERS SHARE THE ARTS
See Primary listing under Multi-Disciplinary Arts

THE ELEVENTEN GALLERY
See Primary listing under Galleries

GALAPAGOS ART SPACE
See Primary Listing under Multi-Disciplinary Arts

GOING COASTAL, INC.
230 Sackett Street, #2L
Brooklyn, NY 11231

Email info@goingcoastal.org
Web www.goingcoastal.org

President: Barbara LaRocco

Going Coastal, Inc. is a nonprofit publishing and educational organization dedicated to connecting people and coastal resources. Through exhibitions, public events, and outreach programs, Going Coastal encourages both adults and children to enjoy and preserve New York City's urban coast.

Secondary Category: Presenting Organizations

HEART OF BROOKLYN
See Primary listing under Arts Services

IFETAYO CULTURAL ARTS
See Primary listing under Multi-Disciplinary Arts

IMAGINE PROJECT, INC.
See Primary listing under Arts for Children/Teens

METAPHOR CONTEMPORARY ART
See Primary listing under Galleries

LITERARY ARTS

NAT CREOLE ONLINE
See Primary listing under Computer Arts/New Media

NY WRITERS COALITION (NYWC)
80 Hanson Place, #603
Brooklyn, NY 11217

Tel 718-398-2883
Email info@nywriterscoalition.org
Web www.nywriterscoalition.org

Founder and Executive Director: Aaron Zimmerman

NY Writers Coalition, Inc. (NYWC) provides free and low-cost creative writing workshops throughout New York City for people from groups that have been historically deprived of a voice in our society. The Writers Coalition also publishes workshop participants' writing and organizes public readings of their work.

Secondary Categories: Arts for Children/Teens, Arts Services

THE OLD AMERICAN CAN FACTORY
See Primary listing under Presenting Organizations

ONE STORY
232 3rd Street, #A111
Brooklyn, NY 11215

Email custserv@one-story.com
Web www.one-story.com

Publisher: Maribeth Batcha

Launched in 2001, *One Story* is a literary magazine that publishes one short story every three weeks and mails it to over 3,000 subscribers. Stories published in *One Story* have been named "best of the year" in anthologies such as the Best American Short Stories and the O. Henry Prize Stories.

PLG ARTS
See Primary listing under Multi-Disciplinary Arts

PROTEUS GOWANUS
See Primary listing under Multi-Disciplinary Arts

REALFORM
See Primary listing under Visual Arts

ROOM 58
168 7th Street
Brooklyn, NY 11215

Tel 347-564-4847
Web www.room58.org

Manager: Erin Courtney

A partnership between Brooklyn Artists Gym and Brooklyn Writers Space, Room 58 provides a work space for researchers, journalists, and other writers. Services include a quiet room with partitioned desks and a phone room with partitioned desks, wi-fi, fax machine, printer, land line, lounge, and bright light from two exposures.

Secondary Category: Arts Services

SOFT SKULL PRESS, INC.
55 Washington Street, #804
Brooklyn, NY 11201

Web www.softskull.com

Publisher: Richard Nash

Soft Skull Press, Inc. is one of the leading independent publishers in North America, with a catalog that encompasses fiction, history, politics and current events, comix, and much more.

SPIRAL THOUGHT
266 12th Street, #10
Brooklyn, NY 11215

Tel 718-832-2310
Email emilyholiday@gmail.com
Web www.geocities.com/emily brooklyn/spiralthought

Founder and Coordinator: Emily Brown

After starting out as a small literary magazine in the mid-1980s, *Spiral Thought* has evolved into an ongoing monthly reading series based in a number of Brooklyn cafes.

Secondary Category: Presenting Organization

ST. JOSEPH'S COLLEGE, NY
See Primary listing under Educational Institution

SUNNY'S
See Primary listing under Music

TWW INC.
See Primary listing under Arts for Children/Teens

UGLY DUCKLING PRESSE (UDP)
c/o The Old American Can Factory
232 Third Street
Brooklyn, NY 11215

Email info@uglyducklingpresse.org
Web www.uglyducklingpresse.org

President: Anna Moschovakis

Ugly Duckling Presse is a nonprofit art and publishing collective producing small to mid-size editions of new poetry, translations, lost works, and artist's books. The Presse favors emerging, international, and "forgotten" writers with well-defined formal or conceptual projects that are difficult to place at other presses.

Secondary Categories: Multi-Disciplinary Arts, Performance Art

VOX POP
See Primary listing under Multi-Disciplinary Arts

LITERARY ARTS

Art hurts. Art urges
voyages—and it is easier
to stay at home.

GWENDOLYN BROOKS

MULTI-DISCIPLINARY ARTS

0.00156 ACRES
See Primary listing under Visual Arts

3RD WARD
195 Morgan Avenue
Brooklyn, NY 11237

Tel 718-715-4961
Fax 718-497-7010
Email info@3rdwardbrooklyn.org
Web www.3rdwardbrooklyn.org

Co-Founder and Executive Director:
Jason Goodman

A 20,000-square-foot workspace and studio facility in East Williamsburg, developed for artists and creative professionals by artists and creative professionals, 3rd Ward provides open-source, cost-effective access to space, facilities, and equipment for contemporary artists and those whose work is often multi-disciplinary.

Secondary Category: Arts Services

651 ARTS
See Primary listing under Presenting Organizations

AFRICUSSION-PERCUSSION DISCUSSION
See Primary listing under Music

AFRO HERITAGE VENTURE
901 Drew Street, #222
Brooklyn, NY 11208

Tel 718-510-5575
Fax 718-647-0254
Email afroheritmag@aol.com

President and Founder:
Olutosin L. Mustapha

Afro Heritage Venture is dedicated to improving cultural and educational services in the community through such innovative programs as its annual Afro Heritage Poetry Day, Black History Month, Kwanzaa, and Women's History Month celebrations, by actively participating in cultural activities that enrich New York City, and by publishing Afro Heritage magazine.

Secondary Categories: Folk Arts, Literary Arts

ALLEN|BODY GROUP (ABG)
327 Sterling Place, #3C
Brooklyn, NY 11238

Tel 877-865-4716
Email m.allen@allenbodygroup.com
Web www.allenbodygroup.com

Director/HNIC: Malinda R. Allen

The Allen Body Group appreciates the human body's potential for communication and constant improvement. Eltesia, the training system developed by Group founder Malinda Allen, increases power, suppleness, and versatility. The company participates in live performance and media projects and also maintains a roster of guest artists from companies as diverse as Pilobolus and Blue Man Group.

Secondary Category: Dance

ART GALLERY AT KINGSBOROUGH COMMUNITY COLLEGE, CUNY
See Primary listing under Galleries

ART PLAZA CULTURAL CENTER
See Primary listing under Arts Services

ART WITHOUT WALLS/FREE SPACE
See Primary listing under Arts for
Children/Teens

ARTICHOKE DANCE COMPANY
See Primary listing under Dance

**ASIAN AMERICAN WOMEN ARTISTS
ALLIANCE**
See Primary listing under Visual Arts

ATTITUDE: THE DANCERS MAGAZINE
See Primary listing under Dance

BAHIA KAO
See Primary listing under Music

BAILEY'S CAFÉ
279 Sterling Place, #3A
Brooklyn, NY 11238

Tel 718-622-4537
Email stefaniesiegel@aol.com

Founder and President: Stefanie Siegel

Bailey's Café is a center for educational
and cultural activity, nurturing individuals in their pursuit of self-knowl-
edge through writing, cooking, music,
dance, and fine arts. Bailey's Café aims
to create an atmosphere of collective
awareness, respect, and responsibil-
ity, built on the talents of the Bedford
Stuyvesant/Crown Heights community.

Secondary Categories: Arts for
Children/Teens, Presenting Organizations

BAM (BROOKLYN ACADEMY OF MUSIC)
30 Lafayette Avenue
Brooklyn, NY 11217

Tel 718-636-4100
Email info@bam.org
Web www.bam.org

President: Karen Hopkins

America's oldest performing arts
institution in continuous operation,
Brooklyn Academy of Music (BAM) is
recognized internationally for innovative dance, theater, and music
programming,including its renowned

Next Wave Festival. BAM also features
an acclaimed repertory film program,
literary and visual art events, and
extensive educational programs.

Secondary Categories: Dance,
Film/Video, Galleries, Literary Arts,
Music, Opera/Music Theater, Presenting
Organizations, Theater, Visual Arts

**BEDFORD STUYVESANT RESTORATION
CORPORATION'S CENTER FOR ARTS
AND CULTURE (CAC)**
1368 Fulton Street, 3rd Floor
Brooklyn, NY 11216

Tel 718-636-6976
Email artws@restorationplaza.org
Web www.restorationplaza.org

President: Colvin Grannum

The Center for Arts and Culture (CAC)
is an incubator for Restoration's multi-
disciplinary arts and cultural programming, which includes the Youth Arts
Academy, Skylight Gallery, and Arts
Residency Program. CAC's mission is
to present, promote, and preserve the
multicultural arts legacy of the African
Diaspora and to encourage the artistic
development of its community.

Secondary Categories: Arts Services,
Presenting Organizations, Theater

**BEDFORD STUYVESANT RESTORATION
CORPORATION'S CENTER FOR ARTS
AND CULTURE - YOUTH ARTS ACADEMY**
See Primary listing under
Visual/ Performing Arts School

BLACK MOON THEATRE COMPANY, INC.
5 North 11th Street
Brooklyn, NY 11211

Tel 718-302-1700
Fax 718-302-9449
Email info@blackmoontheatre
company.org
Web www.blackmoontheatre
company.org

BMTC is a physical theater company
creating original adaptations of novels,

plays, and poetry. The company combines original performance style, expressionistic realism, non-Western dance techniques, visual arts, and original music. BMTC's mission is to develop significant venues and perform in the culturally and economically diverse community of North Brooklyn.

Secondary Categories: Arts for Children/Teens, Theater

BOMB MAGAZINE (NEW ART PUBLICATIONS, INC.)
80 Hanson Place, Suite 703
Brooklyn, NY 11217

Tel 718-636-9100
Web www.bombsite.com

Publisher and Editor-in-Chief: Betsy Sussler

BOMB Magazine was launched in 1981 as a publication in which emerging and established artists could speak openly about the creative process, through conversations between peers. At the forefront of independent publishing for over 26 years, *BOMB* has an archive of over 800 interviews between visual artists, writers, musicians, directors, and actors.

Secondary Category: Literary Arts, Visual Arts

BREEDINGGROUND PRODUCTIONS
300 8th Street, #2C
Brooklyn, NY 11215

Tel 347-683-7698
Web www.breedingground.com

Creative Director: Tomi M. Tsunoda

Founded in 2000, breedingground productions is a collective of self-producing artists. The collective develops collaborative projects in a variety of creative disciplines, and in doing so creates a "breedingground" for innovation that transcends financial limitations and provides exceptional minds with opportunities to take creative risks.

Secondary Categories: Dance, Film/Video, Folk Arts, Galleries, Literary Arts, Music, Opera/Music Theater, Performance Art

BRIC ARTS | MEDIA | BROOKLYN
647 Fulton Street
Brooklyn, NY 11217

Tel 718-855-7882
Fax 718-802-9095
Web www.briconline.org

Executive Director: Leslie G. Schultz

BRIC Arts | Media | Brooklyn is a multi-disciplinary arts and media nonprofit dedicated to presenting visual, performing, and media arts programs that reflect Brooklyn's diversity, and to providing free or low-cost resources and platforms that support the creative process. Programs include Brooklyn Community Access Television, BRIC-studio, BRIC Rotunda Gallery, and the Celebrate Brooklyn! Performing Arts Festival.

Secondary Categories: Arts for Children/Teens, Computer Arts/New Media, Dance, Film/Video, Galleries, Music, Performance Art, Presenting Organizations, Theater

THE BRICK THEATER, INC.
See Primary lisitng under Theater

MULIT-DISCIPLINARY ARTS

BRIGHTON NEIGHBORHOOD ASSOCIATION, INC. (BNA)

1121 Brighton Beach Avenue
Brooklyn, NY 11235

Tel 718-891-0800
Fax 718-891-1163
Email bnapsinger@aol.com
Web www.brightonbeach.com

Founder and Executive Director:
Pat Singer

Founded in 1977 out of a grassroots movement, the Brighton Neighborhood Association has evolved into a multi-service center focused on enhancing the quality of life of its residents. Every summer the BNA presents the Brighton Jubilee, a street festival whose offerings include local crafts, international food, and four stages of entertainment.

Secondary Category: Presenting Organizations

BROOKLYN ARTS EXCHANGE (BAX)

421 Fifth Avenue
Brooklyn, NY 11215

Tel 718-832-0018
Fax 718-832-9189
Email info@bax.org
Web www.bax.org

Executive Director: Marya Warshaw

BAX/Brooklyn Arts Exchange—"arts and artists in progress"—is a multi-disciplinary nonprofit organization in Park Slope, founded in 1991 (as the Gowanus Arts Exchange). Its mission is to provide a nurturing, year-round performance, rehearsal, and educational venue in Brooklyn that encourages artistic risk-taking and stimulates dialogue among diverse constituencies.

Secondary Categories: Arts for Children/Teens, Arts Services, Dance, Galleries, Performance Art, Presenting Organizations

BROOKLYN CENTER FOR THE PERFORMING ARTS AT BROOKLYN COLLEGE (BCBC)
See Primary listing under Presenting Organizations

BROOKLYN PHILHARMONIC
See Primary listing under Music

THE BROOKLYN RAIL

99 Commercial Street, Suite 23
Brooklyn, NY 11222

Tel 718-349-8427
Fax 718-349-1327
Email brooklynrailhq@yahoo.com
Web www.brooklynrail.org

Publisher: Phong Bui

Founded in October 2000, the *Brooklyn Rail* is a nonprofit monthly journal that provides an independent forum for arts, culture, and politics throughout New York City and beyond. In addition to local reporting, art criticism, interviews with artists and writers, fiction, and poetry, it features extensive coverage of music, dance, film, and theater.

Secondary Categories: Arts Services, Dance, Film/Video, Literary Arts, Music, Theater, Visual Arts

BROOKLYN TECHNOLOGY EXCHANGE
See Primary listing under Educational Institutions

BROOKLYN WRITERS SPACE
See Primary listing under Literary Arts

THE BUSHWICK STARR
See Primary listing under Theater

CABINET (IMMATERIAL INCORPORATED)

181 Wyckoff Street
Brooklyn, NY 11217

Fax 718-222-3700
Web www.cabinetmagazine.org

Editor-in-Chief: Sina Najafi

Cabinet is a nonprofit quarterly magazine that approaches art and culture from a perspective similar to that used by artists.

Secondary Categories: Literary Arts, Visual Arts

CAVE
58 Grand Street
Brooklyn, NY 11211

Tel 718-388-6780
Email info@caveartspace.org
Web www.caveartspace.org

Co-Directors: Shige Moriya and Ximena Garnica

Founded in 1996, CAVE is an artists' collective, gallery-performance space, and arts organization whose goal is to maintain an environment that fosters exchange and collaboration among artists of diverse backgrounds. CAVE's primary programs include a gallery, residencies, workshops, a dance studio, an international Butoh festival, and other live productions.

Secondary Categories: Dance, Film/Video, Galleries, Music, Performance Art, Presenting Organizations, Theater, Visual Arts

CENTER FOR INTERNATIONAL ART IN COMMUNITY (FREEDIMENSIONAL)
228 Greene Avenue, #4
Brooklyn, NY 11238

Site address:
677 Lafayette Avenue
Brooklyn, NY 11216

Email inquiry@freedimensional.org
Web www.artincommunity.org

Executive Director: Todd L. Lester

The Center for International Art in Community (CIAC) is a pilot artist residency and community center which serves as the administrative office for freeDimensional's international network of artist residency initiatives. Located at the Magnolia Tree Earth Center, it partners with the Center's

gallery to introduce the local community to international artists in residence.

Secondary Category: Arts Services

CENTER FOR THANATOLOGY RESEARCH AND EDUCATION, INC.
391 Atlantic Avenue
Brooklyn, NY 11217

Tel 718-858-3026
Fax 718-852-1846
Web www.thanatology.org

Director: Roberta Halporn

The Center for Thanatology is a small press, 2,500-book library, and museum with an emphasis on the folk and art history of the graveyard. The collection includes replicas from English cathedrals to rubbings of Colonial, Victorian, and contemporary American memorials.

Secondary Categories: Folk Arts, Literary Arts, Museums, Visual Arts

CHASSIDIC DISCOVERY WELCOME CENTER (CULTURAL WALKING TOURS OF CHASSIDIC NEW YORK)
305 Kingston Avenue
Brooklyn, NY 11213

Tel 718-953-5244
Fax 718-771-6315
Email btours@jewishtours.com
Web www.jewishtours.com

Director: Beryl Epstein

Chassidic Discovery Welcome Center takes guests on an unforgettable interactive journey into the history and culture of an intriguing and welcoming community, through fascinating sites not generally accessible to the public, including the Rebbe's library and synagogue, art galleries, matza bakery, mikva, and the studio of a scribe writing a Torah scroll.

Secondary Categories: Galleries, Music

MULIT-DISCIPLINARY ARTS

CHEZ BUSHWICK
See Primary listing under Dance

CIRCUIT PRODUCTIONS, INC.
635 Carroll Street
Brooklyn, NY 11215
Tel 718-638-4878
Fax 718-638-4878
Web www.circuitproductions.org

Producer and Executive Director:
Susan Goldbetter

Circuit Productions provides booking and managerial services primarily for senior and emerging artists of color in the areas of tap, jazz, world music, and dance. Annual programs include the Tap and Jazz Masters Series, arts in education residencies and workshops, and World Beat—an Emerging Artists Series in world music and dance.

Secondary Categories: Arts for Children/Teens, Arts Services, Dance, Music

CIRCUS AMOK
See Primary listing under Theater

COLLECTIVE OPERA COMPANY
See Primary listing under Opera/Music Theater

CONFLUX FESTIVAL
302 Bedford Avenue
Brooklyn, NY 11211
Email info@confluxfestival.org
Web www.confluxfestival.org

Founder and Director: Christina Ray

Conflux is an annual New York City festival in which visual and sound artists, writers, urban adventurers, and the public gather for four days to explore the physical and psychological landscape of the city.

Secondary Categories: Film/Video, Presenting Organizations

COVENANT DANCE THEATRE OF BROOKLYN
See Primary listing under Dance

CREATE!
See Primary listing under Arts for Children/Teens

CREATIVE WOMEN'S NETWORK
See Primary listing under Arts Services

CRUCIAL ARTS PRODUCTIONS, INC.
P.O. Box 23127
Brooklyn, NY 11202
Tel 718-228-9820
Fax 718-228-9820
Email email@crucialarts.org
Web www.crucialarts.org

Executive Director: Carmen Neely

Crucial Arts' mission is to support, produce, promote, and present performances and visual media that celebrate the diverse artists and artistry of people of color. Crucial Arts' activities include, but are not limited to, theater and film production, digital media and visual art exhibits, fiscal sponsorship, production management, and consultation.

Secondary Categories: Film/Video, Literary Arts, Music, Performance Art, Theater, Visual Arts

DANCE GIANT STEPS, INC.
(ATTITUDE: THE DANCERS' MAGAZINE)
93 Montague Street
Brooklyn, NY 11201
Email dance_giant_steps@yahoo.com
Web www.geocities.com/dance attitude

Executive Director: Bernadine Jennings

Founded in 1979, Dance Giant Steps, Inc. is a service organization and presenter that documents the diverse dance community of New York while exploring ways to obtain parity and leadership for artists of color. Dance Giant Steps also offers personalized consulting and archival research and documentation through *Attitude: The Dancers' Magazine*.

Secondary Categories: Dance, Literary Arts

DANCE THEATRE ETCETERA
480 Van Brunt Street, Suite 203
Brooklyn, NY 11231

Tel 718-643-6790
Fax 718-643-6790
Email info@dancetheatreetcetera.org
Web www.dancetheatreetcetera.org

Executive Director: Martha Bowers

Premised on the belief that the arts are an effective vehicle for social transformation, Dance Theatre Etcetera unites artists and community members as co-creators in dynamic cultural activities. Through site-specific performances, festivals, parades, and performing arts/media education programs, DTE stimulates the social imagination through acts of informed creative expression.

Secondary Categories: Dance, Theater

DANCES AND DRUMS OF AFRICA, INC.
See Primary listing under Dance

DARMSTADT
See Primary listing under Music

DIGITAL STORY WORKSHOP
See Primary listing under Film/Video

DRUMSONG AFRICAN BALLET THEATRE, INC. (SABAR AK RU AFRIQ)
1299 Carroll Street
Brooklyn, NY 11213

Site address:
127 West 127th Street
New York, NY 10027

Tel 718-953-5584
Email drumsong7@yahoo.com
Web www.drumsongsociety.com

Artistic Director: Obara Wali A. Rahman Ndiaye

The Drumsong African Ballet Theatre performs and presents professional and community African folkloric dance, music, drama, and poetry which also makes reference to AfricanAmerican and world cultures. In addition to its stage performances, the company offers lectures and workshops in school as well as after school programs to give young audiences exposure, training, and development.

Secondary Categories: Art for Children/Teens, Dance, Folk Arts, Music, Presenting Organizations

DUMBO ARTS CENTER
See Primary listing under Visual Arts

EGRESS THEATRE COMPANY
See Primary listing under Theater

EL PUENTE
211 South 4th Street
Brooklyn, NY 11211

Tel 718-387-0404
Fax 718-387-6816
Email flucerna@elpuente.us
Web www.elpuente.us

Executive Director: Frances Lucerna

El Puente offers young people training in dance, theater, visual arts, music, and video in the context of a holistic leadership program, and also partners with schools for integrated arts in education programs. Home to two long-standing resident companies—Teatro El Puente and the El Puente Muralistas—El Puente hosts arts events year-round.

Secondary Category: Arts for Children/Teens

MULIT-DISCIPLINARY ARTS

ELDERS SHARE THE ARTS (ESTA)
138 South Oxford Street
Brooklyn, NY 11217
Tel 718-398-3870
Fax 718-398-3864
Web www.estanyc.org

Executive Director: Carolyn Zablotny

Elders Share the Arts (ESTA) upholds the time-honored role of elders as bearers of history and culture through its signature "living history arts" programs, which encourage the recalling of memories and the transmitting of wisdom through storytelling and the arts. ESTA works in diverse settings throughout greater New York, including senior centers, libraries, schools, and nursing homes.

Secondary Categories: Folk Arts, Literary Arts, Visual Arts

THE ELEVENTEN GALLERY
See Primary listing under Galleries

FAMILY TREE COLLECTIVE
See Primary listing under Presenting Organizations

FIVEMYLES
See Primary listing under Galleries

FLATBUSH DEVELOPMENT CORPORATION
See Primary listing under Arts for Children/Teens

FREE103POINT9
302 Bedford Avenue, #261Y
Brooklyn, NY 11211
Site address:
338 Berry Street
Brooklyn, NY 11211
Tel 917-297-1537
Email info@free103point9.org
Web www.free103point9.org

Executive Director:
Galen Joseph-Hunter

free103point9 is a nonprofit arts organization focused on transmission arts, a genre encompassing experimental practices in radio art, video art, light sculpture, installation, and performance utilizing the electromagnetic spectrum. free103point9's programs include performances, exhibitions, an online radio station and distribution label, an education initiative, an artist's residency, and a study center.

Secondary Categories: Arts Services, Computer Arts/New Media, Performance Art, Presenting Organizations, Visual Arts

GALAPAGOS ART SPACE
16 Main Street
Brooklyn, NY 11201
Tel 718-222-8500
Email patrick@galapagosartspace.com
Web www.galapagosartspace.com

Director: Robert Elmes

Awarded an OBIE in 2003 for its support of the emerging arts, Galapagos Art Space presents a full schedule of the performing arts. Unique in New York City's cultural landscape, Galapagos does not accept public or foundation funding of any kind, and functions solely on its earned income.

Secondary Categories: Architecture & Urban/Environmental Design, Arts for Children/Teens, Computer Arts/New Media, Dance, Film/Video, Galleries, Literary Arts, Opera/Music Theater, Performance Art, Presenting Organizations

THE GALLERY AT HARRIET'S ALTER EGO
See Primary listing under Galleries

THE GOWANUS STUDIO SPACE, INC.
285 Pacific Street, #4
Brooklyn, NY 11201
Site address:
8th Street between 2nd and 3rd Avenues, Brooklyn, NY 11251
Email info@gowanusstudio.org
Web www.gowanusstudio.org

Director: Angela Conant

The Gowanus Studio offers space, equipment, and much-needed support to emerging designers, artists, and craftspeople. Located in the historically industrial neighborhood along the Gowanus Canal, the Studio houses a large printmaking and industrial arts workshop as well as private studio and exhibition space.

Secondary Categories: Architecture & Urban/Environmental Design, Arts for Children/Teens, Arts Services, Computer Arts/New Media, Film/Video, Galleries, Performance Art

HEART OF BROOKLYN
See Primary listing under Arts Services

HIP-HOP THEATER FESTIVAL
See Primary listing under Theater

THE HOGAR COLLECTION
See Primary listing under Galleries

IFETAYO CULTURAL ARTS FACILITY, INC.
629-A East 35th Street, Suite 2
Brooklyn, NY 11203

Tel 718-856-1123
Fax 718-856-1192
Email info@ifetayoculturalarts.org
Web www.ifetayoculturalarts.org
President and CEO: Kwayera Archer-Cunningham

Ifetayo Cultural Arts Facility, Inc. is an arts and cultural organization dedicated to supporting the creative, educational, and vocational development of youth and families of African descent. Ifetayo provides programs in cultural awareness and performing and visual arts, as well as academic instruction, health and wellness, and professional skills development.

Secondary Categories: Arts for Children/Teens, Arts Services, Dance, Literary Arts, Music, Presenting Organizations

ILAND, INC.
See Primary listing under Dance

INI NYC
277 Nostrand Avenue, #1B
Brooklyn, NY 11216

Tel 646-361-4765
Email natasha@ininyc.org
Web www.ininyc.org

InI NYC is a nonprofit organization dedicated to providing a supportive environment for artists in the community. The group's mission is to educate, foster growth, inspire creativity, and encourage free flow of expression. InI's main event is the Eclipse, a night of eclectic performance—part showcase, part open mic—presented by a diverse group of artists.

Secondary Category: Performance Art

INTERNATIONAL AFRICAN ARTS FESTIVAL
See Primary listing under Arts Services

ISSUE PROJECT ROOM (IPR)
232 3rd Street, 3rd Floor
Brooklyn, NY 11215

Tel 718-330-0313
Email info@issueprojectroom.org
Web www.issueprojectroom.org

A nonprofit, multidisciplinary arts space in Brooklyn, ISSUE Project Room (IPR) aims to expose under-accessible art from local, national, and international artists who challenge and expand conventional practices in art. IPR presents weekly contemporary art events which involve music, performance, visual art, poetry, literature, dance, and artisan cuisine.

Secondary Categories: Computer Arts/New Media, Dance, Film/Video, Galleries, Music, Performance Art

KINGS BAY YM-YWHA
See Primary listing under Presenting Organizations

MULIT-DISCIPLINARY ARTS

THE KURDISH HERITAGE FOUNDATION OF AMERICA
See Primary listing under Museums

LIKE THE SPICE
See Primary listing under Galleries

MARQUIS STUDIOS, LTD.
45 Main Street
Brooklyn, NY 11201

Tel 718-694-9400
Fax 718-694-0106
Email david@marquisstudios.org
Web www.marquisstudios.org

Executive Director: David G. Marquis

Marquis Studios, Ltd. has provided a variety of arts in education services to New York City public schools for the last 30 years. Marquis' team of 30 artists provides residencies and staff development and parent/child workshops in disciplines as diverse as puppetry, circus arts, mural-making, music, drawing, painting, storytelling, and movement.

Secondary Category: Arts for Children/Teens

METAPHOR CONTEMPORARY ART
See Primary listing under Galleries

MICRO MUSEUM
See Primary listing under Museums

MIXED BAG & COMPANY, INC.
See Primary listing under Dance

MONKEY TOWN
See Primary listing under Film/Video

NEW GENERAL CATALOG
See Primary listing under Visual Arts

THE NIETZSCHE MUSIC PROJECT
See Primary listing under Music

NORA STEPHENS / NORANEWDANCE
See Primary listing under Dance

NOT AN ALTERNATIVE, INC.
See Primary listing under Presenting Organizations

OBRUMANKOMA SANKOFA TRADITIONALS OF GHANA
See Primary listing under Dance

OFFICEOPS
57 Thames Street, 2nd Floor
Brooklyn, NY 11237

Tel 718-418-2509
Fax 718-418-9282
Email info@officeops.org
Web www.officeops.org

Managing Partner: Kevin Lindamood

OfficeOps is an East Williamsburg arts center that rents out studio and performance space at affordable rates, and also hosts classes, rehearsals, rooftop screenings, and other events.

Secondary Categories: Dance, Film/Video, Performance Art, Theater, Visual Arts

THE OLD AMERICAN CAN FACTORY
See Primary listing under Presenting Organizations

PARIJAT DESAI DANCE COMPANY
See Primary listing under Dance

PDM PERFORMING ARTS CORPORATION (PERSHAY DANCE MINISTRY)
219-26 138th Road
Laurelton, NY 11413

Site address:
392 Blake Avenue
Brooklyn, NY 11207

Tel 718-341-3388
Email trevipershay@aol.com
Web www.pdmperformingarts.com

President and Executive Director:
Trevolia M. Pershay

PDM is a community theater workshop and dance organization that works with inner city children, young adults, seniors, and other community residents. A faith-based organization,

PDM provides inspirational theater, dance performances, and other artistic programs at the Van Dyke Community Center in Brownsville.

Secondary Categories: Arts for Children/Teens, Dance, Theater

PERIPHERAL MEDIA PROJECTS, INC.

See Primary listing under Visual Arts

PHILIPPA KAYE COMPANY

Email pkc@philippakayecompany.org
Web www.philippakayecompany.org

President: Kerith Gardner

Philippa Kaye Company supports the innovative dance work and artistic vision of choreographer Philippa Kaye, company dancers, and multimedia collaborators. Performances celebrate the epic, wonderful, and absurd forces that shape our existence. The company connects with the public through concerts, teaching residencies, and lecture/demonstrations.

Secondary Category: Dance

PLACE IN HISTORY

See Primary listing under Architecture & Urban/Environmental Design

PLG ARTS

163 Ocean Avenue, #M5
Brooklyn, NY 11225

Email info@plgarts.org
Web www.plgarts.org

Co-Founder: Laura Frenzer

PLG Arts promotes the arts, supports local artists, and builds community by celebrating the vibrant creativity of the residents of Prospect Lefferts Gardens and surrounding Brooklyn neighborhoods.

Secondary Categories: Arts for Children/Teens, Literary Arts, Music, Theater, Visual Arts

PROSPECT PARK & PROSPECT PARK ALLIANCE

95 Prospect Park West
Brooklyn, NY 11215

Tel 718-965-8951
Web www.prospectpark.org

Administrator and Alliance President: Tupper Thomas

Prospect Park is a 585-acre urban oasis with a stunning array of natural features, including Brooklyn's only forest and a 60-acre lake. Activities include the nation's first Audubon Center, pedal boats, an ice skating center, a tennis center, and fields for baseball, soccer, and football.

Secondary Categories: Architecture & Urban/Environmental Design, Arts for Children/Teens, Galleries, Museums, Music, Presenting Organizations, Visual Arts

PROTEUS GOWANUS

543 Union Street
Brooklyn, NY 11217

Tel 718-243-1572
Email info@proteusgowanus.com
Web www.proteusgowanus.com

Founder and Director: Sasha Chavchavadze

Proteus Gowanus is a gallery and reading room located on the Gowanus Canal. The gallery develops interdisciplinary exhibits and programs that revolve around an annual theme. Proteus Gowanus incorporates the rich and diverse cultural resources of seven nonprofit organizations into its exhibits and programming.

Secondary Categories: Film/Video, Galleries, Literary Arts, Visual Arts

THE PUPPETEERS COOPERATIVE

See Primary listing under Theater

MULIT-DISCIPLINARY ARTS

THE PUPPETRY ARTS THEATRE, INC. (TPAT)
339 2nd Street, #1R
Brooklyn, NY 11215

Tel 718-768-3703
Email info@puppetryarts.org
Web www.puppetryarts.org
Executive Director: Timmy Young

The Puppetry Arts Theatre, Inc. offers creative outlets and cultural exploration through the multi-disciplinary art of puppetry, fostering youth development and enriching family activity. While upholding this mission, TPAT provides opportunities to arts teachers and emerging visual and performing artists of all backgrounds, from every corner of New York City.

Secondary Category: Visual/Performing Arts Schools

PUPPETWORKS
See Primary listing under Theater

RADIOHOLE
See Primary listing under Performance Art

RAIZES DO BRASIL CAPOEIRA BROOKLYN
See Primary listing under Folk Arts

REVELATION PERFORMING ARTS STUDIO, INC.
See Primary listing under Visual/Performing Arts School

RHYTHM VISIONS PRODUCTION COMPANY, INC.
See Primary listing under Arts for Children/Teens

RUDDER BLADE PRODUCTIONS, INC.
See Primary listing under Film/Video

RUSH PHILANTHROPIC ARTS FOUNDATION
See Primary listing under Arts for Children/Teens

SABA-THE ASSOCIATION OF YEMENI AMERICANS
464 3rd Avenue
Brooklyn, NY 11215

Web www.saba-ny.org

SABA-The Association of Yemeni-Americans is a nonprofit, community-based, multi-service organization committed to serving the unique needs of Yemeni Americans and the broader public through inter-cultural programming, education, and advocacy. SABA celebrates and shares Yemeni culture with all of New York City, as well as on a national basis, through arts programs, community gatherings, workshops, and events.

Secondary Category: Arts for Children/Teens, Arts Services

SABOOGE THEATRE
See Primary listing under Theater

SCENARIOS USA
See Primary listing under Film/Video

THE SHADOW BOX THEATRE, INC.
See Primary listing under Arts for Children/Teens

SOLWORKS, INC.
See Primary listing under Arts for Children/Teens

SOMETHING POSITIVE, INC. (CHERYL BYRON AND SOMETHING POSITIVE)
1655 Flatbush Avenue, Suite C1705
Brooklyn, NY 11210

Tel 718-252-4692
Web www.myspace.com/something positivedanceco

Director: Michael Manswell

Something Positive, Inc. is an African Caribbean performing arts organization dedicated to the art and culture of the African Diaspora. Specializing in multi-media performances, the company utilizes a unique blend of poetry, storytelling, theater, music, and dance, and has been performing both nationally and internationally for over two decades.

Secondary Category: Dance

SOUTHFIRST: ART
See Primary listing under Galleries

SPOKE THE HUB DANCING, INC.
748 Union Street
Brooklyn, NY 11215

Tel 718-408-3234
Fax 718-408-3234
Email spoke@spokethehub.org
Web www.spokethehub.org

Artistic Director and Founder:
Elise M. Long

A multi-purpose community arts organization working out of two Brooklyn spaces, Spoke the Hub Dancing, Inc. offers year-round creative arts, dance, yoga, and fitness classes for all ages, subsidized rehearsal and performance space, exhibits, performance series, festivals, birthday parties, and special community events like the ongoing "Miles of Tiles" community mosaic project.

Secondary Categories: Arts for Children/Teens, Arts Services, Dance, Galleries, Music, Performance Art, Presenting Organizations, Theater

ST. ANN'S WAREHOUSE
See Primary listing under Presenting Organizations

STORYCORPS (SOUND PORTRAITS PRODUCTIONS)
80 Hanson Place, 2nd Floor
Brooklyn, NY 11217

Tel 646-723-7020
Web www.storycorps.net

Executive Director: Dave Isay

StoryCorps is a national oral history project that enables people to interview their loved ones and record these interviews in sound. These oral history interviews are archived at the American Folklife Center at the Library of Congress, and excerpts of a small number of the interviews are broadcast on public radio.

Secondary Category: Folk Arts

STREB LABORATORY FOR ACTION MECHANICS (S.L.A.M.)
51 North 1st Street
Brooklyn, NY 11211

Tel 718-384-6491
Fax 718-384-6491
Email info@strebusa.org
Web www.strebusa.org

Producing Director: Kim Cullen

Opened in January 2003, S.L.A.M. conducts activities year-round at its Williamsburg home, the STREB Lab for Action Mechanics. S.L.A.M. is the company's creative and educational center where new productions are mounted and classes are taught. Founded in 1979, the company STREB Extreme Action tours both nationally and internationally, and all its activities are open to the public.

Secondary Categories:
Arts for Children/Teens, Dance, Music, Performance Art, Presenting Organizations, Theater

TABLA RASA GALLERY
See Primary listing under Galleries

TARGET MARGIN THEATER
See Primary listing under Theater

TIFFANY MILLS COMPANY
See Primary listing under Dance

TRISKELION ARTS
See Primary listing under Dance

MULIT-DISCIPLINARY ARTS

TROIKA RANCH
321 Graham Avenue, #4R
Brooklyn, NY 11211
Tel 718-218-6775
Email info@troikaranch.org
Web www.troikaranch.org

Executive and Artistic Co-Director:
Dawn Stoppiello

Established in 1994, Troika Ranch produces live performances, interactive installations, and digital films, all of which combine traditional aspects of these forms with advanced technologies. The directors regularly offer their Live-I (Live Interactive) Workshop to share their extensive practical and aesthetic knowledge of technology use in contemporary live arts.

Secondary Category: Computer Arts/New Media

UGLY DUCKLING PRESSE
See Primary listing under Literary Arts

UNIONDOCS
See Primary listing under Film/Video

VERTEXLIST
See Primary listing under Computer Arts/New Media

VICTORIAN PLACE CULTURAL CENTER
83 Marlborough Road
Brooklyn, NY 11226
Tel 917-846-7386
Executive Director: Marjorie E. Belson

Sparked by the re-emergence of Brooklyn as an artistic center, the Victorian Place Cultural Center was created to celebrate the delicious mix of its surrounding community. Centrally located, the Cultural Center is dedicated to educating and enriching the lives of Brooklyn's multi-cultural population through diverse cultural programs.

Secondary Category: Presenting Organization

VOX POP (DRENCH KISS MEDIA CORPORATION)
1022 Cortelyou Road
Brooklyn, NY 11218
Tel 718-940-2084
Email sander@voxpopnet.net
Web www.voxpopnet.net

Chief Instigator: Sander Hicks

Vox Pop is a coffeehouse, bookstore, and publishing company with a performance space ideal for acoustic acts, spoken word, author readings, lectures, stand-up, and art openings. Vox Pop's open mic night takes place every Sunday evening, and its book-making operation offers print-on-demand. An event calendar is available at Vox Pop's website.

Secondary Category: Literary Arts

WALKER INTERNATIONAL COMMUNICATIONS GROUP, INC.
293 East 18th Street
Brooklyn, NY 11226
Tel 718-703-2260
Fax 718-703-2464
Email dwkuhne@gmail.com
Web www.walkercommunications group.com

President: Donna Walker-Kuhne

A boutique marketing agency, Walker International Communications Group, Inc. specializes in strategic marketing and audience development for the performing and visual arts, with an emphasis on cultivating long-term relationships with diverse audiences.

Secondary Category: Arts Services

THE WATERFRONT MUSEUM
See Primary listing under Museums

135 Broadway
Brooklyn, NY 11211

Tel 718-486-7372
Fax 718-486-6012
Email wahcenter@earthlink.net
Web www.wahcenter.net

President and Executive Director:
Terrance Lindall

Housed in a landmark 1867 building, the nonprofit Williamsburg Art &
Historical Center (WAH Center) serves
the general public by presenting art
exhibitions, performances, and cultural
events as well as lectures, seminars,
and educational programs of local,
national, and international interest.
The WAH Center also preserves and
displays historical art and artifacts.

*Secondary Categories: Museums,
Presenting Organizations*

WILLIAMSBURG ART NEXUS, INC.
*See Primary listing under Presenting
Organizations*

WORLD EATER RECORDINGS, NYC
See Primary listing under Music

MULIT-DISCIPLINARY ARTS

Art is a spiritual, immaterial respite from the hardships of life.

FERNANDO BOTERO

MUSEUMS

BROOKLYN BOTANIC GARDEN (BBG)
1000 Washington Avenue
Brooklyn, NY 11225

Tel 718-623-7200
Web www.bbg.org

President: Scot Medbury

The Brooklyn Botanic Garden is a 52-acre living museum where beauty, romance, and fun blossom among world-class plant collections and specialty gardens. Admired as an urban horticultural and botanical resource, BBG inspires visitors to discover that plants are essential to life.

Secondary Category: Architecture & Urban/Environmental Design

BROOKLYN CHILDREN'S MUSEUM
145 Brooklyn Avenue
(at St. Marks Avenue)
Brooklyn, NY 11213

Tel 718-735-4400
Fax 718-604-7442
Web www.brooklynkids.org

President: Carol Enseki

The Brooklyn Children's Museum, the world's first museum for kids, provides hands-on learning adventures in natural science and world culture. Nine interactive galleries let children meet live animals, play musical instruments from around the world, examine plants, run a pizza shop, and learn about faraway lands.

Secondary Categories: Arts for Children/Teens, Educational Institutions, Music

BROOKLYN HISTORICAL SOCIETY
See Primary listing under Historical Societies

BROOKLYN MUSEUM
200 Eastern Parkway
Brooklyn, NY 11238

Tel 718-638-5000
Fax 718-501-6134
Email information@brooklynmuseum.org
Web www.brooklynmuseum.org

Director: Arnold Lehman

The mission of the Brooklyn Museum is to act as a bridge between the rich artistic heritage of world cultures, as embodied in its collections, and the unique heritage of each visitor. Dedicated to the primacy of the visitor experience, the Museum aims to serve its diverse public as a dynamic, innovative, and welcoming center for learning through the visual arts.

Secondary Categories: Arts for Children/Teens, Film/Video, Performance Art, Visual Arts

CENTER FOR THANATOLOGY RESEARCH AND EDUCATION, INC.
See Primary listing under Multi-Disciplinary Arts

THE CITY RELIQUARY MUSEUM AND CIVIC ORGANIZATION

P.O. Box 110948
Brooklyn, NY 11211

Site address:
370 Metropolitan Avenue
Brooklyn, NY 11211

Tel 718-782-4842
Email messages@cityreliquary.org
Web www.cityreliquary.org

President: Dave J. Herman

The City Reliquary is committed to serving the people of New York City—natives, newcomers, and passersby. The Reliquary's museum collection displays thoughtfully arranged artifacts of the city's rich history, enticing viewers to learn more about the five boroughs. The Reliquary also hosts an array of special events.

Secondary Category: Architecture & Urban/Environmental Design

DOLL AND TOY MUSEUM OF NYC

157 Montague Street
Brooklyn, NY 11201

Site address:
280 Cadman Plaza, 2nd Floor (inside the Brooklyn Heights Library Branch)
Brooklyn, NY 11201

Tel 718-243-0820
Email mhochmandtofnyc@aol.com
Web www.dtmnyc.org

Founder and Executive Director: Marlene Hochman

A nonprofit educational museum established in 1999, the Doll and Toy Museum of New York City educates the public on the importance of dolls and toys in our culture, through art and play. New York's only museum devoted exclusively to preserving and exhibiting dolls and toys, the Museum also conducts workshops and sponsors traveling exhibits.

Secondary Category: Arts for Children/Teens

THE ENRICO CARUSO MUSEUM OF AMERICA

1942 East 19th Street
Brooklyn, NY 11229

Tel 718-368-3993
Fax 718-368-3993
Email carusomuseumny@aol.com
Web www.enricocarusomuseum.com

President: Aldo R. Mancusi

The Enrico Caruso Museum of America provides lectures and exhibitions on the life and times of legendary tenor Enrico Caruso, both at the Museum and offsite. Visitors to the Museum will see the largest collection of Caruso memorabilia in the United States, including photographs, film, and personal items.

Secondary Categories: Film/Video, Music, Opera/Music Theater

THE GREENPOINT MONITOR MUSEUM

P.O. Box 220378
Brooklyn, NY 11222

Site address:
56 Quay Street
Brooklyn, NY 11222

Tel 718-383-3180
Email admin@greenpointmonitor museum.org
Web www.greenpointmonitor museum.org

President: Janice Lauletta-Weinmann

A state-chartered museum since 1996, the Greenpoint Monitor Museum preserves the memory of the U.S.S. Monitor and the history of Greenpoint, where the legendary Civil War ironclad was built. In 2003, land was donated on Greenpoint's waterfront for the Museum's physical home, and the Museum furthers that work through outreach and education.

Secondary Category: Architecture & Urban/Environmental Design

THE GREEN-WOOD HISTORIC FUND, INC.
See Primary listing under Visual Arts

HARBOR DEFENSE MUSEUM OF FORT HAMILTON
USAG Fort Hamilton,
230 Sheridan Loop
Brooklyn, NY 11252

Tel 718-630-4349
Fax 718-630-4888
Email richard.j.cox1@us.army.mil
Web www.harbordefensemuseum.com

Director: Richard J. Cox

Nestled within Fort Hamilton in Bay Ridge, the Harbor Defense Museum's mission is to preserve the history of New York City's coastal defense systems. As the only Army Museum in New York City, the Harbor Defense Museum has acquired a fine collection of military artifacts from the Revolutionary War to World War II.

Secondary Category: Architecture & Urban/Environmental Design

HEART OF BROOKLYN
See Primary listing under Arts Services

JEWISH CHILDREN'S MUSEUM
792 Eastern Parkway
Brooklyn, NY 11213

Tel 718-467-0600
Email info@jcm.museum
Web www.jcm.museum

Director of Public Relations:
Zev Steinhauser

In the high-tech, fun-filled Jewish Children's Museum, you won't find any "do not touch" or "keep off" signs. Children are encouraged to make full use of the creative, hands-on exhibits, such as a Sabbath dinner table big enough to walk on. Designed to introduce children of all backgrounds to Jewish culture, the museum promotes tolerance through understanding.

Secondary Category: Arts for Children/Teens

THE KURDISH HERITAGE FOUNDATION OF AMERICA (THE KURDISH LIBRARY AND MUSEUM)
345 Park Place
Brooklyn, NY 11238

Site address:
144 Underhill Avenue
Brooklyn, NY 11238

Tel 718-783-7930
Email kurdishlib@aol.com
Web www.kurdishlibrarymuseum.com

Director: Vera B. Saeedpour

The Kurdish Library offers a wide range of research materials on Kurdish history, culture, and contemporary affairs. Collections include books, periodicals, maps, videos, and music collections. The Library also publishes *The International Journal of Kurdish Studies* and *Kurdish Life*. The Kurdish Museum displays a variety of exhibits, including costumes, carpets, jewelry, art, and photographs.

Secondary Categories: Folk Arts, Multi-Disciplinary Arts

MUSEUMS

LEFFERTS HISTORIC HOUSE
95 Prospect Park West
Brooklyn, NY 11215
Site address:
Willink Entrance to Prospect Park,
off Flatbush Avenue
Tel 718-789-2822
Email mcobo@prospectpark.org
Web www.prospectpark.org

Vice-President for Education:
Maria Cobo

Lefferts Historic House represents
more than 200 years of New York
City history. Built by a Dutch family in the 18th-century farming village
of Flatbush, the House interprets the
history of Brooklyn's environment from
pre-Colonial times through the present, using its working garden, historic
artifacts, and documents, as well as
period rooms and exhibits.

*Secondary Categories: Architecture
& Urban/Environmental Design,
Arts for Children/Teens, Folk Arts,
Galleries, Historical Societies*

**MICRO MUSEUM
(PROMOTE ART WORKS, INC.)**
123 Smith Street
Brooklyn, NY 11201
Tel 718-797-3116
Email micromuseum@micro
museum.com
Web www.micromuseum.com

Executive Director: Kathleen Laziza

A "living art center" founded in
1986, Micro Museum hosts weekly
art exhibits year-round along with
monthly special events on Saturdays.
Micro Museum also offers public access
broadcasts, and houses an extensive
archive of video and digital media representing contemporary artists working
in performing, media, and visual arts.

Secondary Category: Multi-Disciplinary Arts

**MUSEUM OF CONTEMPORARY AFRICAN
DIASPORAN ART (MOCADA)**
80 Hanson Place
Brooklyn, NY 11217
Tel 718-230-0492
Web www.mocada.org

Founder and Executive Director:
Laurie A. Cumbo

MoCADA is committed to fostering
a greater awareness of the art and
culture of the African Diaspora as it
relates to contemporary urban issues
through innovative exhibitions, public
programs, and interactive tours.

*Secondary Categories: Arts for
Children/Teens, Arts Services,
Film/Video, Visual Arts*

NEW YORK AQUARIUM
*See Primary liasting under Educational
Institution*

NEW YORK TRANSIT MUSEUM
130 Livingston Street, 10th Floor
Brooklyn, NY 11201
Site address:
Corner of Boerum Place and
Schermerhorn Street
Brooklyn, NY 11201
Tel 718-694-1600
Fax 718-694-1791
Web www.mta.info/museum

Director: Gabrielle Shubert

Opened in 1976, the New York Transit
Museum is home to over 100 years of
transit lore, artifacts, and memorabilia. It is housed in a 1930s subway
station containing vintage subway
and elevated cars, antique turnstiles,
a working signal tower, and more.
Programs include exhibitions, lectures,
screenings, and family workshops.

*Secondary Categories: Arts for
Children/Teens, Historical Societies*

OLD STONE HOUSE OF BROOKLYN (OSH)
P.O. Box 150613
Brooklyn, NY 11215
Site address:
J.J. Byrne Park
3rd Street at 5th Avenue
Brooklyn, NY 11215
Tel 718-768-3195
Fax 718-768-3197
Email oldstonehouse@verizon.net
Web www.theoldstonehouse.org

Executive Director: Kimberly Maier

Built in 1699, the Old Stone House was the site of the Battle of Brooklyn in 1776, and later served as the first clubhouse of the baseball team that became the Brooklyn Dodgers. The OSH offers educational programming for grades 2 through 8, as well as cultural programming in theater, music, and literature.

Secondary Categories: Architecture & Urban/Environmental Design, Music, Presenting Organizations, Theater

PORTSIDE NEWYORK
P.O. Box 195, Red Hook Station
Brooklyn, NY 11231
Site address:
Pier 9B, Brooklyn Marine Terminal, Red Hook
c/o American Stevedoring
70 Hamilton Avenue
Brooklyn, NY 11231
Tel 718-852-0821
Email mail@portsidenewyork.org
Web www.portsidenewyork.org

Director: Carolina Salguero

PortSide NewYork seeks to breathe life into the relationship between land-side communities and the maritime sector—to the advantage of both. The tanker Mary Whalen is PortSide's main physical space at present. PortSide offers waterfront-inspired exhibits, art, performances, film, readings, events, and happenings. PortSide's website delivers significant information about Red Hook, local organizations, and reporting about the waterfront.

Secondary Category: Presenting Organizations

PROSPECT PARK & PROSPECT PARK ALLIANCE
See Primary listing under Multi-Disciplinary Arts

PUPPETWORKS
See Primary listing under Theater

THE WATERFRONT MUSEUM (SHOWBOAT BARGE)
290 Conover Street, Pier 44
Brooklyn, NY 11231
Tel 718-624-4719
Email dsharps@waterfrontmuseum.org
Web www.waterfrontmuseum.org

Founding President: David Sharps

Docked in Red Hook, the Waterfront Museum and Showboat Barge provides waterfront access and affordable cultural and educational programs aboard a historic vessel listed on the National Register of Historic Places. In summer, CIRCUSundays and the Sunset Music Series bring the barge to life as a showboat.

Secondary Categories: Multi-Disciplinary Arts, Music, Presenting Organizations

WILLIAMSBURG ART & HISTORICAL CENTER
See Primary listing under Multi-Disciplinary Arts

MUSEUMS

**WYCKOFF FARMHOUSE MUSEUM
(WYCKOFF HOUSE & ASSOCIATION)**
5816 Clarendon Road
Brooklyn, NY 11203

Tel 718-629-5400
Email info@wyckoffassociation.org
Web www.wyckoffassociation.org

Executive Director: Sean Sawyer

The Wyckoff Farmhouse Museum tells the story of three centuries of agrarian life in western Long Island. The Museum's mission is to educate visitors about the diverse peoples of Brooklyn's Colonial-era farms.

Secondary Categories: Folk Arts, Historical Societies

MUSIC

440 GALLERY
See Primary listing under Galleries

651 ARTS
See Primary listing under Presenting Organizations

AD HOC ART
See Primary listing under Galleries

AFRICUSSION-PERCUSSION DISCUSSION
572 Prospect Place
Brooklyn, NY 11238

Tel 718-230-4997
Email africussion@gmail.com
Web www.ghanasankofaarts.tripod.com

Artistic Director: Harold D. Akyeampong

AFRICUSSION is the multicultural music group of the Centre for World Folkloric Arts. With a name derived from "Africa, percussion, and discussion," AFRICUSSION uses live performance and teaching programs as a foundation for community dialogue, promoting diversity, respect, and unity through music.

Secondary Categories: Arts for Children/Teens, Arts Services, Folk Arts, Multi-Disciplinary Arts, Presenting Organizations

AMERICAN CREATIVE DANCE
See Primary listing under Dance

AMERICAN MUSIC GROUP
285 5th Avenue
Brooklyn, NY 11215

Tel 718-874-6769
Email amgorg@pipeline.com
Web www.americanmusicgroup.org

Artistic Director: Dennis Mitcheltree

A jazz collective, American Music Group fosters collaboration among New York's finest composers and performers. Members are given the opportunity to develop their art through live performances of commissioned works, other original material, and classic jazz standards. Listeners have opportunities to experience this music through low-cost performances and educational programs.

Secondary Category: Presenting Organizations

AMERICAN OPERA PROJECTS (AOP)
138 South Oxford Street, #3B
Brooklyn, NY 11217

Tel 718-398-4024
Fax 718-398-3489
Email info@operaprojects.org
Web www.operaprojects.org

Executive Director: Charles Jarden

American Opera Project's mission is to champion innovative works of music theater, expand the art form, and present new works by emerging and established talent. The Project's goal is to create a lasting legacy of relevant music theater and inspire new audiences with a fresh appreciation for new opera and theater.

Secondary Categories: Opera/Music Theater, Theater

MUSIC

ART LILLARD'S HEAVENLY BAND
(ART LILLARD'S HEAVENLY BIG BAND)
9 Banner 3rd Terrace
Brooklyn, NY 11235-6710

Tel 718-934-6848
Fax 718-934-3637
Email art@artlillard.com
Web www.artlillard.com

Bandleader: Art Lillard

Filling clubs and concert venues since 1987, Art Lillard's Heavenly Band (a 12- to 17-piece ensemble) plays standards and original music with the rich, lush sound of nine horns. The result is a melodic, danceable combination of Latin, swing, blues, and jazz elements.

ART PLAZA CULTURAL CENTER
See Primary listing under Arts Services

ATTITUDE: THE DANCERS' MAGAZINE
See Primary listing under Dance

BAC ARTS IN EDUCATION
See Primary listing under Arts for Children/Teens

BAC FOLK ARTS
See Primary listing under Folk Arts

BAHIA KAO
239 Flatbush Avenue
Brooklyn, NY 11217

Tel 718-783-7189
Fax 718-636-9404
Email ritadexango@aol.com
Web www.brazil-culture.com

President: Rita C. Silva

Through lectures and demonstrations/ performances, Bahia Kao provides a comprehensive introduction to Afro Brazilian culture—its dance and music, its language, traditions, deities, and more.

Secondary Categories: Dance, Multi-Disciplinary Arts

BAM
See Primary listing under Multi-Disciplinary Arts

BAMCAFÉLIVE
30 Lafayette Avenue
Brooklyn, NY 11217

Tel 718-636-4100
Email info@bam.org
Web www.bam.org/events/bamcafe live.aspx

President: Karen Brooks Hopkins

Every Friday and Saturday night, BAMcafé Live showcases renowned and emerging artists, featuring some of the best jazz, R&B, world beat, pop, and experimental music from Brooklyn and beyond. All BAMcafé Live events have a "no cover, no minimum" policy.

Secondary Category: Literary Arts

BANG ON A CAN
80 Hanson Place
Brooklyn, NY 11217

Tel 718-852-7755
Email info@bangonacan.org
Web www.bangonacan.org

Executive Director: Kenny Savelson

Formed in 1987 by composers Michael Gordon, David Lang, and Julia Wolfe, Bang on a Can commissions, performs, creates, presents, and records contemporary music. With an ear for the new and unknown, Bang on a Can strives to expose exciting and innovative music as broadly and accessibly as possible to new audiences worldwide.

Secondary Category: Presenting Organizations

BARGEMUSIC
Fulton Ferry Landing
Brooklyn, NY 11201

Tel 718-624-2083
Fax 718-624-1155
Email info@bargemusic.org
Web www.bargemusic.org

President, Executive Director, and Artistic Director: Mark Peskanov

Bargemusic offers year-round performances of chamber music in a fittingly intimate setting on the East River. To make that unique musical experience available to as many people as possible, Bargemusic presents 220 chamber music concerts annually, and offers free tickets to a variety of groups every week, as well as a monthly free concert open to all.

Secondary Category: Presenting Organizations

BAROQUE ACROSS THE RIVER

87 Columbia Heights, #53
Brooklyn, NY 11201

Tel 718-643-4608
Web www.baroqueacrosstheriver.com

Founder: Kathy McDonald

BaroQue Across the River is a baroque chamber music group that performs on period instruments in historical venues. Known for its attention to detail and historical accuracy, the ensemble has performed in numerous Brooklyn locations, including the Akwaaba Mansion in Stuyvesant Heights and the Lefferts Historic House in Prospect Park.

BELANTHI (BELANTHI ENTERPRISES, INC.)

142 Court Street
Brooklyn, NY 11201

Tel 718-855-2769

President: Paulette Hios

Belanthi Gallery exhibits contemporary art in all styles and media. Music instruction is also available from Belanthi, including piano, voice, music theory, audition coaching, ear training, and sight singing.

Secondary Category: Galleries

BELLA VOCE SINGERS

Email jacorbin@earthlink.net
Web www.bellavocesingers.com

Director: Jessica Corbin

A nonprofit women's choir founded in 2000, Bella Voce Singers is now a 32-member multigenerational group dedicated to excellence. Bella Voce's mission is to enrich and educate its members and audiences alike by performing a diverse repertoire with an emphasis on contemporary composers, and by bringing other, lesser-known works to the community.

BINDLESTIFF FAMILY VARIETY ARTS, INC.
See Primary listing under Theater

BREEDINGGROUND PRODUCTIONS
See Primary listing under Multi-Disciplinary Arts

BRIC ARTS | MEDIA | BROOKLYN
See Primary listing under Multi-Disciplinary Arts

THE BRICK THEATER, INC.
See Primary listing under Theater

BRICSTUDIO
See Primary listing under Presenting Organizations

BROOKLYN CENTER FOR THE PERFORMING ARTS AT BROOKLYN COLLEGE (BCBC)
See Primary listing under Presenting Organizations

THE BROOKLYN CHAMBER ORCHESTRA

1427 71st Street
Brooklyn, NY 11228

Tel 718-259-2772

Artistic Director: Jose A. Guzman

The accompanying orchestra for the Regina Opera Company, the Brooklyn Chamber Orchestra also offers independent performances and school presentations.

Secondary Category: Opera/Music Theater

MUSIC

BROOKLYN CHILDREN'S MUSEUM
See Primary listing under Museums

BROOKLYN CHILDREN'S THEATRE
See Primary listing under Arts for Children/Teens

BROOKLYN COLLEGE CONSERVATORY OF MUSIC (CONSERVATORY OF MUSIC OF BROOKLYN COLLEGE)
2900 Bedford Avenue
Brooklyn, NY 11210
Tel 718-951-5286
Fax 718-951-4502
Email brucem@brooklyn.cuny.edu
Web www.bcmusic.org

Director: Bruce C. MacIntyre

The Brooklyn College Conservatory of Music offers rigorous curricula with first-rate faculty in several music programs, as well as excellent performance opportunities in the College's orchestra, choruses, opera workshop, and wind, jazz, and contemporary ensembles. The Conservatory offers degrees in music education, performance, composition, musicology, and interactive media arts.

Secondary Categories: Computer Arts/New Media, Educational Institutions, Opera/Music Theater

BROOKLYN COLLEGE PREPARATORY CENTER FOR THE PERFORMING ARTS (BC PREP CENTER)
2900 Bedford Avenue, 234 Roosevelt Hall, Brooklyn, NY 11210

Tel 718-951-4111
Fax 718-951-5412
Email bcpc@brooklyn.cuny.edu
Web www.bcprepcenter.org

Director: Diane Newman

Founded in 1978, Brooklyn College's Preparatory Center for the Performing Arts offers outstanding instruction in music, theater, and dance. The foundation of the Preparatory Center's activities is its highly qualified faculty

of professional artist-teachers. In addition to an established reputation as a teacher, each faculty member has distinguished performing credentials.

Secondary Categories: Dance, Theater

BROOKLYN COMMUNITY CHORUS
20 South Oxford Street
Brooklyn, NY 11217
Site address:
Old First Church at 7th Avenue
Brooklyn, NY 11215
Tel 718-534-6540
Email mclary@berkeleycarroll.org
Web www.brooklyncommunitychorus.org

Director: Marlene Clary

A self-governing organization open to singers from diverse backgrounds, ages, and musical experience, the Brooklyn Community Chorus is dedicated to a variety of styles, including classical, spiritual, Motown, show tunes, doo-wop, and jazz. Performances are held three times a year, in both large group and smaller ensemble settings, at its home location and around Brooklyn.

BROOKLYN CONTEMPORARY CHORUS, INC.
P.O. Box 3093
Brooklyn, NY 11202
Web www.brooklyncontemporary chorus.org

President: Diane M. Ward

Brooklyn Contemporary Chorus, Inc. is a neighborhood-based group of singers who have been performing in the Clinton Hill and Fort Greene neighborhoods for 35 years, with music that ranges from works in the great choral tradition to Gilbert and Sullivan to settings of hymns and spirituals and contemporary music.

THE BROOKLYN FOUR PLUS ONE, INC. (B4+1 INC.)

P O Box 22872
Brooklyn, NY 11202

Tel 347-713-5190
Email brooklyn4jazz@hotmail.com
Web www.brooklyn4thearts.org

CEO and President: Wade E. Barnes

Originally a band founded by drummer and educator Wade Barnes in the mid-90's, the Brooklyn Four Plus One, Inc. (B4+1, Inc.) is a nonprofit organization whose mission is to bring the highest quality of America's classical music to all ages, races, ethnic groups, and socioeconomic levels.

BROOKLYN FRIENDS OF CHAMBER MUSIC

140 Bond Street
Brooklyn, NY 11217

Site address:
Lafayette Avenue Presbyterian Church
85 South Oxford Street
Brooklyn, NY 11217

Tel 718-855-3053
Email wflecknaf@aol.com
Web www.brooklynfriendsofchamber music.org

Manager: Wanda Fleck

BFCM presents seven chamber music concerts per season, on Sunday afternoons, at the Lafayette Avenue Presbyterian Church in Fort Greene. World-class musicians perform the classical and contemporary repertoire as well as new works commissioned by BFCM. Tickets are affordably priced, and TDF and High Five vouchers are accepted.

Secondary Category: Presenting Organizations

BROOKLYN MUSIC SCHOOL

See Primary listing under Visual/Performing Arts Schools

BROOKLYN PHILHARMONIA CHORUS

124 Henry Street
Brooklyn, NY 11201

Tel 718-907-9063
Email brooklynchorus@yahoo.com

President: Susan Schindler

Founded in 1955, Brooklyn Philharmonia Chorus is Brooklyn's oldest community chorus, and currently presents a wide variety of choral music to diverse communities around the borough in at least two concerts a year.

BROOKLYN PHILHARMONIC

138-A Court Street
Brooklyn, NY 11201

Tel 718-488-5700
Fax 718-488-5901
Email info@brooklynphilharmonic.org
Web www.brooklynphilharmonic.org

President: Catherine M. Cahill

One of the nation's premiere music ensembles, the Brooklyn Philharmonic celebrates its vital presence in the cultural life of New York, and serves Brooklyn's cultural and educational communities through partnerships with New York City's Department of Education, the Brooklyn Museum of Art, the Brooklyn Public Library, and BAM, among other organizations.

*Secondary Categories:
Arts for Children/Teens, Dance,
Multi-Disciplinary Arts*

THE BROOKLYN RAIL

*See Primary listing under
Multi-Disciplinary Arts*

MUSIC

BROOKLYN SYMPHONY ORCHESTRA (BROOKLYN HEIGHTS MUSIC SOCIETY)

P.O. Box 334
Brooklyn, NY 11202

Email info@brooklynsymphony
orchestra.org
Web www.brooklynsymphony
orchestra.org

Artistic Director: Nicholas Armstrong

The Brooklyn Symphony Orchestra, comprised of talented amateur, semi-professional, and professional musicians, is one of the New York area's finest community orchestras. Founded in 1973 as the "Brooklyn Heights Orchestra," the group joins under the baton of Artistic Director Nicholas Armstrong to present five symphonic concerts per season.

THE BROOKLYN WOMEN'S CHORUS

416 2nd Street
Brooklyn, NY 11215

Tel 718-788-3741
Email bevgrant1@aol.com
Web www.brooklynwomenschorus.com

Director: Bev Grant

Founded by Bev Grant in 1997, the Brooklyn Women's Chorus is a supportive community chorus that fosters creativity and nurtures friendships. Firmly committed to the power of song, the Chorus sings for peace, equality, justice, and the rights of all people. There are no auditions to join.

BROOKLYN YOUTH CHORUS ACADEMY

See Primary listing under Arts for Children/Teens

BROOKLYN-QUEENS CONSERVATORY OF MUSIC (BQCM)

58 7th Avenue
Brooklyn, NY 11217

Tel 718-622-3300
Fax 718-622-3957
Web www.bqcm.org

Executive Director: Alan J. Fox

Founded in 1897, the Brooklyn-Queens Conservatory of Music has been serving the New York musical community for over a century. The Conservatory promotes individual and community growth through music, and is committed to making music accessible to people of all ages, backgrounds, and skill levels.

Secondary Categories: Art for Children/Teens, Opera and Musical Theater, Presenting Organizations

THE BROWNSTONE POETS

See Primary listing under Literary Arts

THE BUSHWICK STARR

See Primary listing under Theater

CAVE

See Primary listing under Multi-Disciplinary Arts

CELEBRATE BROOKLYN PERFORMING ARTS FESTIVAL

See Primary listing under Presenting Organizations

CENTRAL BROOKLYN JAZZ CONSORTIUM (CBJC)

Tel 718-875-1016
Email info@centralbrooklynjazz
consortium.org
Web www.cbjcjazz.org

Founded in 1999, the Central Brooklyn Jazz Consortium is an amalgam of jazz musicians, entertainment venues, music lovers, and faith- and community-based organizations. CBJC produces an annual Spring Jazz Festival, in addition to other events, and has established a Brooklyn Jazz Hall of Fame.

Secondary Category: Presenting Organizations

CHASSIDIC DISCOVERY WELCOME CENTER

See Primary listing under Multi-Disciplinary Arts

CHELSEA STRING BAND
440 Fifth Street
Brooklyn, NY 11215

Tel 718-965-4074
Email alanfriend_music@mind
spring.com
Web www.alanfriendmusic.com

The Chelsea String Band musicians are multi-instrumentalists and singers, specializing in old-time tunes and songs from the Southern Appalachians, as well as contra dance music. Instruments include fiddle, banjo, guitar, concertina, and anything else they can get their hands on. The band plays for square dances, contra dances, and concert venues.

Secondary Category: Folk Arts

CHEZ BUSHWICK
See Primary listing under Dance

CHRISTIANA DRAPKIN JAZZ GROUP
5 Stratford Road, #2
Brooklyn, NY 11218

Tel 718-693-0583
Email chdrapkin@aol.com
Web www.christianadrapkin.com
Director: Christiana Drapkin

Christiana Drapkin has been performing jazz standards with her small combo around New York and the Eastern seaboard for twenty years. The group intersperses original material with standards from the great American songbook. In addition, they present a special "Shakespeare and All That Jazz" program which features Shakespeare's original words set to jazz arrangements by John Dankworth, Duke Ellington, and others.

Secondary Category: Literary Arts

CIRCUIT PRODUCTIONS INC.
*See Primary listing under
Multi-Disciplinary Arts*

CIRCUS AMOK
See Primary listing under Theater

THE CODE FOUNDATION, INC.
See Primary listing under Arts Services

COLLECTIVE OPERA COMPANY
*See Primary listing under Opera/Music
Theater*

CONNECTION WORKS, INC.
*See Primary listing under Arts for
Children/Teens*

COVENANT DANCE THEATRE OF BROOKLYN
See Primary listing under Dance

CREATE!
*See Primary listing under Arts for
Children/Teens*

CREATIVE WOMEN'S NETWORK
See Primary listing under Arts Services

CRUCIAL ARTS PRODUCTIONS, INC.
*See Primary listing under
Multi-Disciplinary Arts*

DAM, STUHLTRAGER GALLERY
See Primary listing under Galleries

DANCES AND DRUMS OF AFRICA, INC.
See Primary listing under Dance

MUSIC

DARMSTADT (DARMSTADT, "CLASSICS OF THE AVANT-GARDE")
253 Cumberland Street, #107
Brooklyn, NY 11205
Tel 347-351-3442
Web www.darmstadtnewmusic.org

Director: Zach Layton

Darmstadt, Classics of the Avant-Garde, is a critically-acclaimed contemporary music series and experimental music listening party led by composer Zach Layton. With its current residency at the Galapagos Arts Space, Darmstadt has been featuring leading experimental composers, performers, and video artists from New York City and around the world since 2005.

Secondary Categories: Computer Arts/New Media, Film/Video, Multi-Disciplinary Arts, Opera/Music Theater, Performance Art, Presenting Organizations

DE NONNO PRODUCTIONS, INCORPORATED
See Primary listing under Film/Video

DRUMSONG AFRICAN BALLET THEATRE, INC.
See Primary listing under Multi-Disciplinary Arts

EGRESS THEATRE COMPANY
See Primary listing under Theater

EL PEQUEÑO ARTISTA
See Primary listing under Arts for Children/Teens

ELECTRIK GODDESS CLUB ORQUESTRA (EGCO)
1515 East 27 Street, 1st Floor
Brooklyn, NY 11229
Site address:
P.O. Box 290-682
Brooklyn, NY 11229
Tel 917-881-5134
Fax 718-951-7218
Email creativwomenntwk@aol.com

Web www.myspace.com/electrikgoddess
and www.sonicbids.com/lisaroma
Director: Lisa Roma

A collaborative musical group led by singer-songwriter-lyricist-musician-composer Lisa Roma, Electrik Goddess Club Orquestra (EGCO) performs at various venues around the tri-state area. Lisa Roma sings original songs, classic jazz, folk, blues, soul, and funk, and performs solo or with the Poetic Notion Chorus, directed by Rob Darnell, vocalist-composer-pianist-arranger.

Secondary Category: Theater

THE ELEVENTEN GALLERY
See Primary listing under Galleries

ELSIE MANAGEMENT
See Primary listing under Arts Services

THE ENRICO CARUSO MUSEUM OF AMERICA
See Primary listing under Museums

FILIPINO ARTS & MUSIC ENSEMBLE (FAME)
1654 Ryder Street
Brooklyn, NY 11234
Email info@famenyc.org
Web www.famenyc.org
President: Belle Locsin

A volunteer-run nonprofit, the Filipino Arts & Music Ensemble (FAME) preserves, presents, and promotes the musical heritage of the Philippines. FAME intends to pass down a rich cultural heritage through a folk dance program and a string ensemble composed of children ages four to sixteen years old.

Secondary Categories: Arts for Children/Teens, Dance, Folk Arts

FORECAST MUSIC
510 Ocean Parkway, #1J
Brooklyn, NY 11218
Tel 212-380-8494

Web www.forecastmusic.org

Artistic Director: Eric Schwartz

Forecast Music is an adventurous, nonprofit, New York City-based new music group. Its mission is to present new and innovative American music of varied aesthetic visions in relaxed, alternative performance spaces, as well as traditional concert venues.

FULTON MALL IMPROVEMENT ASSOCIATION
See Primary listing under Presenting Organizations

GOWANUS WILDCATS
See Primary listing under Presenting Organizations

GRACE & SPIRITUS CHORALE OF BROOKLYN (GRACE CHORAL SOCIETY OF BROOKLYN AND SPIRITUS ET ANIMA)
254 Hicks Street
Brooklyn, NY 11201

Tel 718-707-1411
Email info@graceandspiritus.org
Web www.graceandspiritus.org

President: Donna Epstein

The Grace & Spiritus Chorale of Brooklyn is a 70-member chorus with smaller ensembles drawn from its ranks. Dedicated to performing a wide range of music (including work by living composers), Grace & Spiritus presents two or three concerts a year in brownstone Brooklyn neighborhoods.

HALBERT BARTON AND EL BOMBAZO DE BROOKLYN
See Primary listing under Folk Arts

HEART OF BROOKLYN
See Primary listing under Arts Services

THE HOGAR COLLECTION
See Primary listing under Galleries

IFETAYO CULTURAL ARTS
See Primary listing under Multi-Disciplinary Arts

IMAGINE PROJECT, INC.
See Primary listing under Arts for Children/Teens

ISSUE PROJECT ROOM
See Primary listing under Multi-Disciplinary Arts

THE ITALIAN OPERA COMPANY, INC.
See Primary listing under Opera/Music Theater

JAZZREACH, INC.
55 Washington Street, Suite 509
Brooklyn, NY 11201

Tel 718-625-5188
Fax 718-625-4979
Email jazzreach@earthlink.net
Web www.jazzreach.org

Founder and Executive-Artistic Director: H. Benjamin Schuman

JazzReach, Inc. is a nationally recognized nonprofit organization dedicated to the promotion, performance, creation, and teaching of jazz music. Through the presentation of innovative, live multi-media educational programs, informative clinics, and master-classes for students, and the commissioning, recording, and performance of exciting new works, JazzReach is ardently commited to fostering a greater appreciation, awareness and understanding of this rich, vital, ever-evolving American art form.

MUSIC

THE KINGSBOROUGH MUSICAL SOCIETY CHORUS

1018 East 29th Street
Brooklyn, NY 11210

Tel 718-377-0610
Email brownie55b@aol.com

President: Sandi Pollack

The Kingsborough Musical Society Chorus brings free public music concerts to Kingsborough Community College and its outlying Brooklyn community. Its repertoire includes classical, sacred music, opera and operetta, show tunes, and American and Jewish folk music. The chorus has performed in churches, synagogues, and community centers.

KLEZMER PLUS

2060 East 37th Street
Brooklyn, NY 11234

Tel 718-998-8098
Email klzmrfats@aol.com

Director: Peter D. Sokolow

Klezmer Plus offers historic performances of classic klezmer and early pop and jazz related to Jewish themes, along with lectures and demonstrations concerning this music.

Secondary Category: Arts Services

LA TROUPE MAKANDAL, INC.
See Primary listing under Folk Arts

THE LADSONIAN FOUNDATION

G.P.O. Box 22486
Brooklyn, NY 11202

Site address:
309 Lafayette Avenue
Brooklyn, NY 11238

Tel 718-622-3207
Email v.l.ladson@worldnet.att.net
Web www.neighborhoodlink.com/public/clubhome.html

Executive Music Director and Pianist:
Vivian L. Ladson

The Ladsonian Foundation is dedicated to teaching the gifted and talented of all ages—in piano, music theory, music education, sight-singing, and performance.

Secondary Category: Arts for Children/Teens

LONG ISLAND UNIVERSITY MUSIC DEPARTMENT, BROOKLYN CAMPUS
See Primary listing under Educational Institutions

LONG ISLAND UNIVERSITY, BROOKLYN CAMPUS
See Primary listing under Educational Institutions

LOOP 2.4.3

144 Spencer Street
Brooklyn, NY 11205

Tel 718-254-0483
Email lorne@loop243.com
Web www.loop243.com

Managing Director: Lorne M. Watson

Loop 2.4.3 is an ensemble of gifted percussionists and composers who combine elements of classical, jazz, and ethnic music to create a unique new musical language. In addition to its live performances, Loop 2.4.3 offers recording services, as well as educational outreach and residencies.

LOS BOMBEROS DE BROOKLYN, INC.
See Primary listing under Folk Arts

MANI

Tel 917-670-6029
Email joel@manichambermusic.org
Web www.manichambermusic.org

A performance ensemble focused on classical chamber music and its place in contemporary musical life, Mani presents standard classical concerts as well as concerts in less traditional venues, in collaboration with a variety of artists and organizations, from galleries to pop musicians. Mani's extensive educational programs include music appreciation classes, training, and music education for 4 to 6 year olds.

Secondary Category: Arts for Children/Teens

MANY MOODS PRODUCTION COMPANY
41 Schermerhorn Street, #135
Brooklyn, NY 11201

Tel 718-574-9884
Email mmp7@earthlink.net
Web www.manymoods.com

President: Linda Felder

Many Moods Production Company helps both emerging and veteran musicians, artists, producers, singers, and songwriters further their careers. Offering a sought-after self-help guide, seminars, music promotions, contract assistance, and other resources, Many Moods creates opportunities for the emerging professional artist.

Secondary Category: Arts Services

MARTIN LUTHER KING JR. CONCERT SERIES
31 Prospect Park West
Brooklyn, NY 11215

Site address:
Wingate Field, Winthrop Street and Brooklyn Avenue, Brooklyn, NY 11203

Tel 718-469-1912
Web www.brooklynconcerts.com

Executive Director and Executive Producer: Debra Garcia

The Martin Luther King Jr. Concert Series provides free concerts by top-name entertainers on Monday nights during July and August. Every week highlights a different musical genre, including classic soul, R & B, contemporary, Motown, old-school hip hop, Caribbean, and more.

Secondary Category: Presenting Organizations

MATA FESTIVAL (MUSIC AT THE ANTHOLOGY, INC.)
293 Warren Street # 2
Brooklyn, NY 11201

Tel 212-563-5124
Email info@matafestival.org
Web www.matafestival.org

Executive Director: Missy Mazzoli

MATA is an organization devoted to promoting, presenting and commissioning new works by young composers. MATA presents an annual festival of contemporary music each spring at the Brooklyn Lyceum, and has also initiated a new bi-monthly concert series, as well as a "curatorial associate" program for young composers.

Secondary Category: Presenting Organizations

MBS MUSIC & ENTERTAINMENT
1684 80th Street
Brooklyn, NY 11214

Email mbswebsite@aol.com
Web www.mbsmusic.com

President: Cathy SantoPietro

MBS Music & Entertainment provides entertainment for concerts, weddings, corporate events, and private parties, representing all styles of live music and DJs, including contemporary "name" artists, wedding bands, and oldies specialists.

MUSIC

M'CAHAYA ARTS & EDUCATION FOUNDATION
See Primary listing under Film/Video

MEANRED PRODUCTIONS
249 Smith Street, PMB 184
Brooklyn, NY 11231
Email info@meanredproductions.com
Web www.meanredproductions.com

Creative Director: Jen Lyon

Presenting "arts with a twist," MeanRed Productions is an arts and music event production company that combines genres and media in unlikely contexts. Sample events have featured new media installations and electronic rock in a converted warehouse, skateboarding and live painting in a makeshift park, and dance, illustration, and music in a Japanese restaurant.

Secondary Category: Visual Arts

METROTECH BUSINESS IMPROVEMENT DISTRICT
See Primary listing under Presenting Organizations

MICHAEL ALAN'S DRAW-A-THON
See Primary listing under Arts Services

MONKEY TOWN
See Primary listing under Film/Video

MOUNTAIN REDBIRD MUSIC
See Primary listing under Folk Arts

MOVING THEATER
See Primary listing under Theater

NAT CREOLE ONLINE
See Primary listing under Computer Arts/New Media

NEW YORK BAROQUE (NEW YORK BAROQUE, LTD.)
206 Union Street
Brooklyn, NY 11231
Tel 718-852-4544
Fax 718-852-4544
Email nybaroque@aol.com
Web www.newyorkbaroque.org

Artistic Director: Michael Ishizawa

A professional period instrument and vocal ensemble, New York Baroque performs a repertory of works from the Baroque and Classical periods, and specializes in music from 17th-century Italy. Works performed are carefully checked against original sources and are performed from facsimiles or performing editions specifically created for New York Baroque.

Secondary Category: Opera/Music Theater

THE NIETZSCHE MUSIC PROJECT (NMP, INC.)
37 South Portland Avenue
Brooklyn, NY 11217
Email nmpinc@earthlink.net
Web www.nietzschemusicproject.org

Executive Director: Tali E. Makell

A nonprofit interdisciplinary arts organization, the Nietzsche Music Project examines the interaction between artists and culture. The Project explores the ways in which artists are affected by cultural factors and how artists influence the general culture.

Secondary Category: Multi-Disciplinary Arts

NOEL POINTER FOUNDATION (NPF)
1368 Fulton Street
Brooklyn, NY 11216
Tel 718-230-4825
Fax 718-230-4841
Email info@npsom.org
Web www.npsom.org

Executive Director: Chinita J. Pointer

Established in 1995, the Noel Pointer Foundation (NPF) is premised on the belief that children will be empowered through the learning of string music. NPF's mission is to enrich children's musical and cultural experience by infusing them with a positive sense of who they are and what they may become.

**OBRUMANKOMA SANKOFA
TRADITIONALS OF GHANA**
See Primary listing under Dance

THE OLD AMERICAN CAN FACTORY
*See Primary listing under Presenting
Organizations*

OLD STONE HOUSE OF BROOKLYN
See Primary listing under Museums

THE OMNI ENSEMBLE LTD.
23 Wellington Court
Brooklyn, NY 11230

Site address:
58 Seventh Avenue
Brooklyn, NY 11217

Tel 718-859-8649
Email davewechs@earthlink.net
Web www.omniensemble.org

Music Director: David J. Wechsler

The OMNI Ensemble Ltd. (core players: David Wechsler-flute, Adam Fisher-cello, and Kathleen Supove-piano and synthesizer) presents programs of enormous variety, from the Renaissance to the contemporary avant-garde, designed to provide the audience with a musical experience not ordinarily encountered in a single event. The group performs live electronic music, as well as standard chamber music repertoire.

Secondary Category: Performance Art

ONE WORLD SYMPHONY
209 Argyle Road
Brooklyn, NY 11218

Web www.oneworldsymphony.org

Artistic Director and Conductor:
Sung Jin Hong

One World Symphony actively engages audiences through innovative musical demonstrations, the championing of new music by living composers, and by offering unique and fresh perspectives on the classical repertoire. One World is devoted to serving local and

global communities through music, by performing benefit concerts and raising money for the Children's Fund, the Coalition for the Homeless, and many other organizations.

*Secondary Category: Presenting
Organizations*

OPERA ON TAP
*See Primary listing under Opera/Music
Theater*

PANTONIC STEEL ORCHESTRA
775 East 39th Street
Brooklyn, NY 11210

Tel 718-434-0231
Fax 718-421-2041
Email pantonic1@aol.com
Web www.pantonic.com

President: Glenda V. Gamory

Pantonic Steel Orchestra is a group of approximately 100 gifted, charismatic young players who capture the heart and soul of the urban Caribbean experience. Hailing from varied backgrounds and cultures, and equally comfortable with rap, R&B, and pop as they are with Caribbean music, these versatile musicians represent the next level of the steel band phenomenon.

*Secondary Categories: Arts for
Children/Teens*

MUSIC

PARK SLOPE SINGERS
384A 5th Street
Brooklyn, NY 11215
Email fxbolton@verizon.net
Web www.homestead.com/parkslope
singers
President: Francis X. Bolton

A community chorus founded in 1992, the Park Slope Singers number between 35 to 45 members each semester, and present two concerts each year. Repertoire ranges from Bach to Broadway, and the chorus does not hold auditions—singers join and determine for themselves whether they're up to singing with the group.

PENDU PRODUCTIONS
See Primary listing under Visual Arts

PLG ARTS
See Primary listing under Multi-Disciplinary Arts

POTPOURRI OF COLOR PERFORMING ARTS COMPANY
See Primary listing under Theater

PROSPECT PARK & PROSPECT PARK ALLIANCE
See Primary listing under Multi-Disciplinary Arts

QUEST JR. DRUM & BUGLE CORPS, INC. (QUEST YOUTH ORGANIZATION, INC.)
P.O. Box 26724
Brooklyn, NY 11202
Site address:
272 McDonough Street
Brooklyn, NY 11233
Tel 718-928-7058
Email info@questdbcorps.org
Web www.questdbcorps.org
Executive Director: Thomas Fisher

Rooted in and primarily focused on the community of Bedford Stuyvesant, Quest Jr. Drum & Bugle Corps, Inc. is committed to enriching the lives of its participants through the performing arts. Quest Jr. provides free music lessons, academic assistance for youth, and music mentoring matches.

RAIZES DO BRASIL CAPOEIRA BROOKLYN
See Primary listing under Folk Arts

THE RAY ABRAMS BIG (17-PIECE) SWING BAND
31 Abrams Place
Lynbrook, NY 11563
Site address:
414-1/2 Clinton Street
Brooklyn, NY 11231
Tel 516-680-7670
Email drummerfb@aol.com
Sales Representative: Frank Barbuzza

Swinging since the "Fifties" with a sound and quality reminiscent of the great bands of Basie and Ellington, The Ray Abrams Big Swing Band continues to entertain audiences in jazz and swing-dance venues. Ervin Simpson leads the band, playing the modern works of Netico, Foster, and Hefti, while also keeping Abrams' charts and name alive.

RECORDING ADVENTURE WORKSHOP
20 Jay Street
Brooklyn, NY 11201
Tel 718-624-6300
Email tz@triplezmusic.com
Web www.triplezmusic.com/html/wkshp_FRAM.html
Business Manager: Mary Ellen Bernard

Recording Adventure Workshop offers hands-on recording experience for young musicians, singers, or music-lovers ages 12 through 16. Participants hear (and see) how sound actually works with some acoustic experiments, then take turns behind the microphone and the sound console to lay down some tracks of their own.

Secondary Category: Arts for Children/Teens

REGINA OPERA COMPANY
See Primary listing under Opera/Music Theater

REVELATION PERFORMING ARTS STUDIO, INC.
See Primary listing under Visual/Performing Arts Schools

ROOFTOP FILMS
See Primary listing under Film/Video

S.E.M. ENSEMBLE, INC. (THE ORCHESTRA OF THE S.E.M. ENSEMBLE)
25 Columbia Place
Brooklyn, NY 11201

Tel 718-488-7659
Fax 718-243-0964
Email info@semensemble.org
Web www.semensemble.org

Artistic Director: Petr Kotik

Founded in 1970, S.E.M. Ensemble,Inc. focuses on the performance and advancement of new music, and especially on new works for orchestra. In 1992, the ensemble began performing as the Orchestra of the S.E.M. Ensemble, and today maintains an active concert schedule at the Willow Place Auditorium in Brooklyn Heights.

SCHOOL FOR MUSICAL PERFORMANCE
910 Kings Highway, Top Floor
Brooklyn, NY 11223

Tel 718-339-4989
Fax 718-339-4989
Email kingkovins@aol.com

Musical Director: David S. Kovins

Founded in 1980, the School for Musical Performance offers a wide variety of classes to any age group as well as to the mentally handicapped. The School is dedicated to teaching its students to strive for success and turn their musical goals into reality.

Secondary Categories:
Arts for Children/Teens,
Visual/Performing Arts Schools

SEASIDE SUMMER CONCERT SERIES
31 Prospect Park West
Brooklyn, NY 11215

Site address:
Asser Levy Seaside Park
West 5th Street and Surf Avenue
Brooklyn, NY 11100

Tel 718-469-1912
Web www.brooklynconcerts.com

Executive Director and Executive Producer: Debra Garcia

The Seaside Summer Concert Series provides free concerts by top-name performers on Thursday nights during July and August. Every week features a different musical genre, including classic rock, pop, contemporary, Motown, oldies, and Latin music.

SHIR CHADASH: THE BROOKLYN JEWISH COMMUNITY CHORUS
23 Howard Place
Brooklyn, NY 11215

Tel 718-369-9110
Email bjcc@acedsl.com
Web www.shir-chadash.cfsites.org

President: Lisa Sack

Shir Chadash: The Brooklyn Jewish Community Chorus is a four-part chorus with 50-plus members. Inspired by the richness and diversity of Jewish music from around the globe, the Chorus' repertoire ranges from liturgical offerings to updated arrangements of world folk music in many languages.

MUSIC

SHOSTAKOVICH MUSIC, ART, AND SPORT SCHOOL, INC.
297 Avenue X
Brooklyn, NY 11223

Tel 718-376-8056
Email kaplun21@aol.com
Web www.shostakovichschool.com

Executive Director: Diana Trost

Established in 1981, the Shostakovich School of Music, Art and Sport has grown from a dream envisioned by a small group of Russian immigrants to a vibrant multifaceted institution with three centers in Brooklyn. The School is a nonprofit, non-sectarian institution dedicated to high-quality instruction in art, music, theater, and sport.

Secondary Categories: Arts for Children/Teens, Educational Institutions, Visual/Performing Arts Schools

SLAVIC ARTS ENSEMBLE (EUROPEAN CHAMBER ENSEMBLE)
139 Noble Street
Brooklyn, NY 11222

Tel 718-389-6984
Email slavicartsensemble@earthlink.net
Web www.slavicartsensemble.org

Managing Director:
Mieczyslaw I. Gubernat

The Slavic Arts Ensemble is dedicated to promoting Polish and Slavic chamber music and to giving outstanding young musicians the opportunity to perform and gain the recognition they deserve. The Ensemble gives both formal and informal concerts and offers music for all social events.

SLOPE MUSIC
271 9th Street
Brooklyn, NY 11215

Tel 718-768-3804
Email slopemusic@gmail.com
Web www.slopemusic.com
Director: Charles F. Sibirsky

Slope Music provides music instruction on most instruments and in most genres, including jazz, classical, rock, and folk. Slope Music also offers all kinds of live music for events and functions, including solo piano, violin, or guitar as well as bands playing jazz, classical, or music for dancing.

SONIDO COSTEÑO
570-A 20th Street
Brooklyn, NY 11218

Tel 718-633-1247
Web www.sonidocosteno.com

President: Juan M. Morales

A Latin band with more than 15 years of experience, Billboard Award-winners Sonido Costeño perform in both Spanish and English, with a repertoire that includes music from Latin America, the United States, and the Caribbean. Sonido Costeño has performed at the Brooklyn Public Library and El Museo del Barrio, among other venues.

SOUL TIGERS MARCHING BAND, INC.
Tel 347-482-8578
Email soultigers2006@yahoo.com
Web www.soultigersmarchingband.com

Band Director: Kenyatte L. Hughes

The Soul Tigers Marching Band,Inc. is a nonprofit music education program dedicated to keeping young people safe during after school hours. The program improves academic achievement, increases school attendance, and supports community youth's positive and healthy development while they learn, read, write, and play music as part of a marching band ensemble.

Secondary Category: Arts for Children/Teens

SPOKE THE HUB DANCING, INC.
See Primary listing under Multi-Disciplinary Arts

ST. ANN AND THE HOLY TRINITY CHURCH
157 Montague Street
Brooklyn, NY 11234
Tel 718-875-6960
Email saht@juno.com
Development Associate:
Sandra J. Gilmour

A venue for concerts and organ recitals, St. Ann and the Holy Trinity Church is housed in a National Historic Landmark building that also claims the first figural stained glass windows made in this country and a landmark Skinner organ.

ST. ANN'S WAREHOUSE
See Primary listing under Presenting Organizations

ST. JOSEPH'S COLLEGE, NY
See Primary listing under Educational Institutions

STREB LABORATORY FOR ACTION MECHANICS
See Primary listing under Multi-Disciplinary Arts

SUNNY'S
253 Conover Street
Brooklyn, NY 11231
Owner: Tone Johansen

Dating from the 1890s and currently run by artists, Sunny's Bar is a Red Hook waterfront establishment that features a number of cultural events and activities. The backroom showcases visual art in all disciplines, and, in addition to hosting regular live music and literary readings, Sunny's presents a play for two weeks every spring.

Secondary Categories: Literary Arts, Presenting Organizations, Visual Arts

SWEET ADELINES - BROOKLYN CHAPTER
1659 Kimball Street
Brooklyn, NY 11234
Tel 718-252-0681
Email mag1103@aol.com

President: Marilyn Gaffney

Sweet Adelines is an international women's singing organization. The Brooklyn chapter sings four-part harmony and performs both in the borough and "anywhere we are asked."

TILLIE'S OF BROOKLYN
See Primary listing under Visual Arts

TONEL LAKAY DANCE THEATRE
See Primary listing under Dance

TRIPLE Z MUSIC
20 Jay Street, Suite 306
Brooklyn, NY 11201
Tel 718-624-6300
Email tz@triplezmusic.com
Web www.triplezmusic.com
Creative and Business Manager:
Mary Ellen Bernard

Triple Z Music provides custom scoring and songwriting, recording, and production, as well as musical casting and direction for live theater and special events. Previous projects have included a collaboration with Japanese Imperial Court musicians for the Nagano Olympics and a rock-electronica score for the Greek classic Phaedra.

VERTICAL PLAYER REPERTORY
See Primary listing under Opera/Music Theater

THE WATERFRONT MUSEUM
See Primary listing under Museums

MUSIC

WOMEN IN STEEL
8513 Coventry Road
Brooklyn, NY 11236

Tel 718-629-2471
Email womeninsteel@yahoo.com

CEO and President: Claudette Baptiste

Women In Steel is an all-female steel orchestra and young women's developmental organization. Founded in 1994, its mission is to educate and guide innovative young women, both socially and culturally, through the art form of steel band music.

WORLD EATER RECORDINGS, NYC
434 Putnam Avenue
Brooklyn, NY 11221

Tel 718-443-8126
Fax 718-443-8126
Email worldeatermusic@hotmail.com
Web www.worldeaternyc.com

Producer and Chief Engineer:
Jared H. Foles

Opened by composer, engineer, and instrumentalist Jared Hassan Foles in November 2000, World Eater Recordings, Inc. has grown to become one of New York City's best-known studios for major recording and audio production for independent artists.

Secondary Categories: Arts Services, Computer Arts/New Media, Film/Video, Multi-Disciplinary Arts, Opera/Music Theater, Presenting Organizations

OPERA/MUSIC THEATER

AMERICAN OPERA PROJECTS
See Primary listing under Music

BAM
*See Primary listing under
Multi-Disciplinary Arts*

BREEDINGGROUND PRODUCTIONS
*See Primary listing under
Multi-Disciplinary Arts*

THE BRICK THEATER, INC.
See Primary listing under Theater

**BROOKLYN CENTER FOR THE
PERFORMING ARTS AT BROOKLYN
COLLEGE (BCBC)**
*See Primary listing under Presenting
Organizations*

THE BROOKLYN CHAMBER ORCHESTRA
See Primary listing under Music

BROOKLYN CHILDREN'S THEATRE
See Primary listing under Theater

**BROOKLYN COLLEGE
CONSERVATORY OF MUSIC**
See Primary listing under Music

**THE BROOKLYN THEATRE ARTS
PROJECT, INC.**
See Primary listing under Theater

BROOKLYN WRITERS SPACE
See Primary listing under Literary Arts

BROOKLYN YOUTH CHORUS ACADEMY
*See Primary listing under Arts for
Children/Teens*

**BROOKLYN-QUEENS
CONSERVATORY OF MUSIC**
See Primary listing under Music

**CELEBRATE BROOKLYN PERFORMING
ARTS FESTIVAL**
*See Primary listing under Presenting
Organizations*

COLLECTIVE OPERA COMPANY (COC)
94 Clinton Avenue, #3L
Brooklyn, NY 11205

Web www.collectiveopera.com

Founder and Artistic Director:
Ryan Tracy

Collective Opera Company (COC) is a
multi-disciplinary network of creative
artists, including writers, musicians,
film makers, and visual artists, dedicated to creating original opera works
for a new audience.

*Secondary Categories: Multi-Disciplinary
Arts, Music, Performance Art*

CREATE!
*See Primary listing under Arts for
Children/Teens*

DARMSTADT
See Primary listing under Music

DZIECI
See Primary listing under Theater

EGRESS THEATRE COMPANY
See Primary listing under Theater

ELSIE MANAGEMENT
See Primary listing under Arts Services

**ENCOMPASS NEW OPERA THEATRE
(ENCOMPASS THEATRE COMPANY, INC.)**
138 South Oxford Street, Suite 1A
Brooklyn, NY 11217
Tel 718-398-4675
Fax 718-398-4684
Email encompassopera@yahoo.com
Web www.encompassopera.org
Executive and Artistic Director:
Nancy Rhodes

Encompass New Opera Theatre is
dedicated to creating and producing
new music theater and contemporary opera. Striving to discover and
nurture emerging artists, premiere
groundbreaking new productions, and
revive important 20th-century operas,
Encompass has produced over 50 fully-
mounted operas with an orchestra.

**THE ENRICO CARUSO MUSEUM OF
AMERICA**
See Primary listing under Museums

GALAPAGOS ART SPACE
*See Primary listing under
Multi-Disciplinary Arts*

THE GALLERY PLAYERS
See Primary listing under Theater

IMAGINE PROJECT, INC.
*See Primary listing under Arts for
Children/Teens*

**THE ITALIAN OPERA COMPANY, INC.
(BROADWAY TO OPERA)**
1464 86th Street
Brooklyn, NY 11228
Tel 718-232-8162
Musical Director: Nina Di Gregorio

The Italian Opera Company, Inc.
(Broadway to Opera) helps promote
young and emerging artists' careers in
opera, Broadway, and classical music
by giving them the opportunity to work
with professional directors, musicians,
and vocal coaches. The Italian Opera

Company has performed in theaters,
universities, and other venues throughout New York City.
*Secondary Categories: Arts for
Children/Teens, Music, Theater*

**NARROWS COMMUNITY THEATER,
INC. (NCT)**
9728 3rd Avenue
Brooklyn, NY 11209
Tel 718-482-3173
Email nct@narrowscommunity
theater.com
Web www.narrowscommunity
theater.com
President: Susan Huizinga

The purpose and mission of Narrows
Community Theater, Inc. as stated
in its bylaws, is to further and promote the production of theatrical
plays, musicals, pageants, community
dramas, operas, and scenarios by non-
professional actors and actresses. NCT
has a 36-year history of producing two
shows a year.
Secondary Categories: Dance, Theater

NEW YORK BAROQUE
See Primary listing under Music

OPERA ON TAP (OOT)
1422 Beverley Road
Brooklyn, NY 11226
Tel 917-538-7413
Email operaontap@operaontap.com
Web www.operaontap.com
General Managing Diva: Anne Ricci

Opera on Tap is comprised of young
opera singers and classical instrumen-
talists hell-bent on proving that opera
and classical music can be fun. As a
nonprofit, OOT's mission is to bring
opera to new audiences, support young
singers in their career development
through scholarships and performance
opportunities, and promote works by
contemporary composers.

Secondary Categories:
Arts for Children/Teens, Music,
Presenting Organizations

REGINA OPERA COMPANY
1251 Tabor Court
Brooklyn, NY 11219

Site address:
Regina Hall
1230 65th Street
Brooklyn, NY 11219

Tel 718-232-3555
Fax 718-232-3555
Email reginaopera@yahoo.com
Web www.reginaopera.org

President: Marie L. Cantoni

Brooklyn's only year-round opera company, Regina Opera presents three fully-staged operas and several operatic and popular concerts in its theater, Regina Hall, each season, plus many free-admission "outreach" concerts at public venues. Popular operas are presented in their original language, and with a thirty-piece orchestra.

Secondary Category: Music

RYAN REPERTORY COMPANY
See Primary listing under Theater

THE SHADOW BOX THEATRE, INC.
See Primary listing under Arts for Children/Teens

TARGET MARGIN THEATER
See Primary listing under Theater

THEATER GARDEN, LTD.
304 Windsor Place
Brooklyn, NY 11218

Tel 212-501-6920
Fax 718-788-6217
Email dana@theatergarden.org
Web www.theatergarden.org

Executive Director: Dana L. Goldstein

A nonprofit company committed to the development of new works for new audiences, Theater Garden, Ltd.

produces entertaining, educational theater that brings history to life for students of all ages. All shows have a musical element and are designed to travel to schools, community centers, and theaters.

Secondary Categories: Arts for Children/Teens, Theater

TUCKABERRY PRODUCTIONS
See Primary listing under Theater

VERTICAL PLAYER REPERTORY
219 Court Street
Brooklyn, NY 11201

Tel 212-539-2696
Email VPROpera@aol.com
Web www.vpropera.org

Artistic Director: Judith Barnes

A vital alternative presence on the operatic scene, Vertical Player Repertory is dedicated to the fully-staged performance of operatic works in a chamber setting, embracing operatic repertoire from the 18th to the 21st centuries. VPR's unconventional venue, a factory-turned-sculpture studio-turned-theater, lends itself to imaginative staging and gives the audience an opportunity to experience opera in exciting proximity to the performers.

Secondary Categories: Music, Presenting Organizations, Theater

WORLD EATER RECORDINGS, NYC
See Primary listing under Music

It is through art that we will prevail and we will endure. It lives on after us and defines us as people.

RITA MORENO

PERFORMANCE ART

651 ARTS
See Primary listing under Presenting Organizations

AD HOC ART
See Primary listing under Galleries

ADRIENNECELESTEFADJO DANCE
See Primary listing under Dance

ARTICHOKE DANCE COMPANY
See Primary listing under Dance

ARTMOVINGPROJECTS
See Primary listing under Computer Arts/New Media

BINDLESTIFF FAMILY VARIETY ARTS, INC.
See Primary listing under Theater

BREEDINGGROUND PRODUCTIONS
See Primary listing under Multi-Disciplinary Arts

BRIC ARTS | MEDIA | BROOKLYN
See Primary listing under Multi-Disciplinary Arts

BRIC ROTUNDA GALLERY
See Primary listing under Visual Arts

THE BRICK THEATER, INC.
See Primary listing under Theater

BRICSTUDIO
See Primary listing under Presenting Organizations

BROOKLYN ARTS EXCHANGE
See Primary listing under Multi-Disciplinary Arts

BROOKLYN MUSEUM
See Primary listing under Museums

THE BUSHWICK STARR
See Primary listing under Theater

CAROLYN HULSE DANCE TROUPE
4604 7th Avenue, 2nd Floor
Brooklyn, NY 11220

Tel 347-385-5525
Email carolyn_hulse@hotmail.com
Web www.myspace.com/cahudance

Delivering fun-filled entertainment with a theatrical twist, the Carolyn Hulse Dance Troupe fuses various dance styles, including salsa, Broadway, jazz, modern, and hip hop.

Secondary category: Dance

CAVE
See Primary listing under Multi-Disciplinary Arts

CELEBRATE BROOKLYN PERFORMING ARTS FESTIVAL
See Primary listing under Presenting Organizations

CHEZ BUSHWICK
See Primary listing under Dance

CIRCUS AMOK
See Primary listing under Theater

CIRKULOCK, INC.
See Primary listing under Folk Arts

COLLECTIVE OPERA COMPANY
See Primary listing under Opera/Music Theater

COMMUNICABLE ARTS
See Primary listing under Theater

COMMUNITY THEATRE INTERNATIONALE
755 Washington Avenue, #409
Brooklyn, NY 11238

Tel 718-707-1109
Email info@communitytheatreintl.org
Web www.communitytheatreintl.org

Director: Kate Gardner

Dedicated to creating community through performance, across borders both local and global, Community Theatre Internationale develops multi-media collaborative productions between ensembles in different parts of the world. Mixing live performance with video and Internet technology, the group creates "stages" on which ordinary people from around the globe gather to make theater and art.

Secondary Categories: Computer Arts/New Media, Theater

CONEY ISLAND USA (SIDESHOWS BY THE SEASHORE)
1208 Surf Avenue
Brooklyn, NY 11224

Tel 718-372-5159
Fax 718-372-5101
Email info@coneyisland.com
Web www.coneyisland.com

Artistic Director: Dick Zigun

Coney Island USA seeks to preserve and promote lost forms of American popular culture, contributing to the renaissance of the historic Coney Island neighborhood. Coney Island USA both interprets these art forms for a modern urban audience and presents them in their historic home.

Secondary Category: Presenting Organizations

CONNECTION WORKS, INC.
See Primary listing under Arts for Children/Teens

CONNI CONVERGENCE ENTERPRISES, LLC (CONNI'S AVANT GARDE RESTAURANT)
Email conniconvergence@avant garderestaurant.com
Web www.avantgarderestaurant.com

Producing Director: Connie Hall

Conni's Avant Garde Restaurant is an adventurous theatrical ensemble that performs regularly at the Bushwick Starr and is available for site-specific or private events. At each Restaurant event, guests enter a lively social environment and enjoy five-course, home-cooked meals presented through exquisite performances.

CRUCIAL ARTS PRODUCTIONS, INC.
See Primary listing under Multi-Disciplinary Arts

DAM, STUHLTRAGER GALLERY
See Primary listing under Galleries

DARMSTADT
See Primary listing under Music

DUMBO ARTS CENTER
See Primary listing under Visual Arts

DZIECI
See Primary listing under Theater

THE ELEVENTEN GALLERY
See Primary listing under Galleries

ELSIE MANAGEMENT
See Primary listing under Arts Services

FIREFLY AERIAL ACROBATICS
5 Brewster Street, #142
Glen Cove, NY 11542

Tel 646-291-6364
Fax 212-659-0138
Email info@fireflyaerial.com
Web www.fireflyaerial.com

Artistic Director: Cypher Zero

FireFly Aerial Acrobatics launches precise, highly technical choreography and theater craft into the air, in original performances that fuse the passion and thrill of circus arts with the rhythm and artistry of dance. FireFly offers dynamic feature-length productions as well as special event performances.

Secondary Category: Theater

THE FLYING MACHINE THEATER, INC.
See Primary listing under Theater

FORTY GREENE AVENUE CULTURAL CENTER
See Primary listing under Arts Services

FREE103POINT9
See Primary listing under Multi-Disciplinary Arts

GALAPAGOS ART SPACE
See Primary listing under Multi-Disciplinary Arts

THE GOSSIP FACTORY
See Primary listing under Theater

THE GOWANUS STUDIO SPACE, INC.
See Primary listing under Multi-Disciplinary Arts

HAMPTONIANS NEW YORK
See Primary listing under Arts for Children/Teens

HOPES ALIVE, INC.
See Primary listing under Theater

IMAGINE PROJECT, INC.
See Primary listing under Arts for Children/Teens

IMPACT THEATER
See Primary listing under Theater

INI NYC
See Primary listing under Multi-Disciplinary Arts

ISSUE PROJECT ROOM
See Primary listing under Multi-Disciplinary Arts

LIKE THE SPICE
See Primary listing under Galleries

LMAKPROJECTS
See Primary listing under Galleries

LONG ISLAND UNIVERSITY, BROOKLYN CAMPUS
See Primary listing under Educational Institutions

MICHAEL ALAN'S DRAW-A-THON
See Primary listing under Arts Services

MONKEY TOWN
See Primary listing under Film/Video

MOVING THEATER
See Primary listing under Theater

NORA STEPHENS / NORANEWDANCE
See Primary listing under Dance

NOT AN ALTERNATIVE, INC.
See Primary listing under Presenting Organizations

OFFICEOPS
See Primary listing under Multi-Disciplinary Arts

THE OLD AMERICAN CAN FACTORY
See Primary listing under Presenting Organizations

THE OMNI ENSEMBLE LTD.
See Primary listing under Music

PIEROGI
See Primary listing under Galleries

PROTO-TYPE THEATER, INC.
See Primary listing under Theater

RADIOHOLE
294 Macon Street
Brooklyn, NY 11216

Site address:
146 Metropolitan Avenue
Brooklyn, NY 11211

Tel 718-388-2251
Email wyyy@radiohole.com
Web www.radiohole.com

Co-Artistic Director: Eric Dyer

A collaborative performance ensemble consisting of Erin Douglass, Eric Dyer, Maggie Hoffman, and Scott Halvorsen Gillette, Radiohole has been creating original theatrical assemblages since 1998. Dubbed a "leading innovator in New York's... avant-garde theater" by *Time Out New York*, Radiohole also offers workshops in collaborative performance.

Secondary Categories: Multi-Disciplinary Arts, Theater

SAFE-T-GALLERY
See Primary listing under Galleries

SLATE GALLERY
See Primary listing under Galleries

SPOKE THE HUB DANCING, INC.
See Primary listing under Multi-Disciplinary Arts

STREB LABORATORY FOR ACTION MECHANICS
See Primary listing under Multi-Disciplinary Arts

TARGET MARGIN THEATER
See Primary listing under Theater

THELMA HILL PERFORMING ARTS CENTER
See Primary listing under Dance

TRISKELION ARTS
See Primary listing under Dance

UGLY DUCKLING PRESSE
See Primary listing under Literary Arts

UNDER THE TABLE
See Primary listing under Theater

WILLIAMSBURG ART NEXUS, INC.
See Primary listing under Presenting Organizations

WISELEPHANT
See Primary listing under Arts Services

PRESENTING ORGANIZATIONS

13 PLAYWRIGHTS, INC. (13P)
Email 13playwrights@earthlink.net
Web www.13p.org

Producer: Maria Goyanes

Thirteen Playwrights, Inc.(13P) is a collective of playwrights producing full productions of new plays. The resources of the company are placed at the disposal of the playwright, who serves as the company's artistic director during the production of the play. The company produces 13 plays, one by each member of the group, making use of the texture and ambition of new American plays, produced and performed in-house.

Secondary Category: Theater

651 ARTS
651 Fulton Street
Brooklyn, NY 11217

Tel 718-636-4181
Fax 718-636-4166
Email info@651arts.org
Web www.651arts.org

Executive Director: Georgiana Pickett

651 ARTS develops, produces, and presents arts and cultural programming grounded in the African Diaspora, with a primary focus on contemporary performing arts. 651 ARTS serves the cultural life of Brooklyn and beyond—locally, regionally, nationally, and globally—by informing, nurturing, and connecting artists, audiences, organizations, and communities.

Secondary Categories: Arts Services, Dance, Multi-Disciplinary Arts, Music, Performance Art, Theater

AFRICUSSION-PERCUSSION DISCUSSION
See Primary listing under Music

AMERICAN MUSIC GROUP
See Primary listing under Music

ANNUAL GOWANUS ARTISTS STUDIO TOUR (AGAST)
172 Fifth Avenue, #54
Brooklyn, NY 11217

Tel 718-393-8383
Email info@agastbrooklyn.com
Web www.agastbrooklyn.com

The Annual Gowanus Artists Studio Tour (AGAST) is a self-guided walking tour of artists' studios surrounding the Gowanus Canal. The tour, held each year in October, is open to the public free of charge. Tour maps are available at all studio locations, and may also be downloaded from the AGAST website.

Secondary Category: Visual Arts

BAILEY'S CAFÉ
See Primary listing under Multi-Disciplinary Arts

BAM
See Primary listing under Multi-disciplinary Arts

BANG ON A CAN
See Primary listing under Music

BARGEMUSIC
See Primary listing under Music

BEDFORD STUYVESANT RESTORATION CORPORATION'S CENTER FOR ARTS AND CULTURE
See Primary listing under
Multi-Disciplinary Arts

BILLIE HOLIDAY THEATRE
See Primary listing under Theater

BINDLESTIFF FAMILY VARIETY ARTS, INC.
See Primary listing under Theater

BOOKLYN ARTISTS ALLIANCE
See Primary listing under Visual Arts

BRIC ARTS | MEDIA | BROOKLYN
See Primary listing under
Multi-Disciplinary Arts

THE BRICK THEATER, INC.
See Primary listing under Theater

BRICSTUDIO
647 Fulton Street
Brooklyn, NY 11217

Tel 718-855-7882, ext. 31
Fax 718-802-9095
Email BRICstudio@briconline.org
Web www.briconline.org

Manager: Stephanie Pacheco

This intimate, 4,000 square-foot black-box theater provides a platform for the development of new works in theater, dance, music, and multi-disciplinary performance, as well as subsidized rehearsal, rental, and performance space for non-venue-based artists and arts organizations. BRICstudio is also home to the BRIClab commissioning and residency program for performing artists.

Secondary Categories: Arts Services, Dance, Music, Performance Art, Theater

BRIGHTON NEIGHBORHOOD ASSOCIATION, INC.
See Primary listing under
Multi-Disciplinary Arts

BROOKLYN ARTS COUNCIL
See Primary listing under Arts Services

BROOKLYN ARTS EXCHANGE
See Primary listing under
Multi-Disciplinary Arts

BROOKLYN CENTER FOR THE PERFORMING ARTS AT BROOKLYN COLLEGE (BCBC)
P.O. Box 100163
Brooklyn, NY 11210

Site address:
2900 Campus Road
Brooklyn, NY 11210

Tel 718-951-4600
Web www.brooklyncenteronline.org

Managing Director: Frank Sonntag

Brooklyn Center for the Performing Arts at Brooklyn College (BCBC) has been presenting the finest music, theater, dance, opera, arts education programs, and family events for over 50 years. BCBC is widely known as the borough's largest presenter of arts education programs, serving over 70,000 patrons annually, including 42,000 schoolchildren.

Secondary Category:
Arts for Children/Teens, Dance, Multi-Disciplinary Arts, Music, Opera/Music Theater, Theater

BROOKLYN FRIENDS OF CHAMBER MUSIC
See Primary listing under Music

BROOKLYN JEWISH FILM FESTIVAL
c/o Paul Rothman
99 Berkeley Place
Brooklyn, NY 11217

Tel 718-230-0505
Email paularthur@aol.com
Web www.brjff.org

President: Paul A. Rothman

The Brooklyn Jewish Film Festival is an independent, nonprofit organization committed to showcasing powerful features, challenging documentaries, and exciting experimental and student films by filmmakers from Brooklyn and all over the world that promote public awareness of Jewish identity, history, and culture, as well as the diversity of Jewish life.

Secondary Category: Film/Video

THE BROOKLYN SOCIETY FOR ETHICAL CULTURE (BSEC)
53 Prospect Park West
Brooklyn, NY 11215

Tel 718-768-2972
Fax 718-768-3278
Email bsecoffice@aol.com
Web www.bsec.org

Board President: Eva Kapsis

The Brooklyn Society for Ethical Culture is a religious and educational movement inspired by the ideal that the supreme aim of human life is working to create a more human society. Housed in a landmark mansion on Prospect Park West, the Society regularly sponsors readings, live music, and other events open to the public.

Secondary Category: Historical Societies

BROOKLYN TECHNOLOGY EXCHANGE
See Primary listing under Educational Institutions

BROOKLYN WATERFRONT ARTISTS COALITION
See Primary listing under Visual Arts

BROOKLYN-QUEENS CONSERVATORY OF MUSIC
See Primary listing under Music

CARIBBEAN CULTURAL THEATRE
See Primary listing under Theater

CAVE
See Primary listing under Multi-Disciplinary Arts

CELEBRATE BROOKLYN PERFORMING ARTS FESTIVAL
647 Fulton Street, 2nd Floor
Brooklyn, NY 11217

Site address:
Prospect Park Bandshell
Brooklyn, NY 11215

Tel 718-855-7882
Fax 718-802-9095
Email sgiannelli@briconline.org
Web www.briconline.org/celebrate

Director and Producer: Jack Walsh

A program of BRIC Arts | Media | Brooklyn, Celebrate Brooklyn is New York's longest-running free summer outdoor performing arts festival, offering music, dance, film, and spoken word at the Prospect Park Bandshell. Celebrate Brooklyn presents an 8- to 10-week season of performers from around the world and around the block.

Secondary Categories: Dance, Film/Video, Music, Opera/Music Theater, Performance Art

CENTRAL BROOKLYN JAZZ CONSORTIUM
See Primary listing under Music

CHASSIDIC DISCOVERY WELCOME CENTER
See Primary listing under Multi-Disciplinary Arts

CONEY ISLAND USA
See Primary listing under Performance Art

CONFLUX FESTIVAL
See Primary listing under Multi-Disciplinary Arts

DARMSTADT
See Primary listing under Music

DRUMSONG AFRICAN BALLET THEATRE, INC.
See Primary listing under Multi-Disciplinary Arts

DUMBO ARTS CENTER
See Primary listing under Visual Arts

FAMILY TREE COLLECTIVE
17 South Oxford Street, #7
Brooklyn, NY 11217
Tel 646-784-4193
Email z.foley@familytreecollective.org
Web www.familytreecollective.org

Musical Director: Zack G. Foley

Family Tree is a diverse group of concerned artists whose mission is to produce original, culturally relevant work. In its first year, the group worked with 100 different artists, producing 13 projects which were performed over 29 evenings, including major fundraising events entitled "Outlet: For Artists, For Community."

Secondary Category: Multi-Disciplinary Arts

FIVEMYLES
See Primary listing under Galleries

FORTY GREENE AVENUE CULTURAL CENTER
See Primary listing under Arts Services

FREE103POINT9
See Primary listing under Multi-Disciplinary Arts

FULTON MALL IMPROVEMENT ASSOCIATION (FMIA)
15 MetroTech Center, 19th Floor
Brooklyn, NY 11201
Tel 718-403-1632
Fax 718-403-1650
Email info@fultonstreet.org
Web www.fultonstreet.org

Executive Director: Michael Weiss

Incorporated in 1976, the Fulton Mall Improvement Association (FMIA) is a nonprofit corporation dedicated to improving the economic health and quality-of-life issues in Fulton Mall and nearby downtown Brooklyn communities. The FMIA also hosts special events like the Fulton Street Beat, a free outdoor summer concert series.

Secondary Categories: Architecture & Urban/Environmental Design, Music

GALAPAGOS ART SPACE
Multi-Disciplinary Arts

GOING COASTAL, INC.
See Primary listing under Literary Arts

GOWANUS WILDCATS (VENTURER CREW 588)
198 Bond Street, #6A
Brooklyn, NY 11217
Tel 718-596-9619
Email mamadj7@juno.com
Web www.gowanuswildcats.com

Director: Renee Flowers

The Gowanus Wildcats Drill Team is a nonprofit all-female drill team that originated in 1970 in the Gowanus Houses Community Center. Their instructor, who volunteers her services, is an original member who took over leadership of the drill team in 1972. The present 24 members range from 6 to 21 years of age, and the Wildcats still hold their drill team practices in the community center.

Secondary Category: Music

HAMPTONIANS NEW YORK
See Primary listing under Arts for Children/Teens

IFETAYO CULTURAL ARTS
See Primary listing under Multi-Disciplinary Arts

INTERNATIONAL AFRICAN ARTS FESTIVAL
See Primary listing under Arts Services

IRONDALE ENSEMBLE PROJECT
See Primary listing under Theater

KINGS BAY YM-YWHA
3495 Nostrand Avenue
Brooklyn, NY 11229
Tel 718-648-7703
Email info@kingsbayy.org

Web www.kingsbayy.org

Executive Director: Leonard Petlakh

A Jewish community center serving Sheepshead Bay, Marine Park, Bergen-Beach, Homecrest, and Midwood, the Kings Bay Y offers a variety of educational programs and opportunities in the fine and folk arts (including dance, music, and drama). Many concerts and other events are specifically designed for children, teens, and immigrants.

Secondary Categories: Arts for Children/Teens, Arts Services, Computer Arts/New Media, Dance, Multi-Disciplinary Arts

KLEINBLUE PRODUCTIONS
See Primary listing under Visual Arts

MARTIN LUTHER KING JR. CONCERT SERIES
See Primary listing under Music

MATA FESTIVAL
See Primary listing under Music

METROTECH BUSINESS IMPROVEMENT DISTRICT (METROTECH BID)
15 MetroTech Center
Brooklyn, NY 11201

Tel 718-403-1632
Email info@metrotechbid.org
Web www.metrotechbid.org

Executive Director: Michael Weiss

The MetroTech Business Improvement District (BID) is a nonprofit community development organization founded in 1992 to further downtown Brooklyn's revitalization. The BID provides for public safety, sanitation, economic development, and promotional services throughout a 25-block district, and also hosts the "Arts on the Commons" concert series each spring and fall.

Secondary Categories: Architecture & Urban/Environmental Design, Music

NAT CREOLE ONLINE
See Primary listing under Computer Arts/New Media

**NOT AN ALTERNATIVE, INC.
(THE CHANGE YOU WANT TO SEE GALLERY AND CONVERGENCE STAGE)**
84 Havemeyer Street
Brooklyn, NY 11211

Email winnie@notanalternative.net
Web www.notanalternative.net

Chair: Mary Angela Economopoulos

Not An Alternative, Inc. is a nonprofit arts organization and cultural production company whose mission is to facilitate and engage in the work of creating social change. Not An Alternative operates a multi-purpose space called The Change You Want to See Gallery and Convergence Stage, where it holds workshops, presentations, lectures, panels, and screenings.

Secondary Categories: Multi-Disciplinary Arts, Performance Art

NOT FOR PROFIT PICTURES
57 Thames Street, #2C
Brooklyn, NY 11237

Tel 718-418-2509

Managing Partner: Hannah Spongberg

Not for Profit Pictures' mission is to produce media content of a high caliber and to make art and cultural events more accessible to the community at large. The company services both commercial and nonprofit organizations, as well as independent artists and producers, by providing material resources and through space donation.

Secondary Category: Arts Services

**THE OLD AMERICAN CAN FACTORY
(XØ PROJECTS, INC.)**
232 Third Street, #E3C
Brooklyn, NY 11215

Tel 718-237-4335
Fax 718-237-4534
Email mail@xoprojects.com
Web www.xoprojects.com

Director: Nathan F. Elbogen

The Old American Can Factory, a historic six-building industrial complex in Gowanus, is a curated haven to more than 200 people working in a wide range of disciplines in the arts, culture, and the creative industries.

Secondary Categories: Architecture & Urban/Environmental Design, Dance, Film/Video, Literary Arts, Multi-Disciplinary Arts, Music, Performance Art, Theater, Visual Arts

OLD STONE HOUSE OF BROOKLYN
See Primary listing under Museums

ONE WORLD SYMPHONY
See Primary listing under Music

OPERA ON TAP
See Primary listing under Opera/Music Theater

PAUL ROBESON THEATRE
See Primary listng under Theater

PERFORMING ARTS & SPECIAL EVENTS, KINGSBOROUGH COMMUNITY COLLEGE (LIVELY ARTS & IDEAS AT KINGSBOROUGH)
Performing Arts & Special Events (PA)
Kingsborough Community College
2001 Oriental Boulevard
Brooklyn, NY 11235

Tel 718-368-6680
(Performing Arts Hotline)
Fax 718-368-5785
Email svanburen@kingsborough.edu
Web www.kingsborough.edu

Executive Director: Mona Z. Smith

Kingsborough Community College is proud to serve as southern Brooklyn's premier cultural center, presenting free and affordable performing arts programs for all ages. KCC's year-round performing arts season has expanded to include quality music, dance, and theater performances for adults, a children's theater festival, free summer concerts, free weekday lunchtime concerts, and more.

Secondary Category: Educational Institutions

PORTSIDE NEW YORK
See Primary listing under Museums

PROSPECT PARK & PROSPECT PARK ALLIANCE
See Primary listing under Multi-Disciplinary Arts

PUPPETWORKS
See Primary listing under Theater

REALFORM
See Primary listing under Visual Arts

REVELATION PERFORMING ARTS STUDIO, INC.
See Primary listing under Visual/Performing Arts School

SOL WORKS, INC.
See Primary listing under Arts for Children/Teens

SPIRAL THOUGHT
See Primary listing under Literary Arts

SPOKE THE HUB DANCING, INC.
See Primary listing under Multi-Disciplinary Arts

ST. ANN'S WAREHOUSE (SAW)
45 Main Street, Suite 315
Brooklyn, NY 11201

Site address:
38 Water Street
Brooklyn, NY 11201

Tel 718-834-8794
Fax 718-522-2470
Email info@artsatstanns.org
Web www.stannswarehouse.org

Artistic Director: Susan Feldman

St. Ann's Warehouse (SAW) has been recognized by artists, critics, and audiences as a leading innovator for consistently inventive concert and new music theater presentations. SAW's performance history encompasses two unifying factors: music in a multiplicity of forms and the desire to cross-over among these forms and other disciplines (theater, puppetry, film, and spoken word).

Secondary Categories:
Multi-Disciplinary Arts, Music, Theater

ST. FRANCIS COLLEGE
See Primary listing under Educational Institutions

ST. JOSEPH'S COLLEGE, NY
See Primary listing under Educational Institutions

STREB LABORATORY FOR ACTION MECHANICS
See Primary listing under Multi-Disciplinary Arts

SUNNY'S
See Primary listing under Music

THELMA HILL PERFORMING ARTS CENTER
See Primary listing under Dance

TRISKELION ARTS
See Primary listing under Dance

THE URBAN DIVERS
See Primary listing under Galleries

VERTICAL PLAYER REPERTORY
See Primary listing under Opera/Music Theater

VICTORIAN PLACE CULTURAL CENTER
See Primary listing under Multi-Disciplinary Arts

THE WATERFRONT MUSEUM
See Primary listing under Museums

WEST INDIAN AMERICAN DAY CARNIVAL ASSOCIATION, INC. (WIADCA, INC.)
323-325 Rogers Avenue
Brooklyn, NY 11225

Tel 718-467-1797
Fax 718-778-1808
Email wiadcainc@gmail.com
Web www.wiadca.org

President: Yolanda Lezama-Clark

A nonprofit organization established to develop, promote, and promulgate Caribbean folklore, arts, and culture, WIADCA conducts all aspects of the annual West Indian American Day Carnival Festival and Parade, which represents the rich culture and heritage of the people of the Caribbean islands, and is the largest event of its kind in the United States.

Secondary Categories: Arts for Children/Teens, Arts Services, Folk Arts

WHITE WAVE YOUNG SOON KIM DANCE COMPANY
See Primary listing under Dance

WILLIAMSBURG ART & HISTORICAL CENTER
See Primary listing under Multi-Disciplinary Arts

PRESENTING ORGANIZATIONS

WILLIAMSBURG ART NEXUS, INC. (WAX)

67 Metropolitan Avenue, 4th Floor
Brooklyn, NY 11211

Email info@wax205.com
Web www.wax205.com

Executive Director: Marisa R. Konig Beatty

A multi-disciplinary presenting organization dedicated to emerging artists, WAX believes that the next generation of artists has a valid and imaginative body of work that deserves to be heard and seen in a professional setting. To that end, WAX provides a supportive environment that encourages the creation of new work in all media.

Secondary Categories: Dance, Multi-Disciplinary Arts, Performance Art

WORLD EATER RECORDINGS, NYC
See Primary listing under Music

THEATER

13 PLAYWRIGHTS, INC.
See Primary listing under Presenting Organizations

2 PUNKS PUPPET THEATRE
See Primary listing under Arts for Children/Teens

651 ARTS
See Primary listing under Presenting Organizations

ACTNOW FOUNDATION
See Primary listing under Film/Video

ADHESIVE THEATER PROJECT
448 Court Street, #1R
Brooklyn, NY 11231

Tel 718-596-2565
Email kalle@adhesivetheater.com
Web www.adhesivetheater.com

Executive Director: Kalle Macrides

The Adhesive Theater Project is dedicated to collaborating with artists of all disciplines, particularly those with a non-theatrical background. By challenging these artists to work in theater, Adhesive Theater creates new perspectives for live performance. Adhesive integrates live music, visual arts, metaphor, and narrative storytelling to create epic experiences that excite audiences' imaginations.

ALLIANCE OF RESIDENT THEATRES/NEW YORK
See Primary listing under Arts Services

AMERICAN OPERA PROJECTS
See Primary listing under Music

AMERICAN THEATRE OF HARLEM (ATH)
138 South Oxford Street
Brooklyn, NY 11217

Tel 718-857-2783
Email info@americantheatreof harlem.org
Web www.americantheatreofharlem.org

Artistic Director: Keith Johnston

Committed to quality theater at an affordable price, American Theatre of Harlem (ATH) offers one-act play and film festivals, acting workshops, and arts in education programming. In its acting workshops, ATH provides a healthy environment for developing and maintaining craft through a holistic approach that helps actors discover individual methods of expression, style, and identity.

Secondary Category: Dance

THEATER

ANDHOWTHEATER COMPANY I, INC. (ANDHOW! THEATER COMPANY)
138 South Oxford Street
Brooklyn, NY 11217

Tel 718-398-3690
Fax 718-398-3690
Email andhow@andhowtheater.com
Web www.andhowtheater.com

Artistic Director: Jessica Davis-Irons

Since its founding in 2000, Andhow! Theater Company has presented an annual reading series, full main stage productions, free outdoor plays for children, workshops, experiments, cabarets, and benefits. Andhow! creates completely fictitious worlds straight from the imagination in which unrealistic events are made tangible through strong design and outstanding actors.

Secondary Category: Arts for Children/Teens

ATTITUDE: THE DANCERS' MAGAZINE
See Primary listing under Dance

BAC ARTS IN EDUCATION
See Primary listing Arts for Children/Teens

BAM
See Primary listing under Multi-Disciplinary Arts

BAMSS THEATRE WORKS
See Primary listing under Arts for Children/Teens

BANANA BAG AND BODICE
142 Stockholm Street, Suite 404
Brooklyn, NY 11221

Web www.bananabagandbodice.org

Starting from original text and music in each production, the Banana Bag and Bodice collective challenges notions of genre and tries to redefine its idea of what a theatrical experience is with each show.

BEDFORD STUYVESANT RESTORATION CORPORATION, CENTER FOR ARTS AND CULTURE
See Primary listing under Multi-Disciplinary Arts

BIG DANCE THEATER
Email bigdancetheater@earthlink.net
Web www.bigdancetheater.org

Artistic Director: Annie-B. Parson

An OBIE and Bessie award-winning dance/theater company founded in 1990, big dance theater creates work (often based on literature) with an emphasis on choreography. The company tours nationally and internationally.

Secondary Category: Dance

BILLIE HOLIDAY THEATRE
P.O. Box 470131
Brooklyn, NY 11247

Site address:
1368 Fulton Street
Brooklyn, NY 11216

Tel 718-636-0919
Email billieholidaytheatre@yahoo.com
Web www.thebillieholiday.org

Producer and Executive Director: Marjorie A. Moon

The basic purpose of the Billie Holiday Theatre's major productions is two-fold: 1) to present professional theater of interest and concern to the African/Caribbean American community in a manner which enlightens and entertains, and 2) to sustain a working environment in which talented, trained artists can fully exploit their craft.

Secondary Category: Presenting Organizations

BINDLESTIFF FAMILY VARIETY ARTS, INC. (BINDLESTIFF FAMILY CIRKUS)
P.O. Box 1917
New York, NY 10009

Tel 718-963-2918
Email cirkus@bindlestiff.org
Web www.bindlestiff.org

President: Keith S. Nelson

Part of New York's cultural landscape since 1995, Bindlestiff is dedicated to preserving and enriching the variety arts which include circus, sideshow, vaudeville, burlesque, and Wild West shows. In addition to performances and workshops, Bindlestiff offers resources to variety artists, and its programs are available through schools, theaters, and other cultural institutions.

Secondary Categories:
Arts for Children/Teens, Film/Video, Folk Arts, Music, Performance Art, Presenting Organizations

BLACK MOON THEATRE COMPANY, INC.
See Primary listing under
Multi-Disciplinary Arts

BRAVE NEW WORLD REPERTORY THEATRE
303 Westminster Road
Brooklyn, NY 11218

Email theatre@bravenewworldrep.org
Web www.bravenewworldrep.org

Producing Artistic Director:
Claire Beckman

Brave New World Repertory Theatre is a company of Brooklyn-based theater artists dedicated to bringing affordable, professional theater into the borough. With a focus on classic and neglected plays, as well as original plays by company members, the company strives to nurture Brooklyn's artists and enrich Brooklyn's audiences.

BRIC ARTS | MEDIA | BROOKLYN
See Primary listing under
Multi-Disciplinary Arts

THE BRICK THEATER, INC. (THE BRICK)
170 Norfolk Street, #15
New York, NY 10002

Site address:
575 Metropolitan Avenue
Brooklyn, NY 11211

Tel 718-907-6189
Email info@bricktheater.com
Web www.bricktheater.com

President and Co-Artistic Director:
Robert Honeywell

A nonprofit theater company dedicated to nurturing the work of emerging artists at its performance space in Williamsburg, the Brick Theater, Inc. presents world premieres, a monthly performance series, and seasonal festivals. The Brick continues to seek new artists, and to serve as one of Williamsburg's primary incubators of theater arts.

Secondary Categories: Arts for Children/Teens, Dance, Film/Video, Multi-Disciplinary Arts, Music, Opera/Music Theater, Performance Art, Presenting Organizations

BRICSTUDIO
See Primary listing under Presenting Organizations

BROOKLYN CENTER FOR THE PERFORMING ARTS AT BROOKLYN COLLEGE (BCBC)
See Primary listing under Presenting Organizations

BROOKLYN CHILDREN'S THEATRE
See Primary listing under Arts for Children/Teens

THEATER

BROOKLYN COLLEGE DEPARTMENT OF THEATER

2900 Bedford Avenue
Room 317, Whitehead Hall
Brooklyn, NY 11210

Tel 718-951-5666
Fax 718-951-4606
Web www.depthome.brooklyn.cuny.edu/theater

Chair: Rose Bonczek

Brooklyn College's Department of Theater presents eight to ten full productions annually, in the 500-seat Gershwin Theater and the more intimate New Workshop Theater. Directed and designed by faculty, guest artists, and students, shows feature both BFA and MFA acting majors and occasional guest professionals.

Secondary Category: Educational Institutions

BROOKLYN COLLEGE PREPARATORY CENTER FOR THE PERFORMING ARTS
See Primary listing under Music

THE BROOKLYN RAIL
See Primary listing under Multi-Disciplinary Arts

THE BROOKLYN THEATRE ARTS PROJECT, INC. (BTAP)

2231 East 7th Street, #3A
Brooklyn, NY 11223

Site address:
7301 Ridge Boulevard
Brooklyn, NY 11209

Tel 718-390-7189
Email email@btap.org
Web www.btap.org

Founding Member: Anthony Augello

The Brooklyn Theatre Arts Project, Inc. provides a forum for the development of new works while also presenting the classics to the surrounding community. For the larger community, the Project provides the opportunity to attend and participate in the theatrical arts, aiming not only to entertain but also to enlighten and challenge.

Secondary Category: Opera/Music Theater

BROOKLYN WRITERS SPACE
See Primary listing under Literary Arts

THE BUSHWICK STARR

207 Starr Street, #4
Brooklyn, NY 11237

Email info@thebushwickstarr.org
Web www.thebushwickstarr.org

Managing Director and Curator: Sue Kessler

The Bushwick Starr is a full-scale performance venue dedicated to bringing a continuum of art and artists to the Bushwick community. Focusing on the presentation of theater, dance, and music, the Bushwick Starr welcomes and encourages the exhibition of a broad spectrum of art forms and disciplines.

Secondary Categories: Dance, Film/Video, Multi-Disciplinary Arts, Music, Performance Art

CARIBBEAN CULTURAL THEATRE

138 South Oxford Street, Suite 4Λ
Brooklyn, NY 11217

Tel 718-783-8345
Email caribbeantheatre@yahoo.com
Web www.caribbeantheatre.org

Artistic Director: E. Wayne McDonald

The Caribbean Cultural Theatre presents a balanced rendering of Caribbean culture and the Caribbean American experience in work of a high artistic caliber. The Theatre uses the performing arts to preserve artistic legacies, nurture professional growth, inspire audiences, and empower communities while remaining sensitive to the varied influences that shape Caribbean culture.

Secondary Categories: Arts for Children/Teens, Film/Video, Folk Arts, Literary Arts, Presenting Organizations

CAVE
See Primary listing under Multi-Disciplinary Arts

CIRCUS AMOK
55 South 11th Street, 5th Floor
Brooklyn, NY 11211
Email jennifer@circusamok.org
Web www.circusamok.org

Director: Jennifer Miller

Circus Amok is a New York-based, one-ring, no-animal alternative circus-theater company that provides free, glamorous, raucous, live public art addressing contemporary issues of social justice to diverse neighborhoods and under-served populations throughout the boroughs of New York City.

Secondary Categories: Arts for Children/Teens, Folk Arts, Multi-Disciplinary Arts, Music, Performance Art

COLLAPSABLE GIRAFFE, INC.
P.O. Box 1626
New York, NY 10013

Site address:
146 Metropolitan Avenue
Brooklyn, NY 11211

Tel 718-388-2251
Email info@collapsablegiraffe.org
Web www.collapsablegiraffe.org

Artistic Director: Amy Huggans

An experimental theater collective based in Williamsburg, Collapsable Giraffe, Inc. performs regularly at the Collapsable Hole, its space on Metropolitan Avenue. They have also performed at 3LD, the Performing Garage, the Ontological, and Show World Center.

COMMUNICABLE ARTS
Email communicablearts@gmail.com
Web www.communicablearts.org

Co-Founder: Barrie Gelles

The nonprofit group Communicable Arts is a multi-discipline collaborative whose mission is to create and promote innovative theater work that is current, kinetic, and connective. The group's projects re-contextualize existing pieces and foster original works. Past productions have included Pieces and Parts, the company's original maiden piece, and Shakespeare's "A Midsummer Night's Dream" and "The Comedy of Errors."

Secondary Category: Performance Art

COMMUNITY THEATRE INTERNATIONALE
See Primary listing under Performance Art

CREATE!
See Primary listing under Arts for Children/Teens

CREATIVE WOMEN'S NETWORK
See Primary listing under Arts Services

CRUCIAL ARTS PRODUCTIONS, INC.
See Primary listing under Multi-Disciplinary Arts

DANCE THEATRE ETCETERA
See Primary listing under Multi-Disciplinary Arts

DANCES AND DRUMS OF AFRICA, INC.
See Primary listing under Dance

DE NONNO PRODUCTIONS, INCORPORATED
See Primary listing under Film/Video

THEATER

DRAMA OF WORKS
94 Wyckoff Street, #3R
Brooklyn, NY 11201
Site address:
320 Dean Street
Brooklyn, NY 11217
Tel 917-531-0057
Email gretchen@dramaofworks.com
Web www.dramaofworks.com
Artistic Director: Gretchen E.
Van Lente

Led by Artistic Director Gretchen Van
Lente, Drama of Works is known for
innovative works that are "high on fan-
tastic production values" *(Village Voice)*
and which blur the lines between
actors and puppeteers.

DUŠAN TÝNEK DANCE THEATRE
See Primary listing under Dance

DZIECI (THEATRE GROUP DZIECI)
241 Garfield Place, 1st Floor
Brooklyn, NY 11215
Tel 718-638-6037
Email dzieci@dziecitheatre.org
Web www.dziecitheatre.org
Director: Matt Mitler

Committed to art as a path for transformation, Theatre Group Dzieci blends
work on performance with the work of
service. Dzieci presents performances
and creative interactions in schools,
hospitals, theaters, and sacred spaces.

*Secondary Categories: Art for
Children/Teens, Arts Services,
Opera/Music, Performance Art*

EGRESS THEATRE COMPANY
1803 Beverley Road, Suite 5B
Brooklyn, NY 11226
Email abielski@egresstheatre.org
Web www.egresstheatre.org
Artistic Director: Andrew Bielski

The mission of the Egress Theatre
Company is to restore an urgent vitality

to the theater by returning the performance of the creative ensemble to its
position at the heart of the theatrical
experience.

*Secondary Categories:
Arts for Children/Teens, Literary Arts,
Multi-Disciplinary Arts, Music,
Opera/Music Theater*

ELECTRIK GODDESS CLUB ORQUESTRA
See Primary listing under Music

FALCONWORKS ARTISTS GROUP
P.O. Box 310283
Brooklyn, NY 11231
Tel 718-395-3218
Email info@falconworks.com
Web www.falconworks.com
General Manager: Christopher
Hammett

Falconworks Artists Group supports
and empowers communities and individuals through theater that addresses
personal and local issues. The group
also leads workshops in playwriting
and performance that offer individuals
the skills and resources to tell their
own stories.

*Secondary Category: Arts for
Children/Teens*

FIREFLY AERIAL ACROBATICS
See Primary listing under Performance Art

THE FLYING MACHINE THEATER, INC.
293 North 7th Street, #2L
Brooklyn, NY 11211
Tel 718-937-6804
Web www.theflyingmachine.org
Executive Director: Joshua Carlebach

The Flying Machine Theater, Inc. is a
highly acclaimed, international collaboration formed in Paris in 1996 by
a group of performers and educators
from various theatrical backgrounds,
under the auspices of legendary
teacher Jacques Lecoq. Using a
global array of theatrical styles, the

Theater creates works from original and adapted narratives while expanding theatrical possibilities to tell the most vibrant stories possible.

Secondary Categories: Arts for Children/Teens, Performance Art

FORTY GREENE AVENUE CULTURAL CENTER
See Primary listing under Arts Services

FREEDOM TRAIN PRODUCTIONS
Email andre@freedomtrain productions.org
Web www.freedomtrainproductions.org

Freedom Train promotes new work written by up-and-coming Black playwrights. All plays feature Black LGBT hero and shero characters. Freedom Train playwrights have had their work staged at Fresh Fruit Festival, Blue Heron Theatre, HERE Arts Center, Nuyorican Poets Cafe, WOW CaféTheatre, and other New York City theaters.

THE GALLERY PLAYERS
199 14th Street
Brooklyn, NY 11215

Tel 718-595-0547
Email info@galleryplayers.com
Web www.galleryplayers.com

Executive Director: Matt Schicker

Brooklyn's premier Off-Off Broadway theater since 1967, the Gallery Players brings plays and musicals to Brooklyn audiences, as well as a new play festival and a musical theater adventure camp for kids.

Secondary Category: Opera/Music Theater

THE GLASS CONTRAPTION
360 Clinton Avenue, Suite 6D
Brooklyn, NY 11238

Tel 718-399-0163
Email justine@glasscontraption.org
Web www.glasscontraption.org

Founder and Co-Artistic Director: Justine Williams

The Glass Contraption is a theater company and arts outreach organization that produces lovingly handcrafted clown theater. The company promotes clown theater and its related forms (commedia, physical comedy, games, bouffon) to support and revitalize communities.

Secondary Category: Arts for Children/Teens

THE GOSSIP FACTORY
221 South 3rd Street
Brooklyn, NY 11211

Email thegossipfactory@gmail.com
Web www.thegossipfactory.org

President: Ryan H. McWilliams

The Gossip Factory, a theater collective, was created to explore new ideas in contemporary performance. Influenced by historical conventions, pop culture, and social themes, the Gossip Factory sets out to both enlighten and entertain.

Secondary Categories: Dance, Film/Video, Performance Art, Visual Arts

THEATER

HIP-HOP THEATER FESTIVAL
57 Thames Street, #4B
Brooklyn, NY 11237

Tel 718-497-4282
Fax 718-497-4240
Email info@hiphoptheaterfest.org
Web www.hiphoptheaterfest.org

Executive Director: Clyde Valentin

The Hip-Hop Theater Festival invigorates the fields of theater and hip hop by nurturing innovative work within the hip hop aesthetic, presenting American and international artists whose work addresses the issues relevant to the hip hop generation, and serving young, urban communities through outreach and education that celebrates contemporary language and culture.

Secondary Category: Multi-Disciplinary Arts

HOPES ALIVE, INC.
379 Jefferson Avenue, 2nd Floor
Brooklyn, NY 11221

Tel 718-757-6526
Email hopesaliveinc2@aol.com

Executive Director: Nicole Michele Guide

The mission of Hopes Alive, Inc. is to create theatrical performances that enlighten the hearts of the community. The group presents painful experiences with theater pieces, in hopes that the audience will learn from these productions, and take a journey with the performers, as positive change begins to take shape in working through these human experiences.

Secondary Category: Performance Art

I.D.E.A.S. (INTERACTIVE DRAMA FOR EDUCATION AND AWARENESS IN THE SCHOOLS, INC.)
98 4th Street
Brooklyn, NY 11231

Tel 718-387-5055
Fax 718-222-0945
Email info@ideasdrama.org
Web www.ideasdrama.org

Director: Lisa B. Dennett

I.D.E.A.S. was established in order to bring drama as a teaching and learning tool to disadvantaged youth and youth with disabilities, ages 8 through 21. Participants have the opportunity to experience a variety of situations creatively, through improvisation, and respond to themes through characters they create, with props and costumes at hand.

Secondary Category: Arts for Children/Teens

IMAGINE PROJECT, INC.
See Primary listing under Arts for Children/Teens

IMMIGRANTS' THEATRE PROJECT (ITP)
44 Douglass Street
Brooklyn, NY 11231

Tel 718-237-4545 or 347-512-5572
Fax 718-237-4545
Email immigrantstheat@aol.com
Web www.immigrantstheat.org

Artistic Director: Marcy Arlin

Founded in 1988 by Artistic Director Marcy Arlin, Immigrants' Theatre Project is a multicultural professional theater company that gives a theatrical voice to those who are marginalized, promotes "immigrant theater" as an artistic model for intercultural relations, and introduces immigrant and native-born audiences to challenging theater works. Programs include productions, readings, workshops, and international artists' exchanges.

IMPACT THEATER

54 South Elliot Place, #18
Brooklyn, NY 11217

Site address:
190 Underhill Avenue
Brooklyn, NY 11238

Email impacttheaternyc@yahoo.com
Web www.geocities.com/impact
theaternyc

Theater Owner: Tim Lewis

Impact Theater, Prospect Heights' neighborhood theater, supports theater and performance artists new to New York by offering directing, acting, and producing opportunities as well as inexpensive rehearsal space. The theater exists as a space where young and emerging artists are able to grow artistically and gain experience that will help further their careers.

Secondary Category: Performance Art

IRONDALE ENSEMBLE PROJECT (IRONDALE CENTER FOR THEATER, EDUCATION, AND OUTREACH)

85 South Oxford Street
Brooklyn, NY11217

Tel 718-488-9233
Email terry@irondale.org
Web www.irondale.org

Executive Director: Terry L. Greiss

A theater company that creates and presents original work, the Irondale Ensemble Project engages the wider community through partnerships with schools, prisons, and shelters, and at its home, the Irondale Center. Irondale's plays and education programs are socially relevant, challenge the status quo, and inspire fresh perspectives in its audiences.

Secondary Categories: Arts for Children/Teens, Presenting Organizations

THE ITALIAN OPERA COMPANY, INC.
See Primary listing under Opera/Music Theater

KUMBLE THEATER FOR THE PERFORMING ARTS, LONG ISLAND UNIVERSITY BROOKLYN CAMPUS

One University Plaza
Brooklyn, NY 11201

Tel 718-488-1624
Fax 718-780-4066
Email kumble@brooklyn.liu.edu
Web www.kumbletheater.org

Managing Director: Rodney K. Hurley

The Kumble Theater for the Performing Arts at Long Island University's Brooklyn Campus is a state-of-the art performance venue. Impeccably crafted for the dramatic and technical demands of dance, music, and theatrical productions, this elegant 320-seat theater provides finely-tuned acoustics and top-tier lighting, projection, and other electronic capabilities.

Secondary Category: Educational Institutions

LONG ISLAND UNIVERSITY, BROOKLYN CAMPUS
See Primary listing under Educational Institutions

MICHAEL ALAN'S DRAW-A-THON
See Primary listing under Arts Services

MONKEY TOWN
See Primary listing under Film/Video

THEATER

MONTAUK THEATRE PRODUCTIONS (MTP)
35 Pierrepont Street, #7C
Brooklyn, NY 11201
Site address:
40 Peck Slip
New York, NY 10038
Tel 718-852-7773
Email wkbadv1@aol.com
Web www.shootingstartheatre.org
Executive Director: William K. Brown, Jr.

Montauk Theatre Productions is a performing arts organization offering year-round programs, with an emphasis on the development of new performing, writing, and technical talent.

MOVING THEATER
304 Boerum Street, #23
Brooklyn, NY 11206
Tel 917-553-6484
Fax 718-418-4405
Email brennan@movingtheater.org
Web www.movingtheater.org
Co-Director: Brennan Gerard

Moving Theater, the company-in-residency at Chez Bushwick, is an ensemble of artists who have been collaborating since 2002 to produce new work at the crossroads of dance, theater, music, and the visual arts. Moving Theater facilitates international exchange to create new and potentially transformative opportunities for artists and audiences.

Secondary Categories: Dance, Music, Performance Art, Visual Arts

MY VOICE THEATRE
See Primary listing under
Arts for Children/Teens

NARROWS COMMUNITY THEATER, INC.
See Primary listing under
Opera/Music Theater

NEW YORK DEAF THEATRE, LTD. (NYDT)
138 South Oxford Street
Brooklyn, NY 11217
Tel 718-398-5227
Fax 718-398-2794
Email nydt@juno.com
Web www.nydeaftheatre.org
President: Dorothy L. Cohler

A nonprofit, professional theater organization, New York Deaf Theatre, Ltd. was established in 1979 by a group of deaf actors and theater artists who wanted to create opportunities for the production of a dramatic art form that was not found elsewhere in New York City: plays in American Sign Language (ASL).

NIA THEATRICAL PRODUCTION
COMPANY, INC.
138 South Oxford Street
Brooklyn, NY 11217
Tel 718-346-6591
Artistic Director and President:
Les E. Ford

nia theatrical production company, inc. entertains and educates. It provides production pathways for emerging playwrights and performing arts programs to school systems. The company produces at least two main stage productions annually, and works with public and private schools year-round to improve the arts acumen of their students, teachers, and parents.

Secondary Category: Arts Services

OFFICEOPS
See Primary listing under
Multi-Disciplinary Arts

THE OLD AMERICAN CAN FACTORY
See Primary listing under Presenting
Organizations

OLD STONE HOUSE OF BROOKLYN
See Primary listing under Museums

PAGE 73 PRODUCTIONS

138 South Oxford Street
Brooklyn, NY 11217

Tel 718-398-2099
Fax 718-398-2794
Web www.p73.org

Executive Director: Liz Jones

Page 73 Productions seeks out, develops, and produces the work of emerging playwrights who have shown substantial merit and professional commitment but who haven't yet achieved widespread recognition. Programs include the P73 Playwriting Fellowship, summer residencies and development programs, a writing group, and an annual full-scale Actors' Equity production.

Secondary Category: Arts Services

PAUL ROBESON THEATER

54 Greene Avenue
Brooklyn, NY 11238

Tel 718-783-9794

Director: Ramik J. Williams

The Paul Robeson Theater is an arts organization which serves as a forum for arts and community to create, develop, and preserve artistic and cultural expressions which reflect the experiences of people of African descent.

Secondary Categories: Arts for Children/Teens, Arts Services, Dance, Presenting Organizations

PDM PERFORMING ARTS CORPORATION
See Primary listing under Multi-Disciplinary Arts

PETER KYLE DANCE
See Primary listing under Dance

PLG ARTS
See Primary listing under Multi-Disciplinary Arts

POTPOURRI OF COLOR PERFORMING ARTS COMPANY

1570 East 102nd Street
Brooklyn, NY 11236

Tel 718-444-0290
Email pocpacs@yahoo.com
Web www.potpourriofcolor.4t.com

Founder and Director: Leslie Green

Potpourri of Color Performing Arts Company was expressly created to deliver messages through dramatic performance. A collaborative effort, Potpourri of Color provides an opportunity for people of various age groups to utilize their God-given talents and express themselves artistically.

Secondary Categories: Dance, Music

PROTO-TYPE THEATER, INC.

Tel 212-252-5526
Email info@proto-type.org
Web www.proto-type.org

Artistic Director: Peter S. Petralia

Proto-type Theater, Inc. creates new works of live performance that give equal weight to form and content. Physical theater, text, circus, original music, and evocative lighting merge into an unpredictably dynamic form through which Proto-type dissects modernity. Proto-type's audience expects to have a strong reaction—to love it, to hate it, to be inspired into conversation or silence.

Secondary Category: Performance Art

THEATER

THE PUPPETEERS COOPERATIVE
3396 12th Avenue
Brooklyn, NY 11218
Tel 718-853-7350
Email puppetco@gis.net
Web www.gis.net/~puppetco

Producer: Theresa Linnihan

The Puppeteers Cooperative is a group of puppeteers and musicians whose mission is to provide the public with hands-on experience in puppetry. The Cooperative specializes in giant puppets and outdoor parades and pageants, and its practice is to align with community organizations to build these puppets and performances.

Secondary Category: Multi-Disciplinary Arts

PUPPETWORKS
P.O. Box 150562
Brooklyn, NY 11215
Site address:
338 6th Avenue
Brooklyn, NY11215
Tel 718-965-3391
Email puppetworks@verizon.net
Web www.puppetworks.org

Artistic Director: Nicolas Coppola

Founded in 1980, Puppetworks is dedicated to the preservation and presentation of classic puppet theater entertainment, with special emphasis on the hand-carved wooden marionette. Puppetworks plays are as faithful as possible, in language and situations, to their original source material—primarily children's literature and international folk and fairy tales.

Secondary Categories: Arts for Children/Teens, Multi-Disciplinary Arts, Museums, Presenting Organizations, Visual Arts

QIIQ PRODUCTIONS
27 South Portland Avenue, #2
Brooklyn, NY 11217
Site address:
334 Grand Avenue
Brooklyn, NY 11238
Tel 917-402-3717
Email q2q4u@aol.com
Web www.qiiqproductions.com

Executive Director: Jennifer J. Davis

QIIQ Productions offers introductory theater classes for youth ages 8 through 18. Sessions last for 12 weeks and cycle Native American, African, and Latino folkloric plays as well as contemporary, youth-inspired work. All programs are fee-based, culminate in a public performance, and are held on Sundays at Danny Simmons' Corridor Gallery in Clinton Hill.

Secondary Category: Arts for Children/Teens

RABBIT HOLE ENSEMBLE
1668 42nd Street
Brooklyn, NY 11204
Tel 718-686-6624
Web www.rabbitholeensemble.com

Artistic Director: Edward Elefterion

Rabbit Hole Ensemble emphasizes the communal nature of theater through a distinctly minimalist aesthetic that focuses on space, audience, and the performer (especially the basic tools of physicality and voice) to produce a uniquely direct and candid experience. Strong stories, told simply and theatrically, without much technology, are the result.

RADIOHOLE
See Primary listing under Performance Art

REVELATION PERFORMING ARTS STUDIO, INC.
See Primary listing under Visual/Performing Arts School

RYAN REPERTORY COMPANY
2445 Bath Avenue
Brooklyn, NY 11214

Tel 718-996-4800
Email ryanrep@juno.com

Executive Director: Barbara Parisi

Ryan Repertory Company produces two family-time and two adult productions per season. Material ranges from new playwrights to classic works with a social message. RRC makes an effort to showcase local playwrights (Brooklyn talent in particular) as well as writers from across the USA.

Secondary Categories: Arts for Children/Teens, Opera/Music Theater, Visual/Performing Arts Schools

SABOOGE THEATRE
2515 Glenwood Road, #6G
Brooklyn, NY 11210

Web www.sabooge.org

Co-Artistic Director: Adrienne S. Kapstein

SaBooge Theatre is an award-winning international ensemble whose mission is the creation and development of original work. The company creates highly theatrical and strikingly visual performances with text that is distilled into the poetic. Comprised of artists from the US, Canada, and the UK, SaBooge produces work from Montreal and New York City.

Secondary Categories: Multi-Disciplinary Arts, Visual/Performing Arts Schools

THE SACKETT GROUP
126 Saint Felix Street
Brooklyn, NY 11217

Tel 718-638-7104
Email dan@sackettgroup.org
Web www.sackettgroup.org

Managing Director: Dan Haft

The Sackett Group produces ensemble-based American plays. Recent productions have included works by Sam Shepard and Lanford Wilson.

SHADOW PUPPET THEATRE
592 Manhattan Avenue
Brooklyn, NY 11222

Tel 718-383-3839
Email brendacolling@earthlink.net

Artistic Director: Brenda J. Colling

Founded in 2001, and the offspring of a design career spanning three decades, Shadow Puppet Theatre presents both original plays and adaptations of world fables and folklore for audiences of all ages.

Secondary Category: Arts for Children/Teens

SHARON'S DANCE THEATRE
See Primary listing under Dance

SPOKE THE HUB DANCING, INC.
See Primary listing under Multi-Disciplinary Arts

ST. ANN'S WAREHOUSE
See Primary listing under Presenting Organizations

ST. JOSEPH'S COLLEGE, NY
See Primary listing under Educational Institutions

STAGES OF LEARNING
See Primary listing under Arts for Children/Teens

THEATER

STREB LABORATORY FOR ACTION MECHANICS
See Primary listing under Multi-Disciplinary Arts

TARGET MARGIN THEATER
138 South Oxford Street, #5A
Brooklyn, NY 11217

Tel 718-398-3095
Web www.targetmargin.org

Artistic Director: David Herskovits

Target Margin Theater is founded on the principle that works of art return us to real truths more powerfully by their divergence from a strict illustration of reality. Through classic as well as contemporary texts, Target Margin seeks continuously to expand audience conceptions of what can take place in a theater.

Secondary Categories: Multi-Disciplinary Arts, Opera/Music Theater, Performance Art

THEATER GARDEN, LTD.
See Primary listing under Opera/Music Theater

THELMA HILL PERFORMING ARTS CENTER
See Primary listing under Dance

TONEL LAKAY DANCE THEATRE
See Primary listing under Dance

TRISKELION ARTS
See Primary listing under Dance

TUCKABERRY PRODUCTIONS, INC.
85 Eastern Parkway, #6E
Brooklyn, NY 11238

Tel 845-797-1320
Email tuckaberry@yahoo.com
Web www.tuckaberry.com

Managing Director: Dianna T. Baritot

Tuckaberry Productions' objective is to present high-quality, intelligent, entertaining musical and non-musical theater to children and their families. The company believes "children's theater" should meet the same expectations as adult theater, and hopes to entertain and inspire anyone who delights in live music, compelling characters, comic pratfalls, or even Sondheim references.

Secondary Categories: Arts for Children/Teens, Opera/Music Theater

TWW INC.
See Primary listing under Arts for Children/Teens

UNDER THE TABLE
1045 Union Street, #5F
Brooklyn, NY 11225

Tel 347-693-7630
Email us@underthetabletheatre.org
Web www.underthetabletheatre.org

Under the Table is dedicated to creating original, hilarious, relevant, and accessible physical theater. Its work is fueled by a commitment to the collaborative process of the ensemble. The company was founded in 2001 and has mounted seven original productions, touring and teaching across the city and the nation.

Secondary Category: Performance Art

VAMPIRE COWBOYS THEATRE COMPANY
111 Conselyea Street, #2L
Brooklyn, NY 11211

Tel 212-696-7806
Email news@vampirecowboys.com
Web www.vampirecowboys.com

Vampire Cowboys Theatre Company creates and produces new works of theater based on stage combat and dark comedy with a comic book aesthetic. The company aims to bridge the gap between mass media entertainment and the performing arts, exposing the community to thought-provoking live entertainment rooted in today's pop culture vernacular.

VERTICAL PLAYER REPERTORY
See Primary listing under Opera/Music Theater

VOLCANO LOVE
See Primary listing under Dance

WHITE BIRD PRODUCTIONS
138 South Oxford Street, Suite 3A
Brooklyn, NY 11217

Tel 718-398-3658
Email registration@whitebird productions.org
Web www.whitebirdproductions.org

Since 1987 White Bird Productions has been producing plays, commission-ing new work, and collaborating with musicians at such theaters as BRICstu-dio, HERE Arts Center, and the Ohio Theater. Housed in the ART/NY build-ing in Fort Greene, White Bird offers children's summer theater and after school programs through its Creative Theatrics classes.

Secondary Category: Arts for Children/Teens

WRIGHT NOW!
PERFORMANCEXPERIENCE
See Primary listing under Dance

THEATER

I found I could say
things with color and
shapes that I couldn't
say any other way—
things I had no
words for.

GEORGIA O'KEEFE

VISUAL ARTS

0.00156 ACRES
114 Smith Street
Brooklyn, NY 11201

Tel 718-935-1412
Email veronicamijelshon@yahoo.com

Founder and Director:
Veronica Mijelshon

0.00156 is an art space showing emerging, mid-career, and established artists whose work builds awareness of social issues such as immigration, urbanism, demographics, the environment, education, health, et cetera. All media are included in 0.00156 acres' exhibition program.

Secondary Categories: Architecture & Urban/Environmental Design, Computer Arts/New Media, Film/Video, Galleries, Multi-Disciplinary Arts

10 GRAND PRESS
See Primary listing under Arts Services

440 GALLERY
See Primary listing under Galleries

5+5 GALLERY
See Primary listing under Galleries

A SPACE GALLERY
See Primary listing under Galleries

AD HOC ART
See Primary listing under Galleries

AG GALLERY
See Primary listing under Galleries

A.M. RICHARD FINE ART
See Primary Listing under Galleries

ANNUAL GOWANUS ARTISTS STUDIO TOUR
See Primary listing under Presenting Organizations

ART101
See primary Listing under Galleries

ART GALLERY AT KINGSBOROUGH COMMUNITY COLLEGE, CUNY
See Primary listing under Galleries

ART GLASS STUDIO (ERNEST PORCELLI/ART GLASS)
543 Union Street, #3A
Brooklyn, NY 11215

Tel 718-586-4353
Fax 718-596-4353
Email eporcelliart@cs.com
Web www.ernestporcelli.com

Owner: Ernest Porcelli

A stained glass and glass fusing studio, Ernest Porcelli/Art Glass works in both contemporary and traditional designs.

Secondary Category: Arts Services

ART PLAZA CULTURAL CENTER
See Primary listing under Arts Services

ARTMOVINGPROJECTS
See Primary listing under Computer Arts/New Media

ARTWORKS FOR YOUTH
See Primary listing under Arts for Children/Teens

VISUAL ARTS

ASIAN AMERICAN WOMEN ARTISTS
ALLIANCE (AAWAA)
136 15th Street, Ground Floor
Brooklyn, NY 11215

Tel 718-788-6170
Fax 718-788-6170
Email info@aawaa.org
Web www.aawaa.org

Executive Director: Yan Kong

A unique women's collective that
organizes two to four exhibitions
a year, the Asian American Women
Artists Alliance (AAWAA) has enabled
emerging women artists, especially
those of Asian descent, to create art
and present their works to diverse
communities around New York City.

Secondary Categories:
Arts for Children/Teens, Folk Arts,
Multi-Disciplinary Arts

BAC ARTS IN EDUCATION
See Primary listing under Arts for
Children/Teens

BAC GALLERY
See Primary listing Galleries

BAM
See Primary listing under
Multi-Disciplinary Arts

BEDFORD STUYVESANT RESTORATION
CORPORATION'S CENTER FOR ARTS
AND CULTURE - SKYLIGHT GALLERY
See Primary listing under Galleries

BEDFORD-STUYVESANT ARTISTS'
ASSOCIATION
See Primary listing under Arts Services

BOMB MAGAZINE
See Primary listing under
Multi-Disciplinary Arts

BOOKLYN ARTISTS ALLIANCE
(BOOKLYN, INC.)
37 Greenpoint Avenue, 4th Floor
Brooklyn, NY 11222

Tel 718-383-9621
Email staff@booklyn.org

Web www.booklyn.org
President: Mark Wagner

Founded in 1999, Booklyn is an artist-
run nonprofit whose mission is to
promote artist books as an art form
and educational resource, to provide
educational institutions and the public
with programming involving contemporary artist books, and to assist artists in
exhibiting, distributing, and publishing
innovative bookwork.

Secondary Categories: Arts for
Children/Teens, Arts Services, Literary
Arts, Presenting Organizations

BRIC ROTUNDA GALLERY
33 Clinton Street
Brooklyn, NY 11201

Tel 718-875-4047
Fax 718-488-0609
Email rotunda@briconline.org
Web www.briconline.org

Director of Visual Arts: Elizabeth Ferrer

The visual arts program of BRIC Arts
| Media | Brooklyn, BRIC's Rotunda
Gallery presents contemporary art,
public events, and an innovative arts
education program. The Gallery aims to
increase the visibility and accessibility
of contemporary art while bridging the
gap between the art world and global
culture in Brooklyn and beyond.

Secondary Categories: Arts for
Children/Teens, Arts Services,
Film/Video, Galleries, Performance Art

BROOKLYN ARTISANS GALLERY
See primary Listing under Galleries

BROOKLYN ARTISTS GYM (BAG)
168 7th Street, 3rd Floor
Brooklyn, NY 11215

Tel 718-858-9069
Fax 718-768-1719
Email info@brooklynartistsgym.com
Web www.brooklynartistsgym.com

Executive Director: Peter Wallace

Brooklyn Artists Gym provides a fully-equipped communal artists' studio and private and semi-private studio spaces, and has a gallery available for rent. Artists-in-Residence receive special invitations to events and discounts on workshops and figure drawing, and are eligible for health insurance. BAG also houses Room 58, a writer's space.

Secondary Categories: Arts for Children/Teens, Arts Services, Galleries

BROOKLYN ARTS COUNCIL
See Primary listing under Arts Services

BROOKLYN COLLEGE ART GALLERY
See Primary listing under Galleries

BROOKLYN FILM & ARTS FESTIVAL
See Primary listing under Film/Video

BROOKLYN MUSEUM
See Primary listing under Museums

THE BROOKLYN RAIL
See Primary listing under Multi-Disciplinary Arts

BROOKLYN TECHNOLOGY EXCHANGE
See Primary listing under Educational Institutions

BROOKLYN WATERCOLOR SOCIETY
454 Second Street
Brooklyn, NY 11215

Tel 718-965-3024
Email baxelrod@nyc.rr.com
Web www.bws.org

President: Robert Axelrod

The Brooklyn Watercolor Society was founded in 1975 by a group of dedicated watercolor painters living in Brooklyn. The organization is dedicated to excellence in watercolor media, sharing knowledge and skills, and exhibiting. Membership is by portfolio review (twice yearly). The Society currently has 40 members; inquiries are invited.

BROOKLYN WATERFRONT ARTISTS COALITION (BWAC)
c/o OHM
76 Degraw Street
Brooklyn, NY 11231

Site address:
499 Van Brunt Street
Brooklyn, NY 11231

Tel 718-596-2506/2507
Email bwacinfo@aol.com
Web www.bwac.org

President: John Strohbeen

The Brooklyn Waterfront Artists Coalition has been helping emerging Brooklyn artists by presenting their work in free art exhibits for over 25 years. BWAC sponsors three huge art exhibitions inside a Civil War-era warehouse on the Red Hook Pier each year, as well as an outdoor sculpture show in DUMBO.

Secondary Categories: Galleries, Presenting Organizations

CABINET
See Primary listing under Multi-Disciplinary Arts

CAVE
See Primary listing under Multi-Disciplinary Arts

CENTER FOR THANATOLOGY RESEARCH AND EDUCATION, INC.
See Primary listing under Multi-Disciplinary Arts

THE CENTER FOR URBAN PEDAGOGY
See Primary listing under Architecture & Urban/Environmental Design

CHASSIDIC ART INSTITUTE
See Primary listing under Galleries

VISUAL ARTS

CH'I CONTEMPORARY FINE ART
See Primary listing under Galleries

CINDERS GALLERY
See Primary listing under Galleries

CLINTON HILL ART GALLERY
See primary Listing under Galleries

CLINTON HILL SIMPLY ART &
FRAMING GALLERY
See primary Listing under Galleries

THE CODE FOUNDATION, INC.
See Primary listing under Arts Services

CONJUNCTIONARTS, INC.
62 Washington Avenue
Brooklyn, NY 11205

Tel 718-246-2464
Email brad@conjunctionarts.org
Web www.conjunctionarts.org

ConjunctionArts, Inc. supports compelling, socially progressive art within the public sphere. The organization is committed to developing new forms of artistic agency, critical discourse, and public outreach by acting as a venue for fiscal sponsorship and international, cross-cultural exchange, specifically with a studio-based residency program in China.

Secondary Category: Arts Services

CORRIDOR GALLERY
See Primary listing under Galleries

CREATE!
See Primary listing under Arts for Children/Teens

CREATIVE WOMEN'S NETWORK
See Primary listing under Arts Services

CRUCIAL ARTS PRODUCTIONS, INC.
See Primary listing under Multi-Disciplinary Arts

CTS (CREATIVE THRIFTSHOP)
See primary Listing under Galleries

DABORA GALLERY
See primary listing under Galleries

DAM, STUHLTRAGER GALLERY
See Primary listing under Galleries

DIGITAL STORY WORKSHOP
See Primary listing under Film/Video

DOBBIN MILL
50-52 Dobbin Street
Brooklyn, NY 11222

Email dobbinmill@earthlink.net

Established in 1989 by book and paper artist Robbin Ami Silverberg, Dobbin Mill/Dobbin Books is a hand papermaking mill and collaborative artist book studio in Greenpoint. Its facilities are comprised of a fully-equipped papermaking studio, a large book bindery, a printmaking area, and a papermaker's garden. An outdoor courtyard area is available for larger work.

Secondary Category: Arts Services

DOUG MEYER FINE ART
1775 East 34th Street
Brooklyn, NY 11234

Tel 718-375-8006
Email dmfineart@aol.com
Web www.dougmeyerfineart.com

President: Doug Meyer

Doug Meyer Fine Art is a secondary market specialist buying, selling, and trading previously enjoyed works of art in paper, bronze, and canvas. Servicing the art market, Doug Meyer wholesales to fine art galleries across the nation, often buys from private parties to fill orders, and has also published and guided up-and-coming artists.

DUMBO ARTS CENTER (DAC)
30 Washington Street
Brooklyn, NY 11201

Tel 718-694-0831
Email office@dumboartscenter.org
Web www.dumboartscenter.org

Executive Director: Breda Kennedy

The Dumbo Arts Center presents a year-round exhibition program in its gallery, hosts an annual Artists' Opportunity Workshop, and commissions editions, multiples, and public space works. DAC also produces the Annual Dumbo "Art Under the Bridge" Festival, the largest forum for experimentation in public art by emerging artists in the country.

Secondary Categories: Arts Services, Film/Video, Galleries, Multi-Disciplinary Arts, Performance Art, Presenting Organizations

ELDERS SHARE THE ARTS
See Primary listing under Multi-Disciplinary Arts

THE ELEVENTEN GALLERY
See Primary listing under Galleries

ESTHERGRACE DESIGNS
See Primary listing under Architecture & Urban/Environmental Design

ETGALLERIES
See primary Listing under Galleries

EX GALLERY
See Primary listing under Galleries

FIVEMYLES
See Primary listing under Galleries

FLAVORS OF HAITI FINE ARTS & CRAFTS GALLERY
See Primary listing under Galleries

FORT GREENE PHOTOGRAPHY ORGANIZATION (FGPO)
858 Greene Avenue
Brooklyn, NY 11221

Email info@fgpo.org
Web www.fgpo.org

Founder: Ocean Morisset

Founded in 2001, the Fort Greene Photography Organization is open to anyone who has an interest in the art of photography. The Fort Greene Photography Organization is not a class, or a camera club, but rather an informal environment in which creative photographers share their knowledge of photography and learn from others.

FORTH ESTATE
See Primary listing under Arts Services

FRANKLIN FURNACE ARCHIVE, INC.
80 Hanson Place, #301
Brooklyn, NY 11217

Tel 718-398-7255
Fax 718-398-7256
Email mail@franklinfurnace.org
Web www.franklinfurnace.org

Founding Director: Martha Wilson

Born in 1976 in TriBeCa, Franklin Furnace presented artists' books, installation, and performance art for 20 years. The organization "went virtual" on its 20th anniversary, and now provides grant support to emerging performance and Internet artists. Additionally, Franklin Furnace is transforming its physical archives into a research resource on the ephemeral art practices it pioneered.

Secondary Category: Arts for Children/Teens

FREE103POINT9
See Primary listing under Multi-Disciplinary Arts

FRONT ROOM GALLERY
See Primary Listing under Galleries

GALERIA GALOU
See primary Listing under Galleries

GALERIA JANET KURNATOWSKI
See Primary listing under Galleries

THE GALLERY AT HARRIET'S ALTER EGO
See Primary Listing under Galleries

VISUAL ARTS

GALLERIES AT LONG ISLAND
UNIVERSITY BROOKLYN CAMPUS
See Primary listing under Galleries

GEORGE WASHINGTON CARVER GALLERY
See Primary listing under Galleries

GITANA ROSA GALLERY
See Primary listing under Galleries

GLORIA KENNEDY GALLERY
See Primary listing under Galleries

GOLOBOROTKO'S STUDIO
68 Jay Street
(entrance at 147 Front Street)
Brooklyn, NY 11201

Tel 718-722-2772
Fax 718-722-2772
Email goloborotko@yahoo.com
Web www.goloborotko.com

Director: Sheila Goloborotko

In DUMBO since 1989, Goloborotko's
Studio is a printmaking center established to encourage individual visions
within a nurturing environment that
supports the creation of works that
push the boundaries of printmaking.
Workshops are available for a range of
skill levels, from emergent to working artists, from specific projects to
experimental sessions.

*Secondary Categories: Arts for
Children/Teens, Arts Services, Galleries,
Visual/Performing Arts Schools*

THE GOSSIP FACTORY
See Primary listing under Theater

THE GREEN-WOOD HISTORIC FUND, INC.
500 25th Street, #1
Brooklyn, NY 11232

Site address:
5th Avenue and 25th Street
Brooklyn, NY 11232

Tel 718-788-7850
Fax 718-788-7782
Email info@green-wood.com
Web www.greenwoodcemetery.org

President: Richard J. Moylan

The mission of the Green-Wood
Historic Fund is to share the spectacular resources of the Green-Wood
Cemetery, a National Historic Landmark, with the public, to interpret the
cemetery's 478 acres of architecture,
gardens, signs, tombs, monuments,
bird and animal habitats, and to
educate the public on the more than
560,000 individuals interred there.

*Secondary Categories: Architecture &
Urban/Environmental Design, Museums*

GROUNDSWELL COMMUNITY
MURAL PROJECT
See Primary listing under Arts for
Children/Teens

HEART OF BROOKLYN
See Primary listing under Arts Services

HENRY GREGG GALLERY
See Primary listing under Galleries

THE HOGAR COLLECTION
See Primary listing under Galleries

HOLLAND TUNNEL
See Primary listing under Galleries

HQ
See Primary listing under Galleries

JEWISH FOLK CRAFTS GUILD
See Primary listing under Galleries

KENTLER INTERNATIONAL DRAWING
SPACE
See Primary listing under Galleries

KLAUS VON NICHTSSAGEND GALLERY
See Primary listing under Galleries

KLEINBLUE PRODUCTIONS
63 Stagg Street, #4B
Brooklyn, NY 11206

Email sarah@kleinblueproductions.com
Web www.kleinblueproductions.com

Creative Director: Sarah Stanley

Kleinblue Productions creates curatorial projects with a focus on urbanism,

architecture, conceptual photography, performance art, and the intersection between art and design.

Secondary Category: Presenting Organizations

KLOMPCHING LLC
See Primary listing under Galleries

LAND GALLERY AND STUDIO (LEAGUE ARTISTS NATURAL DESIGN)
See Primary Listing under Galleries

THE LAUNDROMAT PROJECT
c/o 275 Macdonough Street
Brooklyn, NY 11233

Tel 718-574-0798
Email info@laundromatproject.org
Web www.laundromatproject.org

Founder: Risë Wilson

The Laundromat Project is committed to making visual art more accessible to communities of color. Believing that art-making is an invaluable tool for self-determination, social critique, and problem-solving, each year the Project invites like-minded artists of color to mount public art projects that inspire active participation from their neighbors.

Secondary Category: Arts for Children/Teens

LEWIS GALLERY
See Primary listing under Galleries

LIKE THE SPICE
See Primary listing under Galleries

LMAKPROJECTS
See Primary listing under Galleries

LONG ISLAND UNIVERSITY, BROOKLYN CAMPUS
See Primary listing under Educational Institutions

LOTHAR OSTERBURG STUDIO
See Primary listing under Arts Services

MCCAIG-WELLES GALLERY
See Primary listing under Galleries

MEANRED PRODUCTIONS
See Primary listing under Music

METAPHOR CONTEMPORARY ART
See Primary listing under Galleries

MICHAEL ALAN'S DRAW-A-THON
See Primary listing under Arts Services

MILL BASIN DELI AND FINE ART GALLERY
See Primary Listing under Galleries

MOMENTA ART
See Primary listing under Galleries

MONKEY TOWN
See Primary listing under Film/Video

MOVING THEATER
See Primary listing under Theater

THE MUDPIT
See Primary listing under Arts Services

MUSEUM OF CONTEMPORARY AFRICAN DIASPORAN ART
See Primary listing under Museums

NAT CREOLE ONLINE
See Primary listing under Computer Arts/New Media

NEIL STEVENSON FINE ART LLC
See Primary Listing under Galleries

NELSON HANCOCK GALLERY
See Primary listing under Galleries

VISUAL ARTS

NEW GENERAL CATALOG
140 Franklin Street
Brooklyn, NY 11222

Tel 917-687-9747
Web www.newgeneralcatalog.com

Executive Director: Trong G. Nguyen

Located in Greenpoint, New General Catalog is a project space dedicated to hosting exhibitions and programs of contemporary art in all media, with a focus on showing challenging works and ideas of exceptional quality.

Secondary Category: Multi-Disciplinary Arts

NURTUREART (THE NURTUREART GALLERY & EMERGING CURATORS' RESOURCE CENTER)
910 Grand Street
Brooklyn, NY 11211

Tel 718-782-7755
Fax 718-569-2086
Web www.nurtureart.org

Executive Director: Karen Marston

NURTUREart nurtures new contemporary art by providing exhibition opportunities and resources for both emerging artists and curators. NURTUREart's motto reads, "Our name is our mission."

Secondary Categories: Arts for Children/Teens, Arts Services

NUNU GALLERIE
See Primary listing under Galleries

OBJECT IMAGE GALLERY
See Primary listing under Galleries

OFFICEOPS
See Primary listing under Multi-Disciplinary Arts

THE OLD AMERICAN CAN FACTORY
See Primary listing under Presenting Organizations

ORANGE VECTOR
See Primary listing under Arts Services

PAINT ACROSS AMERICA
312 Carlton Avenue, #2B
Brooklyn, NY 11205

Email kara@paintacrossamerica.org
Web www.paintacrossamerica.org

Co-Founder and Treasurer:
Kara L. Hultin

Paint Across America organizes and hosts interactive art festivals, "Paint Outs," where communities create art together under the instruction of artists. Individuals of all walks and stages of life, as well as all levels of artistic aptitude and experience, work together to celebrate and participate in artistic expression.

Secondary Category: Arts for Children/Teens

THE PAINTED POT
See Primary listing under Arts Services

PARKER'S BOX
See Primary listing under Galleries

PARK SLOPE GALLERY
See Primary listing under Galleries

PENDU PRODUCTIONS (PENDU GALLERY)
1117 8th Avenue, 1st Floor
Brooklyn, NY 11215

Email info@pendu.org
Web www.pendu.org

Director: Todd D. Brooks

Founded in 2003, Pendu Productions is an arts organization dedicated to the collusion of multi-/interdisciplinary, eclectic, outsider, and experimental media. Pendu is comprised of Pendu Gallery, Pendu Sound Recordings, and Pendu Bookshop.

Secondary Category: Music

PERIPHERAL MEDIA PROJECTS, INC. (PMP)
49 Bogart Street, Unit 1G, Buzzer 22
Brooklyn, NY 11206

Tel 718-366-2466
Fax 866-599-7270
Email info@peripheralmedia projects.com
Web www.peripheralmediaprojects.com

CEO and Co-Founder:
Garrison H. Buxton

Peripheral Media Projects, Inc. (PMP) collaborates with artists, architects, designers, musicians, and performers, producing prints for the street, apparel, galleries, festivals, and more. PMP is committed to promoting awareness and social transformation through the creation of art and clothing, both inside and outside traditional gallery and fashion systems.

Secondary Categories: Arts Services, Film/Video, Multi-Disciplinary Arts

PIER GLASS
See Primary listing under Arts Services

PIEROGI
See Primary listing under Galleries

PLG ARTS
See Primary listing under Multi-Disciplinary Arts

PLUTO
See Primary listing under Galleries

POLIZZI FINE ART
See primary Listing under Galleries

PROSPECT PARK & PROSPECT PARK ALLIANCE
See Primary listing under Multi-Disciplinary Arts

PROTEUS GOWANUS
See Primary listing under Multi-Disciplinary Arts

PUPPETWORKS
See Primary listing under Theater

REALFORM (ARTICLE PROJECTS)
205 East 78th Street, #19L
New York, NY 10021

Site address:
218 Bedford Avenue
Brooklyn, NY 11211

Tel 212-772-2351
Fax 212-772-6304
Email articleprojects@gmail.com
Web www.articleprojects.blogspot.com and www.realform.blogspot.com

Director: David M. Gibson

Article Projects is an independent curatorial initiative presenting gallery exhibitions, literary readings, educational lectures by artists and art world professionals, cultural tours, and mixed-media salons.

Secondary Categories: Arts Services, Film/Video, Literary Arts, Presenting Organizations

REVELATION PERFORMING ARTS STUDIO, INC.
See Primary listing under Visual/Performing Arts Schools

THE RIVIERA
See Primary listing under Galleries

RUBELLE AND NORMAN SCHAFLER GALLERY AT THE PRATT INSTITUTE
See Primary listing under Galleries

RUSH PHILANTHROPIC ARTS FOUNDATION
See Primary listing under Arts for Children/Teens

S.E.E.D GALLERY
See Primary listing under Galleries

SAFE-T-GALLERY
See Primary listing under Galleries

SANKARANKA GALLERY
See Primary listing under Galleries

VISUAL ARTS

SANKOFA ART CENTRE
See Primary listing under Galleries

SARAH BOWEN GALLERY
See Primary listing under Galleries

SECRET PROJECT ROBOT
210 Kent Avenue
Brooklyn, NY 11211

Tel 917-860-8282
Email secrets@secretprojectrobot.org
Web www.secretprojectrobot.org
Founders: Erik Zajaceskowski and
Rachel Nelson

Secret Project Robot is an installation-
and performance-centered experimental art space that believes in creating a
supportive environment outside of the
usual commercial sphere, where artists
are free to experiment, create, and
develop styles that aren't contingent
upon their ability to sell.

Secondary Category: Film/Video

SLATE GALLERY
See Primary listing under Galleries

SMACK MELLON
92 Plymouth Street
Brooklyn, NY 11201

Tel 718-834-8761
Email info@smackmellon.org
Web www.smackmellon.org
Executive Director: Kathleen Gilrain

Smack Mellon's mission is to nurture
and support emerging, under-recognized mid-career and women artists
in the creation and exhibition of new
work by providing exhibition opportunities, studio workspace, and access to
equipment and technical assistance for
the realization of ambitious projects.

Secondary Category: Galleries

SMUDGE STUDIO
372 2nd Street, #4C
Brooklyn, NY 11215

Web www.smudgestudio.org
Co-Directors: Elizabeth Ellsworth and
Jamie Kruse

smudge studio is a nonprofit collaborative art practice that smudges the
intersections between art practices
and life practices. smudge uses various
media (video, photography, audio,
Super 8, the Internet) to document
how topographies of place, landforms,
and people (including themselves)
look, sound, feel, and move when they
are addressed as "in the making."

*Secondary Category: Architecture &
Urban/Environmental Design*

SOAPBOX GALLERY
93 Wyckoff Street
Brooklyn, NY 11201

Site address:
636 Dean Street
Brooklyn, NY 11238

Email jimmygee777@aol.com
Web www.soapboxgallery.org
Founder: Jim Greenfield

Soapbox Gallery is a street-level display window measuring 10'x10'x7' and
dedicated to providing visual artists in
all media an uncensored opportunity
to express themselves about the world
and any of the compelling issues of the
day. Soapbox Gallery challenges artists
to speak out and be relevant.

Secondary Categories: Film/Video, Galleries

SOUTHFIRST: ART
See Primary Listing under Galleries

**SOUTH OF THE NAVY YARD ARTISTS
(SONYA)**
P.O. Box 381082
Brooklyn, NY 11238

Site Address:
SONYA at ElevenTen Gallery
1110 Fulton St.
Brooklyn, NY 11238

Tel 718-789-2545
Fax 718-789-2545
Email kathleenhayek@verizon.net
Web www.sonyaonline.org

President: Kathleen Hayek

South Of The Navy Yard Artists (SONYA) ia a nonprofit organization of diverse and dynamic visual artists living, creating, and exhibiting in the Fort Greene, Clinton Hill, Wallabout, and Bedford Stuyvesant neighborhoods. SONYA's mission is to recognize, support, and celebrate the visual art and artists within these diverse communities.

Secondary Category: Galleries

SPRING
See Primary listing under Galleries

ST. JOSEPH'S COLLEGE, NY
See Primary listing under Educational Institutions

STACY STEWART SMITH GALLERY (STACY STEWART SMITH ENTERPRISES)
P.O. Box 570
New York, NY 10018

Site address:
972 Atlantic Avenue
Brooklyn, NY 11238

Tel 718-230-5165
Email stacy.smith4@verizon.net
Web www.stacystewartsmith.com

President: Stacy Stewart Smith

Stacy Stewart Smith Gallery represents artists (including Stacy Smith himself) from his studio and gallery through special events and private showings. Visits are by appointment only, unless there is an open exhibit advertised.

Secondary Categories: Arts Services, Galleries

STRIPEMAN GALLERY LTD.
See Primary listing under Galleries

STUDIO 354, INC.
See Primary listing under Galleries

SUNNY'S
See Primary listing under Music

TWW INC.
See Primary listing under Arts for Children/Teens

TABLA RASA GALLERY
See Primary listing under Galleries

TILLIE'S OF BROOKLYN
248 DeKalb Avenue
Brooklyn, NY 11205

Tel 718-783-6140
Fax 718-783-8691
Email mail@tilliesofbrooklyn.com
Web www.tilliesofbrooklyn.com

President: Patricia L. Mulcahy

Tillie's of Brooklyn is a Fort Greene coffeehouse/cafe with open mic night every other Thursday, in addition to frequent musical events, literary readings, and art exhibitions that change every five weeks. All events are listed on the Tillie's website.

Secondary Category: Music

TRIANGLE ARTS ASSOCIATION
20 Jay Street, Suite 318
Brooklyn, NY 11201

Fax 718-858-1260
Email mail@triangleworkshop.org
Web www.triangleworkshop.org

Executive Director: Sarah L. Walko

The Triangle Arts Association sets out to promote dialogue and experimentation among contemporary visual artists. Triangle does this by providing year-round residency programs and a biennial two-week workshop for working, professional artists at various stages of their careers.

VISUAL ARTS

UNDERBRIDGE PICTURES
See Primary listing under Galleries

THE URBAN DIVERS
(UDEC ENVIRO MEDIA)
See Primary Listing under Galleries

URBANGLASS
647 Fulton Street, Third Floor
Brooklyn, NY 11217

Site address:
57 Rockwell Place
Brooklyn, NY 11217

Tel 718-625-3685
Fax 718-625-3889
Email info@urbanglass.org
Web www.urbanglass.org

Executive Director: Dawn Bennett

UrbanGlass is an international center
that advances the use and appreciation of glass as a creative medium and
makes glass accessible to a diverse
audience through programs, educational initiatives, and publications.
Programs include the open-access
studio, classes and workshops, *GLASS:
The UrbanGlass Art Quarterly*, on-
and off-site exhibitions, and a gallery
and store.

Secondary Category: Galleries

VERTEXLIST
See Primary listing under Computer
Arts/New Media

VISUAL ART STUDIO
See Primary listing under Film/Video

WAGMAG (WILLIAMSBURG AND
GREENPOINT MONTHLY ART GUIDE)
147 Roebling Street
Brooklyn, NY 11211

Email info@wagmag.org
Web www.wagmag.org

WAGMAG has been serving the art community in Williamsburg and Greenpoint
since 2001, producing a monthly listing
service for galleries, as well as

an up-to-date map, an arts events
page, listings, and critical reviews.

Secondary Category: Arts Services

WESSEL + O'CONNOR FINE ART
(WESSEL + O'CONNOR GALLERY)
See Primary listing under Galleries

WISELEPHANT
See Primary listing under Arts Services

ZION GALLERY
See Primary listing under Galleries

VISUAL/PERFORMING ARTS SCHOOLS

VISUAL/PERFORMING ARTS SCHOOLS

ART'S HOUSE SCHOOLS, INC.
See Primary listing under Arts for Children/Teens

BEDFORD STUYVESANT RESTORATION CORPORATION'S CENTER FOR ARTS AND CULTURE – YOUTH ARTS ACADEMY (YAA)
247 Herkimer Street
Brooklyn, NY 11216

Tel 718-636-6969
Fax 718-636-0511
Email artws@restorationplaza.org
Web www. restorationplaza.org

President: Colvin Grannum

Restoration's Youth Arts Academy (YAA) is the only comprehensive arts education institution in Bedford Stuyvesant. YAA offers classes each year in dance, drumming, and theater to youth ages 3-19, and conducts residencies and workshops in the New York City schools through its Arts-In-Action program. YAA is also home to the renowned Restoration Dance Theater Junior Company.

Secondary Categories:
Arts for Children/Teens, Dance,
Multi-Disciplinary Arts

BROOKLYN MUSIC SCHOOL
126 Saint Felix Street
Brooklyn, NY 11217

Tel 718-638-5660
Email contact@brooklynmusic
school.org
Web www.brooklynmusicschool.org

Interim Executive Director:
Jeffrey Tannenbaum

The mission of the Brooklyn Music School is to provide the highest level of music and dance training to the community, serving students regardless of age, income, race, or professional aspiration. The Music School offers programs for both children and adults, and classes in all levels of proficiency.

Secondary Categories: Dance, Music

GOLOBOROTKO'S STUDIO
See Primary listing under Visual Arts

THE MEDGAR EVERS COLLEGE PREPARATORY SCHOOL CONTEMPORARY DANCE THEATRE
1186 Carroll Street
Brooklyn, NY 11225

Tel 718-703-5400, ext. 1615

Artistic Director: Valerie McLeod-Katz

The Contemporary Dance Theatre is a professional dance company that performs a fusion of modern, jazz, hip hop, and Afro Caribbean dance forms. The company is housed in the Medgar Evers College Preparatory School, a secondary school for math, science, and technology, with a strong visual and performing arts curriculum.

Secondary Category: Educational Institutions

NEW YORK CIRCUS ARTS ACADEMY
5 Brewster Street, #142
Glen Cove, NY 11542
Site address:
227 4th Avenue
Brooklyn, NY 11215
Tel 646-291-6364
Fax 212-659-0138
Email info@nycircusarts.com
Web www.nycircusarts.com

President: Cypher Zero

The New York Circus Arts Academy is dedicated to providing high-quality professional and recreational training for adults. Training with NYCAA is an exhilarating, artistic, and unique experience for people of all fitness levels and body types. In each course, students build competency in the technical and creative aspects of the art form.

THE PUPPETRY ARTS THEATRE, INC.
See Primary listing under Multi-Disciplinary Arts

REVELATION PERFORMING ARTS STUDIO, INC. (RPAS, INC.)
5712 Church Avenue
Brooklyn, NY 11203

Tel 718-342-1908
Email info@rpas.org
Web www.rpas.org

Founder, CEO, and Executive Artistic Director: Bridgette Chapman

A faith-based, nonprofit youth development and performing arts organization, Revelation Performing Arts Studio, Inc. (RPAS) educates and uplifts communities through dance, theater, and music. RPAS has an artist-in-residency program, a performance repertoire, and a dance company.

Secondary Categories: Arts for Children/Teens, Arts Services, Dance, Galleries, Multi-Disciplinary Arts, Music, Presenting Organizations, Theater, Visual Arts

RYAN REPERTORY COMPANY
See Primary listing under Theater

SABOOGE THEATRE
See Primary listing under Theater

SCHOOL FOR MUSICAL PERFORMANCE
See Primary listing under Music

SHOSTAKOVICH MUSIC, ARTS, AND SPORT SCHOOL, INC.
See Primary listing under Music

STAGG STREET CENTER FOR CHILDREN
77-83 Stagg Street
Brooklyn, NY 11206

Tel 718-388-1395/96
Email daycare77@aol.com

Director: Lawrence A. Provette

The Stagg Street Center for Children is a childcare center with concentrations in art, drama, music, and dance.

Secondary Category: Arts for Children/Teens

BAC BOARD AND STAFF

BOARD OF DIRECTORS

Honorary Chairman
Marty Markowitz,
Brooklyn Borough President

Chairman
Dr. Thomas F. Schutte

Vice Chairmen
Peter Aschkenasy
Marvin Numeroff

Treasurer
Sylvia Lanka Barone

Secretary
Michael A. Armstrong

Audrey Frank Anastasi
George Andreozzi
Carol Enseki
Theodore Gunn
Radiah Harper
Dan Holt
Arnold N. Kriss
Rodney J.E. Leon
Terence J. Mitchell
Erminia Rivera
Ada Rodriguez
Susan Rowland
Carl Self
Sharon E. Simmons
Donna Walker-Kuhne
I. Donald Weston
Antonia Yuille Williams

STAFF

Ella J. Weiss, *President*

Agnes Murray, *Art Services Director*

Marisa Cerio, *Administrative Assistant*

Kathleen Christie, *Arts in Education Manager*

Sara DeRose, *Communications Director*

Melissa Estro, *Fiscal Assistant*

Deborah Field, *Arts in Education Coordinator*

Thomas Fordham, *Finance Director*

Angela Fatou Gittens, *Program Coordinator*

Katherine P. Higgins, *Development Manager*

Nicole Macotsis, *Folk Arts Associate*

Tricia Mire, *Development Consultant*

Mozhgan Motamedi, *Fiscal Manager*

Carol Sterling, *Arts in Education Director*

Kay Turner, *Folk Arts Director*

Ethany Uttech, *Regrant Coordinator*

Courtney J. Wendroff, *Executive Assistant and BAC Gallery Coordinator*

BAC SUPPORTERS

Council programs are made possible, in part, with public funds from:

National Endowment for the Arts

U.S. Department of Justice, Office of Juvenile Justice and Delinquency Prevention

New York State Council on the Arts, a State Agency

New York State Department of Education

New York State Office of Parks, Recreation and Historic Preservation

Brooklyn Delegation of the New York State Assembly

Brooklyn Delegation of the New York State Senate

New York City Department of Cultural Affairs

New York City Department of Youth and Community Development

New York City Department for the Aging

The New York City Council

Brooklyn Delegation of The New York City Council

Brooklyn Borough President Marty Markowitz

Major corporate, foundation and in-kind support is provided by:

American Express

Baisley Powell Elebash Fund

Booth Ferris Foundation

Carnegie Corporation of New York

Commerce Bank

Con Edison

Concert Foods

Courier-Life Publishing

Experimental Television Center

Fidelity Investments

Health Plus

Independence Community Foundation

JPMorgan Chase

KeySpan

Maimonides Medical Center

Merrill Lynch

Mertz Gilmore Foundation

Milton and Sally Avery Arts Foundation

Robert Sterling Clark Foundation

Rockefeller Brothers Fund

Rush Philanthropic Arts Foundation

Sovereign Bank

The Heckscher Foundation for Children

The Mary Duke Biddle Foundation

The New York Community Trust

The New York State Music Fund, established by the New York State Attorney General at Rockefeller Philanthropy Advisors

Two Trees Management Co., LLC

United Homes

Washington Mutual

Major individual supporters are:

Pamela Brier and Peter Aschkenasy

Sylvia Lanka and William Barone

Linda Endres Greco

Marvin Numeroff

Erminia and Gilbert Rivera

Additional support comes from Materials for the Arts and WNYC, New York Public Radio.

LOG ON

DIRECTORY CREDITS

Editor/Researcher	Jeff Tompkins
Associate Editor	Linda Zerella
Consulting Editor	Eleanor Ruth Geryk
Proofreader	Vanessa Petrillo
Production Coordinator	Sara DeRose
Supervisory Editor	Ella J. Weiss
Design	WWW.GOODESIGNNY.COM
Printing	Galvanic Printing

The 2008 *Directory of Brooklyn Arts Organizations* is generously underwritten by JPMorgan Chase.

 JPMorganChase